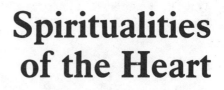
Spiritualities of the Heart

APPROACHES TO PERSONAL WHOLENESS IN CHRISTIAN TRADITION

edited by
Annice Callahan, R.S.C.J.

PAULIST PRESS
New York/Mahwah, N.J.

ACKNOWLEDGEMENTS

Portions of Elizabeth Dreyer's chapter have been previously published in "*Affectus* in St. Bonaventure's Theology" in *Franciscan Studies*, 42 (1982), 5–20.

The Collected Works of St. John of the Cross. Tr. Kieran Kavanaugh, O.C.D., and Otilio Rodriguez, O.C.D. 2nd ed. Washington, D.C.: Institute of Carmelite Studies, 1979.

.

Linocut and cover design by Aileen Callahan

Library of Congress Cataloging-in-Publication Data

Callahan, Annice, 1945–
    Spiritualities of the heart / by Annice Callahan.
      p. cm.
    Includes bibliographical references and index.
    ISBN 0-8091-3101-3
    1. Spirituality—Catholic Church—History of doctrines. 2. Heart—
Religious aspects—Christianity—History of doctrines. 3. Catholic
Church—Doctrines—History.   I. Title.
    BX2350.65.C35 1989
    248.4'82—dc20   89-36861
                                                          CIP

Published by Paulist Press
997 Macarthur Boulevard
Mahwah, New Jersey 07430

Printed and bound in the
United States of America

Contents

Introduction

The heart is the center where our freedom, affectivity, and consciousness most intimately dwell. It is the place where we surrender to or resist the mystery of God, the mystery of ourselves, and the mystery of life. It is the place of our orientation to God, our openness to the transcendent in our daily lives. It is the core of our being whereby the presence of God touches us. It is the blood-pumping muscle of the body as well as the center of our interiority. As such, it is an appropriate symbol of the center of the human person.

A spirituality of the heart is necessarily incarnational and holistic. It views the heart as a uniquely human reality that is both corporeal and spiritual. It represents the total mystery of the human person. It reflects on what it means to be human in light of what it means to become divine. A spirituality of the heart is also redemptive and unitive. It describes a particular way of living the paschal mystery in our daily lives, that is, accepting the sufferings and joys that we and others experience. It is concerned with what can unify our fragmented selves, with what can heal our brokenness. It points to communion at a deep level, heart-to-heart.

This book is an attempt to explore and express the different ways in which several spiritual writers have viewed and incorporated the heart into their work. They do not all necessarily use the word "heart," but they all treat in some way the mysterious center of the human person. We present chronologically representative writers from different periods of history who make explicit references to the heart or who imply that they work with a notion of the heart in their approach to the person's relationship to God. The selection is partial and incomplete.

We begin with two patristic writers, Irenaeus and Augustine. Mary Ann Donovan, S.C., from the Jesuit School of Theology at Berkeley,

1

discusses Irenaeus' theological anthropology and his conviction that the glory of God is the human person fully alive, that is, living the life of the Spirit. Instead of speaking the language of heart, he writes about the wholeness of the person and the fullness of life. The divine physician brings us to the fullness of life in the vision of God, which is the glory of humankind at the heart of life.

Mary T. Clark, R.S.C.J., at Manhattanville College, in Purchase, New York, describes how Augustine uses the image of the eyes of the heart and concludes that faith and love of neighbor heal and enlighten our hearts so that we can see God. Although we are made in God's image and likeness, the image and likeness are authentic only when we remember, understand, and love the trinitarian God. The mind is the source of the image of the Trinity and the heart is the source of the affective likeness of self-giving love. This love enlightens the eyes of the heart. Augustine emphasizes the spiritual dimension of the heart, its capacity for understanding, desiring, and loving others and God.

We continue with three representatives of the middle ages: Bonaventure, Thomas Aquinas, and Catherine of Siena. Elizabeth Dreyer of the Washington Theological Union in Silver Spring, Maryland, reflects on the role of *affectus* or affectivity in Bonaventure's thought on the Holy Spirit and in his spirituality. For him, the Holy Spirit is the mutual love, the unity or bond between the Father and the Son. The Holy Spirit's role unites forms of knowledge of God in the bond of charity and orders them to contemplative union with God. Bonaventure reveals the significance of the heart when he uses the image of the believer beholding Christ on the cross with faith, hope, love, devotion, praise, and joy. He uses heart-language to describe devotion. For him, the contemplation of wisdom is love, *affectus*, the experience of God as divine sweetness.

Walter Principe, C.S.B., of the Pontifical Institute of Medieval Studies in Toronto, maintains that for Thomas Aquinas, the heart implies affective, cognitive, and volitional dimensions. The heart is the driving force of the other acts and powers of the person. Thomas, then, champions human affectivity as being at the center of our strivings for the perfect happiness to be found only in God. For him, when a lover is united with the beloved by love, the lover acquires a connatural knowledge of the beloved; when the beloved is God, union with God by charity gives the person a connatural knowledge of God that is experiential and mystical in character. For Thomas, the Holy Spirit is the Love breathed forth by the Word of God, and so is the loving heart of Christ, the life-giving heart of the church.

Suzanne Noffke, O.P., at the University of Chicago, Illinois, discusses how Catherine of Siena focuses on the human heart responding to the heart of Jesus revealing the heart of God. Thus for Catherine, the heart is the physical reality and the locus of human response, the place where truth and love meet and are unified. The open heart of Jesus crucified assures us that we are loved boundlessly and invites us to drink and rest. Catherine is drawn to drink from the wounded side of Jesus, from the secret of his heart, in order to be open to his love of others. Using the image of the eye of the heart that Augustine uses, she wants us to look into the open heart of Jesus crucified in order to see the truth that God loves us and to be transformed into the kiss of peace. She encourages the gift of friendship, which is perfect in proportion as we drink it within the fountain that is the heart of Christ and the fire of the Holy Spirit.

Next, we consider seven sixteenth, seventeenth, and nineteenth-century European writers: Martin Luther, Ignatius of Loyola, Teresa of Avila, John of the Cross, Francis de Sales, Jane de Chantal, and Madeleine Sophie Barat. Jared Wicks, S.J., of the Gregorian University, Rome, discusses Martin Luther's insight into the believing heart clinging to God's word of grace. He indicates Luther's changing points of emphasis: first, the heart's confrontation with Christ's call to conversion, second, the heart's consolation by Christ's sacramental word of forgiveness, and, finally, the heart's submission to the words and signs of the Christian community. For Luther, the heart is the cognitive and affective center of the person where God's grace works its transformation of desires. Praying before the cross, the perceiving heart sees the loving-kindness of Christ's own heart, which reveals the very heart of God.

Harvey D. Egan, S.J., of Boston College, calls Ignatius of Loyola a mystic at the heart of the Trinity and at the heart of Jesus Christ. Ignatius enjoyed a mystical relationship with each person of the Trinity, as well as a mystical grasp of the incarnation. Ignatius' spirituality of the heart combines a mystical distinction between the persons of the Trinity, an experiential taste of the Trinity's indwelling in our hearts, and Augustine's intuitive grasp of the Trinity's oneness. On hearing the name of Jesus, Ignatius' heart felt love, assurance, and an intensified desire to follow Jesus. Egan suggests that this mysticism of the name of Jesus might underlie the Jesuit devotion to the heart of Christ. Ignatius mystically experiences Jesus' divine and human sonship and so stands at the heart of Jesus, one with him in the mystery of his identity. Ignatius is also given a mysticism of the Holy Spirit who confirms and consoles him in powerful ways. For him, the heart is the place of our encounter with the Trinity, of our identification with Christ.

Margaret Brennan, I.H.M., at Regis College, Toronto, describes the significance of desire in Teresa of Avila. Although Teresa did not have an explicit spirituality of the heart, she certainly lived and prayed from her heart, from her experience of God which led her to critique societal and cultural structures in her day. She desired to read the book of her life mediated by the humanity of Christ. She desired to help others to find the center of God's presence within themselves. Teresa based her Carmelite reform on her desire for the honor of serving God in imitation of Christ, holding in contempt the prestige of titles or pure blood. She affirmed women's deep desire to contribute to the building up of the church, in spite of man's low regard for them. She fostered a spirituality of empowerment and embodiment as habits of the heart which are relevant today.

Keith J. Egan at Saint Mary's College, Notre Dame, finds in John of the Cross a marvelous resource in the contemporary effort to retrieve the heart as a religious symbol. Mystical experience, poetic genius, and familiarity with the scriptures converge in the poetry and commentaries of John of the Cross to offer a rich mine in which the heart is used effectively as a religious symbol. Once attuned to John's use of the heart imagery, one is drawn to a new awareness of the wonderful potential of the heart as an effective religious symbol. John of the Cross reminds one to value language and symbol. Such care for language and symbol can be a powerful agent in retrieving the heart as a symbol that both moves and instructs.

Wendy M. Wright at Creighton University, Omaha traces the imagery of the heart in the writings of Francis de Sales and Jane de Chantal. For both, it is the central dynamism of human and divine living, the core of the person, and the seat of love begetting love. The heart of God is the center of trinitarian life and the source of love. The mediator between the human and divine hearts is the heart of Christ which is the model and catalyst of interior transformation. They viewed the vocation of the Visitation Sisters to be a life of the surrender of the heart, a way to live Jesus by loving gently and humbly, a way to be opened and crucified for the beloved. This life, then, is a martyrdom of love identifying with Jesus in his paschal mystery.

Mary Quinlan, R.S.C.J., formerly at Newton College of the Sacred Heart in Newton and currently doing research on the Society of the Sacred Heart in Cambridge, Massachusetts, develops Madeleine Sophie Barat's doctrine of the interior life. This doctrine is based on the heart's surrender to the guidance of the Holy Spirit, in union and conformity with the heart of Christ, the source and symbol of God's love. It focuses, in fact, on devotion to the Sacred Heart, in particular on love, trust, and adoration of the Blessed Sacrament. The educational mission of the Society of the Sacred Heart which she founded is to discover and manifest God's love by contemplation in the midst of action. Her spirituality of the heart, then, is a spirituality of loving adoration, surrender, trust, and compassion. It fosters interior spirit, which is joyful freedom in dependence on God.

We end this book by reflecting on three contemporary writers: Pierre Teilhard de Chardin, S.J., Jean Vanier, and Henri Nouwen. Robert Faricy, S.J., at the Gregorian University in Rome, discusses Pierre Teilhard de Chardin's spirituality of the heart which is based on a spirituality of the heart of Christ. For Teilhard, the heart of the risen Christ is the heart of matter, energy, and fire, penetrating everything. At the same time, this heart universalizes God's love by radiating it everywhere. His union with the heart of the cosmic Christ evokes his loving surrender to God's will. The heart of Christ is the center of the world's movement into the future, radiating the creative force of Christ's love from his presence in the eucharist. Teilhard's devotion to the Sacred Heart is his way of living his personal relationship with Jesus in trust and abandonment. This heart is not only the center of the person of Christ, but also the center of every person and of the universe: it is the heart of the world, a center of convergence.

Michael Downey at Loyola Marymount University in Los Angeles plumbs the depths of Jean Vanier's spirituality of the heart, a spirituality of vulnerability and wisdom. For Vanier, the heart is the center of the person enabling us to love God and so enter into the life of God. The vulnerability of our hearts opens us to experience God's strength in our weakness and suffering. Handicapped people live this wound of weakness and suffering in an open way. At the center of each person is the heart, that most basic level of human existence, which is more intent on building communion through shared vulnerability than on building empires through efficient productivity. In fact, for Vanier, a person is the heart, that is, the uniquely human combination of understanding, choice, and affect. Our heart's personal relationship with Christ is a solid foundation for building community in faith with others, especially with people who are marginalized by society because of handicaps.

I outline Henri Nouwen's spirituality of the compassionate heart by describing six attitudes of heart that recur in his writings: solitude, service, prayer, compassion, gratitude, and communion. For Nouwen, the heart is home, the place where we encounter ourselves, God, and others.

The heart, then, is the symbol of the center of the person. It represents and reveals our feelings, thoughts, and choices. It is both corporeal and spiritual. As such, it is an appropriate symbol of the incarnational structure of our human reality. It is the place where we encounter the Trinity and where God transforms us. It is the place where we mediate God's love to others in faith, friendship, and service. It is the place of our gratitude and surrender, for through it we are open to the transcendent. It is also the locus of our shared vulnerability, for through it we are open to one another.

These spiritualities of the heart are approaches to personal wholeness in Christian tradition. We turn to God with the loving eyes of the heart. God turns to us in the heart of Christ through the Holy Spirit. The heart of Christ is both the heart of matter and the heart of the church. May your reading of this collection help you to recognize and affirm your way of the heart, a way that leads to the heart of Christ.

Lawrence Boadt, C.S.P., our editor at Paulist Press, contributed much by his persistent availability, advice, and encouragement. Aileen Callahan, my sister, designed the striking linocut and cover.

Annice Callahan, R.S.C.J.
Regis College, Toronto

Contributors

Margaret Brennan, I.H.M., professor of pastoral theology, teaches courses on spirituality and ministry at Regis College, Toronto, and has published articles in *America, Concilium,* and *The Way.*

Annice Callahan, R.S.C.J., professor of spiritual theology, teaches courses on spirituality and theology at Regis College, Toronto, and is the author of *Karl Rahner's Spirituality of the Pierced Heart: A Reinterpretation of Devotion to the Sacred Heart,* as well as articles in *Barat Review, Horizons, Irish Theological Quarterly, RSCJ: A Journal of Reflection,* and *The Way.*

Mary T. Clark, R.S.C.J., emeritus professor of philosophy at Manhattanville College and Visiting Professor in the Theology/Spirituality Program of the University of San Francisco, is the author of numerous books and articles, including *Augustine, Philosopher of Freedom, Augustinian Personalism,* and *Augustine of Hippo.*

Mary Ann Donovan, S.C., professor of historical theology at the Jesuit School of Theology at Berkeley, is the author of *Sisterhood As Power: The Past and Passion of Ecclesial Women.* She has published articles in *Horizons, Second Century, Toronto Journal of Theology, Studia Patristica,* and *Theological Studies.*

Michael Downey, professor of theology at Loyola Marymount University, Los Angeles, teaches courses in sacramental theology, spirituality, and ministry, and is the author of *A Blessed Weakness: The Spirit of Jean Vanier and l'Arche, Clothed in Christ: The Sacraments and Christian Living,* and articles in *Doctrine and Life, Horizons, Liturgy, Spiritual Life, Spirituality Today, Philosophy and Theology,* and *Theology Today.*

Elizabeth Dreyer, professor of spirituality at Washington Theological Union, teaches courses in the history of Christian spirituality, is the author

7

of *Manifestations of Grace* and *Passionate Women: Two Medieval Mystics.*
She has published articles in *Franciscan Studies, Spirituality Today, Spiritual Life, Westminster Dictionary of Christian Spirituality, New Catholic World, Horizons, Emmanuel,* and *America.*

Harvey D. Egan, S.J., professor of systematic and mystical theology
at Boston College, is the author of numerous books and articles, including
Ignatius Loyola the Mystic, Karl Rahner in Dialogue (ed.), *Karl Rahner—I
Remember* (tr.), *Christian Mysticism: The Future of a Tradition, What Are
They Saying About Mysticism?* and *The Spiritual Exercises and the Ignatian
Mystical Horizon.*

Keith J. Egan, chair of the religious studies department and director
of the center for spirituality at Saint Mary's College, Notre Dame, has
published *What Is Prayer?*, monographs, and articles in journals such as
Carmelus, Carmelite Studies, American Benedictine Review, Horizons, Review for Religious, Spiritual Life, Sisters Today, and *Peaceweavers: Medieval
Religious Women.*

Robert Faricy, S.J., professor of spiritual theology at the Pontifical
Gregorian University, Rome, is the author of numerous books and articles
including *The Spirituality of Teilhard de Chardin, Teilhard de Chardin's Theology of the Christian in the World, Seeking Jesus in Contemplation and Discernment, Wind and Sea Obey Him: Approaches to the Theology of Nature,* and *The
Lord's Dealing: The Primacy of the Feminine in Christian Spirituality.*

Suzanne Noffke, O.P., visiting scholar at the University of Chicago,
is translator of *Catherine of Siena: The Dialogue, The Prayers of Catherine of
Siena,* and currently her *Letters,* as well as the author of several articles.

Walter Principe, C.S.B., professor of history of theology at the Pontifical Institute of Medieval Studies, Toronto, has published four volumes
on *The Theology of the Hypostatic Union in the Early Thirteenth Century,* a
book on *Introduction to Patristic and Medieval Theology,* and articles in
Franciscan Studies, Gregorianum, Medieval Studies, Studia Patristica, Studies in Religion, and *The Way.*

Mary Quinlan, R.S.C.J., former professor of history and academic
dean at Newton College of the Sacred Heart, and author of *Mabel Digby
and Janet Erskine Stuart: Superiors General of the Society of the Sacred Heart,
1895–1914* and *Ursula Benziger, RSCJ,* is now working on a volume dealing with the history of the Society of the Sacred Heart from 1914 to 1964.

Jared Wicks, S.J., professor of theology at the Gregorian University,
Rome, is the author of *Luther and His Spiritual Legacy,* as well as articles
in *Theological Studies, Catholic Historical Review,* and the *Dictionnaire de
Spiritualité.*

Wendy M. Wright, visiting professor of Christian spirituality and
theology at Creighton University, Omaha, is the author of *Bond of Perfec-*

tion: Jeanne de Chantal and François de Sales, Silent Fire: An Invitation to Western Mysticism, and *Francis de Sales and Jane de Chantal: Letters of Spiritual Direction,* as well as articles and reviews in such journals as *Praying, Studia Mystica, Theology Today,* and *Weavings.* She is married to Roger Bergman and they have three children.

Mary Ann Donovan, S.C.

Irenaeus: At the Heart of Life, Glory

Irenaeus models one of the earliest Christian forms of spirituality. He speaks with a voice unique in patristic literature. His spirituality respects the dynamism of human living and incorporates the totality of the human person. It is centered on the glory that is the divine presence and vibrates with the life lit by that glory. For him God's glory is the human person fully alive. His is indeed a spirituality of the heart for our day.

However, Irenaeus lived and worked in the late second century. To hear him rightly we need a minimal grasp of his project. Valentinian gnosticism, against which he strove to defend Christian belief, provides a basic context for interpretation of his thought. A brief look at this context will acquaint us with his point of departure, and lead into our main task, which is to explore the aspects of Irenaeus' work that support a dynamic spirituality respecting and valuing the materiality in and through which, with Christ, we follow the Spirit to the Father.

Valentinian gnosticism[1] was a popular second century movement which understood the human situation in terms of a radical dualism. The supreme unknown, unknowable God is totally remote from matter. The creator of this world is the product of the fall of the least of the "aeons" (emanations of the supreme God). Each of the elect, known as the "pneumatic" or "spiritual," contains a spark of the heavenly world. Salvation is by knowledge or gnosis of the heavenly world whence came that inner spark, and to which the predestined will return, once free of matter. These teachings were circulated in the form of myths, often interpreting stories found in Genesis or the four gospels. While various ways of life found

11

justification in elements of gnostic doctrine, all reflect a sharp antipathy to the material cosmos.

What way of life does the Irenaean doctrine support? Evidence comes from review of his teaching on creation, on incarnation-salvation, and on the human person as image of God. Thus, four questions shape the remainder of this chapter: (1) What is our God like? (2) How do we come to know our God? (3) How does God's action for us affect our living? (4) Is what is described here truly a spirituality, and a spirituality of the heart?

What Is Our God Like?

Our God is not distant and remote, but immersed to the elbows in our materiality. In fact, God is as close as our breath. True, as the gnostics teach, one cannot apprehend the greatness and the depths of God. (Like a good debater, Irenaeus is always willing to concede such common ground as he shares with his opponent.) In those areas God is immeasurable, and quite literally out of our reach. On this point, Irenaeus and his opponents are in agreement with what will develop into the great tradition of apophatic theology typified by Pseudo-Dionysius. There has always been a place in the Christian tradition for emphasis on the transcendence of God that exceeds the limits of our thought and speech. In this sense God is indeed unknowable. It is the distorted claim that presents an absolutely transcendent and unknowable God hostile to the cosmos which Irenaeus rejects.

Consequently, our bishop turns to the other dimension, the immanence of God. While God remains unknown in greatness, God is always known in love. God is like a loving parent, whose strength and wisdom far exceed the comprehension of an infant, but who yet speaks tender words of love to that infant. Indeed, as the baby comes forth from its mother, so the world, in its very beginnings, came directly from the hands of the creator. The one God, the Father, used God's hands, the Word and the Wisdom (the Son and the Spirit), to create, to shape, and to adorn all things (*AH* 4, 20,1).[2] So too, God shaped the first human; it was God—and no lesser being—who breathed the breath of life into the face of that first human being and imprinted the divine image in its very flesh (*AH* 5, 6, 1). Far from being remote, God is immediate to us in our very materiality.

Not satisfied with molding us in our physicality and loving us in it, in the ripeness of time God's Word became one of us so as to join the end of creation, humankind, to its beginning, God. As Irenaeus expresses it, this "mixing and communion of God and humanity was done according to the good pleasure of the Father." Why was this done? "So that *homo*, embraced by the Spirit of God, might come into the glory of the Father" (*AH*

4, 20,4). As creation was a trinitarian work involving the Father and the two hands of God, so too the incarnation has roles for Word, Spirit, and Father. Also, note that in this text there is a deliberate surplus of meaning in the use Irenaeus makes of *homo;* this term designates at once the man Jesus, and all of humanity who are "summed up" or "recapitulated" in Jesus. The point at issue here is that the Word became a human being so that in the embrace of the Spirit we might enter the glory of the Father.

As Irenaeus develops his thought, it becomes clear that our entry into glory is central to experiencing the fullness of life, and it is equally clear that that entry into glory is dependent on the vision of God. In biblical terms, some may say this poses a dilemma, for on the one hand "Blessed are the pure of heart, for they will see God" (Mt 5:8), but on the other hand "No one will see God and live" (Ex 33:20). Here the bishop, confident of his insight into the biblical tradition, returns to his principle: God cannot be comprehended according to greatness, but only according to love. The fullness of God's majesty is unbearable for the creature; in that sense we will never see God. Yet because of the love that desires fullness of life for us, God has devised a way for us to enter into the vision little by little and according to our capacity. So the paradox: God remains unseen— but we do see God, and shall see God! Thus we come to glory.

Glory and vision are here connected like life and light. As the bishop of Lyons points out, those who see light are within light and share in its brightness; so, too, those who see God are within God and share God's brightness. As light gives life, so the brightness of God vivifies those on whom it shines. Life, true life, comes from participation in God. Thus Irenaeus tells us that "participation in God is to see God and to enjoy God's bountifulness" (*AH* 4, 20,5).

Just as our earthly eyes vary in their capacity to see, so too the capacity to see God varies, both for the human race across the span of time and for the individual across a lifetime. In terms of the race, the God who was seen once prophetically through the mediation of the Spirit is now seen adoptively through the mediation of the Son. In the kingdom of heaven, God will be seen paternally. This leading into vision is a work that God does directly, but of course with the help of the divine hands! Word and Wisdom have their essential roles to play (*AH* 4, 20,5–6).

The pattern holds not only for the human race, but also for each individual member. The Spirit prepares us for the Son, and it is the role of the Son to lead us to the Father, who delights in giving us the vision of God and the gifts associated with it. What are these gifts? The vision of God results in sharing the divine life, eternal life. For us mortals it means a share in what Irenaeus calls "incorruptibility."[3] When we look on the Father we will finally be wholly alive. It is along these lines that Irenaeus intends the famous text which in its entirety reads: "The glory of God is the living human person, and the life of the human person is the vision of God" (*AH* 4, 20,7).

In this understanding of God, the Father remains invisible to us until we enter the kingdom of heaven. The Son, his way prepared by the Spirit, makes the Father visible to us "adoptively" while on earth. Even on earth we carry the image of God in our flesh as an endowment from creation. Fullness of life for us consists in the vision of God. The path to that vision has been gradual for our race, and is so for each one of us. Before we look at the dynamic it entails in our daily living, it will be helpful if we understand the role of the Son in showing us the Father.

How Do We Come To See Our God?

We come to see our God in seeing Jesus. Jesus stands, as it were, in the doorway between two worlds. Through him time flows into eternity, and eternity into time. The Father sees in the man Jesus, who is his Son, *homo*—all of humanity. We, humankind, see in the man Jesus, who is our brother, the Son of God. Another way of putting this is that Jesus sums up or recapitulates in himself all of humanity. At the same time he makes visible and comprehensible the invisible and incomprehensible God. The majesty of God may remain remote, but the love of God has drawn so near as to suffer with and for us in the Word become a man. We know and see our God as we know and see Jesus Christ, God's Son, the Word made flesh (*AH* 3,16,6).

How is the Son the "visibilization" of the Father? Here Irenaeus turns to the text "No one knows the Son but the Father, nor does anyone know the Father but the Son, and those to whom the Son wishes to reveal him" (Mt 11:27). He draws an analogy between the human word, which articulates our knowledge (including self-knowledge), and the divine Word. The Father, who is invisible and inexpressible to us, is yet known and expressed by his own Word. Reciprocally, the divine Word is known in its fullness by the Father alone. This is the twofold truth Irenaeus finds in the text of Matthew 11:27 explaining how the Son reveals the Father in revealing himself (*AH* 4,6,1–3).

We come to know God, then, not by ourselves but with God's help. The initiative in revelation is on the side of God. On our side is freedom of choice, a freedom respected by divine judgment. The Father reveals the Son, and manifests himself through the Son, to all of humankind in order justly to welcome into eternal delight all who believe in him. (In this context to believe is to do the will of God.) With equal justice, the Father will cast into darkness those who do not believe and so flee the light. There is a fitting irony in the condemnation to darkness of those who fled light!

While fullness of life in the lightsome vision of God is our destiny, we are not compelled to accept it. It is possible to blind our eyes to the vision revealed by the Word. In molding the world, the creative Word revealed the creator, but not all believed. Through the law and the prophets the Word announced both himself and the Father, but not all believed. Finally, the Word became visible and palpable in Jesus Christ. Those who still fail to believe do not see the Father in the Son. Belief opens our eyes so that we recognize that "the invisible of the Son is the Father and the visible of the Father is the Son" (AH 4,6,6).

Those who do believe accept the gift won for us by Jesus Christ. Human like us, he was tested; Word of God, he had the capacity for the glorified life of incorruptibility and immortality. Only because the Son of God became Son of Man could we become children of God. Only because incorruptibility and immortality were united to us in Christ are we able to participate in them (AH 3,19,1). Irenaeus reminds us that as Christ the head has risen from the dead, so too the rest of the body will rise; all those found truly alive at the time of death will come to full vigor in resurrection thanks to the increase given by God (AH 3,19,3).

It is God's intent that we pass through all that life contains, including death, to come to resurrection, so that we learn by experience the evil from which we have been freed. In accepting the gifts of God we learn where our own glory lies. It is not just that God's glory is a living human person, so that God's presence shines out in giving life to us. It is also that our glory is the very God who works this way in us. So in receiving the action of God we come into the splendor that is ours, at the same time becoming most truly ourselves as we become what God has designed us to be.

God is the one in whom we reach this radiance, for we are the ones in whom God labors like a doctor among patients. To the extent that we submit to the divine physician's work in us we will receive from God who is our glory an even greater glory, progressively becoming like the one who died for us. The Son of God after all became Son of Man "to accustom humankind to know God and to accustom God to dwell in humankind, according to the good pleasure of the Father" (AH 3,20,2).

Notice how from creation through the coming of Jesus Christ all is ordered in the same direction: the entire divine plan or economy is designed to bring humankind to the life-giving vision of God. Every step of the way, from creation through the law and the prophets to Jesus Christ, is the work of the one same God who acts from love of us, calling us freely to believe and do the will of God that we might enter into full life. Our growth toward life is a healing and maturing process under the immediate care of a loving God.

All of this is quite different from the gnostic notion of an unknowable God remote from matter, distinct from the creator God of the Old Testament, with separate aeons named Jesus, Christ, Savior, Son, and Word. So, too, Irenaeus' stress on our freedom of choice contradicts the Valentinian concept of predestination, in the same way that the continuous growth of humankind through time toward eternal life contradicts the Valentinian discontinuity between life here and in the heavenly world. These divergences in characteristic positions on creation and the saving incarnation imply different spiritualities, different approaches to daily living. This leads us to our next topic.

How Does God's Action Affect Us in Our Daily Living?

Our glory is God who works within us to heal and to whole us, and God's glory is us, become completely alive. We come to this fullness of life by our growing in conformity with the Son of God, by our allowing the presence of God to touch the core of our daily life. To understand how this happens we must permit Irenaeus to teach us his understanding of the two key notions of image and likeness.

What Irenaeus teaches about these notions has as backdrop the Valentinian position that he is refuting. Remember that in the Valentinian view, each of the elect contains a spark from the heavenly world to which it will return once freed from matter and so from flesh. The spark, which is the Valentinian version of likeness to the divine, is spiritual and of the spirit. Granted this it should be no surprise to find Irenaeus holding that from the moment of creation the image of God rests in our very flesh. He accepts the biblical notion of a triadic composition of the human person; we are a union of flesh, soul, and spirit (1 Thes 5:23). For the bishop of Lyons "the perfect human being is the mingling and union of the soul which has received the Spirit of the Father and which has been united to the flesh which has been modeled according to the image of God" (*AH* 5,6,1). It is the very stuff that the creator shaped in the divine image which will glorify God.

Within this composition Irenaeus distinguishes image from likeness, and utilizes two meanings for likeness. One must analyze these distinctions to grasp the dynamic unfolding of the interior life in Irenaeus' view.[4]

To begin with there is the distinction between image and likeness. While the image is in the flesh, likeness is produced in the composite by the Spirit. The image and the likeness must both be present for there to be a complete human being. Lacking the Spirit, a person remains imperfect though possessing the image of God in the flesh. How could anyone without the likeness be whole? On the other hand, supposing one should seek to destroy the image and reject the flesh, what would the situation be then? In such a case it would not be possible even to recognize a human being, but only part of one. To reject the flesh is to reject precisely that which is central to our humanity.

Flesh, soul, and Spirit each has a role to play in making a complete human being. The flesh and the soul are each part of the human being whereas the Spirit is and remains the Spirit. The joining of the flesh made in the image of God and the soul forms the whole person made into the likeness by the Spirit (AH 5,6,1).

Quite obviously, without the flesh we are incomplete. This is so self-evident that to state it would demand apology, were it not for the repression and denial of the flesh that has haunted so much of Christian thought and practice. It is thus important to pause to notice the very high value Irenaeus attaches to the flesh. Not for him a body-rejecting spirituality! On the contrary, in his view our humanity in its very fleshliness is a dominant motif in every chapter of the story of humankind's relationship with God. In creation God's hands shaped the plasma we are into the divine image. Throughout revelation the Word came to us in ways increasingly palpable, until finally the invisible God became visible when the Word of God took humanity to himself, becoming a man in flesh like ours. The Son of God become Son of Man lived, suffered, died, and rose in human flesh. He nourishes us with his very flesh and blood in the eucharist.

How splendid is our flesh imprinted with the divine image! How beautiful is the flesh borne by the Son of God! How wondrous is our flesh made member of Christ in the baptismal water and fed with Christ in the eucharistic meal! How fitting it is that flesh so honored should be transformed by the Spirit and at last be raised up to taste incorruptibility and shine with the glory of God! It is the Spirit that is at work to bring this about, and it is through the work of the Spirit that the divine likeness is effected in us.

The notion of likeness in Irenaeus has two meanings (depending on the form of the underlying Greek word)[5] and carries with it the principle of growth that gives dynamism to his description of the Christian life. The first sense of likeness, here termed "similitude," refers to the way in which we are like the Father. The similitude between us and the Father is in freedom. He is free in his actions, and so we too have at our command the disposition of our actions (AH 4, 37,4). This is in contradistinction to the gnostic view that understands some humans as good by nature. We resemble the Father in our freedom in the same way the Son is like us in his humanity. The Son is truly human, and passed through every stage of our life, from newborn through childhood, youth, and maturity to death (*AH* 2, 22,4). As the Son knew true human growth, so we experience true divine freedom of choice.

Irenaeus notes that, if we were not free, there would be no meaning in God having imposed commandments on us. But God has done so, and, as the bishop remarks, "humankind is free from the beginning, for God is free in whose similitude humankind is made" (*AH* 4,37,4). Our freedom extends even to faith, which is why those who believe are rewarded with eternal life (*AH* 4, 37,5). Would we really enjoy communion with God acquired without effort or care? Irenaeus thinks not. Effort and care, after all, are the price of freedom (*AH* 4,37,6). Even if we use our freedom to sin, the similitude to the Father is ours inalienably; sin does not destroy it.

There is, however, a second sense in which likeness is affected by sin. Likeness in that sense is conferred by the presence of the Spirit, and it was lost to us in Adam; it was the task of the incarnate Word to restore the likeness (*AH* 5,9,1; 5,16, 2; 4,33,4). The call to greater glory is the call to grow into the likeness of the one who died for us (*AH* 3,20,2). In his death we were remade, and we receive from him the likeness to himself, as well as the gift that is his to bestow, the gift of incorruptibility (*AH* 5, pref-5,1,1).

In the similitude which is the principle of self-determination and the likeness which involves the call of the Spirit to growth—in these two factors lies the dynamism of the spiritual life.

Such are the basics of our constitution: we are so made that our flesh is in the image of God, our souls are imprinted with an inalienable similitude to the Father in our freedom of action, and—to the extent that we are whole—we bear an all too alienable likeness to God. Sin cost humanity its divine likeness, but Christ's redemptive incarnation and death has won it back.

How then do we live out our call and exercise our freedom? Is it possible for humans in their entirety, including flesh and blood, to enter the kingdom? "Not so" answer the gnostics, who base their position on Paul: "flesh and blood will not inherit the kingdom of God" (1 Cor 15:50). In response to this gnostic position, Irenaeus develops his interpretation of that text, working from his understanding of the threefold composition of the human person, with the dynamic role of the Spirit which he holds this composition includes.

The dynamic of Christian life is the dynamic of life in the Spirit. It is the work of the Spirit to model humankind into the likeness of God (Pr.5).[6] The Spirit is the lifegiver. Our flesh is weak, but when we are docile to the Spirit, the Spirit absorbs our weakness, and those who look on us see instead the power of the Spirit shining forth, as happened, for instance, with the martyrs (*AH* 5, 9, 2).[7]

Be that as it may, he holds that the Spirit, absorbing our weakness, in turn possesses the flesh for itself. Our very flesh is joined to the Spirit. So Irenaeus tells us: "From the two comes the living human being: living, because of the participation of the Spirit; human, because of the substance of the flesh" (*AH* 5, 9, 2). This is the human person in the likeness of God. Such is what we are called to become as we grow toward the fullness of life that will be ours in glory.

The process of growth in the image and likeness of God is a key concept, since we began as children (both as a race and as individuals). In this process we come to know good, which consists in obeying God, keeping the commandments in docility. Here is life in response to the Spirit. Yet we also come to know evil. Irenaeus explains that, just as the tongue learns by tasting to distinguish sweet from bitter and the eye by looking comes to discern black from white, so the spirit acquires the knowledge of good by experiencing both good and evil. Wiser, then, from knowledge of both, one will be most attentive to obeying God, for knowing where sweetness lies one will not want to taste again the bitterness of disobedience (*AH* 4, 39,1). Irenaeus is ever the optimist.

Humans as human, and so fleshly, are called to the fullness of resurrection life. Dead flesh cannot enter the kingdom of God; dead flesh will not see God or share in glory. However, "where there is the Spirit of the Father, there there is a living human being" (*AH* 5,9,3); flesh possessed by the Spirit in a sense forgets its mortality to become what the Spirit is. Then it becomes capable of the gift of incorruptibility won for it by the death of Jesus Christ.

Basic to our life in the Spirit is submission to God; from this ultimately comes incorruptibility, and so glory. What is the pattern of our life? Irenaeus summarizes it in this beautiful extended passage:

> Such is then the order, such the rhythm, such is the movement by which shaped and formed humankind is made according to the image and likeness of the uncreated God: the Father decides and commands, the Son executes and models, the Spirit nourishes and gives increase, and humankind progresses little by little, and grows toward perfection; that is, it comes near to perfection, for the only perfect is the uncreated, and that is God. As to humankind, it is necessary that first it should be made, that having been made it should grow, that having grown it become adult, that having become adult it multiply, that having multi-

plied it become strong, that having become strong it should be glorified, and finally that having been glorified it should see its Lord: for it is God who must be seen, for the vision of God gives incorruptibility, and "incorruptibility brings one near to God (Wis 6:19)." (*AH* 4, 38, 3).

Father, Son, and Spirit work to bring the race and each member of the race to glory. The Father commands, the Son executes, and the Spirit nurtures. Humankind, and each human being, grow little by little toward God. Every stage of the journey marks a step on the path leading to the glorification which comes from the vision of God and the gift of incorruptibility.

A Spirituality of the Heart?

What Irenaeus describes is a life subject to the Spirit leading humans to God. Father, Son, and Spirit, while remaining transcendent in majesty, are yet intimately involved in the human drama from the moment of creation until its dénouement in the face to face vision of the Father. The Father, using only his hands, the Son and the Spirit, who are the Word and Wisdom of God, shapes and models the first humans imprinting the divine image in their very flesh. Not only is humankind directly made by God; the Word became one of us so that in the embrace of the Spirit we might enter into the glory of the Father.

The glory to which we are destined is connected with vision as life is connected with light. True life comes from participation in God through vision. This is a gradual thing for us; once God was seen by the Spirit through the prophets' work, then God became visible in the Son, and in heaven God will be seen "paternally." The Spirit prepares each of us for the Son who leads us to the Father; the Father gives us the vision and the fullness of life in incorruptibility connected with it. Then, sharing in the vision of God, we will be the glory of God that is the human person fully alive for we will be living by the life of the Spirit.

Jesus Christ, the Word made flesh, being one of us presents us to the Father in his own person, and being Son of God makes the Father visible to us. God wills that we accept the revelation offered us in Jesus and believe in him, but we remain free to reject it. If we believe, we will become able to share in the gifts he won for us, including the incorruptibility that is eternal life. Accepting his gifts teaches us where our glory is; our glory is God for we are the ones in whom God, working like a good physician, exercises the divine wisdom and power to bring us to wholeness of life. What is thus described is certainly a spirituality if by that we mean a way of life subject to the Spirit and leading humans to God.

Is this spirituality a spirituality of the heart? Yes, it incorporates the totality of the human person and respects the dynamism of human living. Irenaeus holds that in our completeness we are the union of the soul which has received the Spirit of the Father with the flesh shaped in the image of God. It is this complete formation of soul, Spirit, and flesh which is the human person in the likeness of God. As the flesh is in the image of God so the soul bears a similitude to the Father in its freedom, the freedom by which it knows good and evil and so in coming to maturity comes to accept the Spirit who molds the totality of the person into the divine likeness.

At the core of the dynamism of human living there is a twofold action. On our side, the action is that of human freedom maturing under God. On God's side, it is the action of the divine physician, Father, Son, and Spirit at work in us to bring us in all we are, through the knowledge of good and evil, to the fullness of life in the vision of God. It is clear that both the completeness of the human person and the dynamism of human living are accounted for in this spirituality which is truly a spirituality of the heart.

At the heart of life is glory: the glory of humankind, which is the living God, and the glory of God, which is a human being come fully alive in the vision of God. At the heart of life, glory!

NOTES

1. For a useful presentation of gnosticism, see Kurt Rudolph, *Gnosis*, translated and edited by Robert McLachlan Wilson (Edinburgh: Clark, 1983).

   The concern here is not with whether or not Irenaeus is a reliable witness to gnostic teaching, but with the way in which he presented his own thought, shaped by what he understood gnostic teaching to be.

2. Reference is to *Adversus haereses*, identified here and throughout by the sigla *AH*, and then by book, chapter, and section.

   Adversus haereses is Irenaeus' major extant work. The critical edition is Adelin Rousseau, ed., with Bertrand Hemmerdinger, Louis Doutreleau, and Charles Mercier, *Contre les Hérésies* 4, tomes 1 and 2, Sources Chrétiennes 100 (Paris: Cerf, 1965). Adelin Rousseau, Louis Doutreleau, and Charles Mercier, eds., *Contre les Hérésies* 5, tomes 1 and 2, Sources Chrétiennes 152, 153 (Paris: Cerf, 1969). Adelin Rousseau and Louis Doutreleau, eds., *Contre les Hérésies* 3, tomes 1 and 2, Sources Chrétiennes 210, 211 (Paris: Cerf, 1974); ibid., 1, tomes 1 and 2, Sources Chrétiennes 263, 264 (Paris: Cerf, 1979); and ibid., 2, tomes 1 and 2, Sources Chrétiennes 293, 294 (Paris: Cerf, 1982).

The only available English translation is that in Alexander Roberts and James Donaldson, editors, *The Ante-Nicene Fathers*, vol. 1 (Grand Rapids, Michigan: Eerdmans, reprinted 1973), pp. 309–567. The fragments of the lost works of Irenaeus are also translated here, pp. 568–578.

3. See Ysabel de Andia's recent study: *Homo Vivens: Incorruptibilité et divinisation de l'homme selon Irénée de Lyon* (Paris: Etudes Augustiniennes, 1986).

4. For selection of texts as well as interpretation in this section, I am indebted to Jacques Fantino *L'homme image de Dieu chez saint Irénée de Lyon* (Paris: Cerf, 1986), pp. 110–143.

5. The distinction is between *homoiotes* (similitude) and *homoiosis* (likeness). Fantino writes: "Le terme similitudo, dans le cas de la relation de l'homme à Dieu, peut avoir plusieurs significations. En référence à l'humanité du Christ, il traduit la similitude (*homoiotes*) de celle-ci avec celle de tous les hommes (cf. adv 2, 22,4). En rapport avec Dieu le Père, similitudo exprime la similitude (*homoiotes*) existant entre la liberté humaine et la liberté divine (cf. adv 4,37,4). Cette liberté rend possible le don fait à l'homme de la ressemblance (*homoiosis*) (cf. adv 3, 20, 2): celle-ci est établie entre l'homme et le Fils incarné (cf. adv 4,33,4/ 5,16, 2) et par celui-ci il est à la ressemblance du Père" (p. 116; see also pp. 106–118).

6. The reference is to the *Proof of the Apostolic Preaching*, a minor work, available in the Ancient Christian Writers edition: Joseph P. Smith, S.J., translator and annotator, *St. Irenaeus: Proof of the Apostolic Preaching*, Ancient Christian Writers, No. 16 (New York: Newman, 1952).

7. Here Irenaeus could easily have been thinking of the powerful example of Blandina, martyred at Lyons in 177 just before he became bishop. This woman in her Spirit-given strength inspired her martyr companions to courage. The story of Blandina's heroism is told by Eusebius, *Ecclesiastical History* 5,1,4–61.

Mary T. Clark, R.S.C.J.

Augustine:
The Eye of the Heart

In religious art Augustine is frequently pictured with a book and heart. This heart signifies his own religious experience as an evolution into human wholeness in his approach to God. Through a long conversion he was able to unify his mind and will and feelings into a single-hearted desire for God. In Augustine's spirituality the heart stands for the totality of the human being as responsive to God's love in Christ and in the indwelling Spirit: it is a tenderness toward God. Only gradually did Augustine realize that affection was more effective than knowledge for union with God. He then held out hope for the seeing of God even in this life through the eye of the heart, through human interiority opened by love to respond to God's presence in all things. Augustine's approach to God became the prayer of the heart—a desire, a longing to be one with Christ, open to the Father.

Early Efforts

The book in portraits of Augustine has its own significance. Early in life Augustine was directed by the *Libri Platonicorum* to the eyes of his mind. In following this direction he left his exterior pursuits to discover his "interiority" which at that time meant for him the finding of his own mind, and, by means of it, making an effort to encounter God. The entire Greek tradition had likened the mind to the eye, the organ of seeing and looking. This act of seeing was accomplished, however, only in the presence of light, and what was accomplished was the imaging of the object seen, dependent upon the self-disclosure of being, the truth of being. Acts of knowing lead the human being into the realm of the universal. There is a certain desertion of the body in the act of knowing, a fusion of the knower and the known. We have Augustine's own account of his efforts to follow the directives of the philosophers.

> And admonished by all this to return to myself, I entered into my inmost part, with You as leader . . . and saw, with my mind's eye, an unchangeable light. . . . And you beat back the weakness of my gaze. . . . And I knew myself to be far from You in the region of unlikeness.[1]

This famous passage of the *Confessions* is a classic description of the attempt, prompted by the Platonic books, to see God only with the eye of the mind; and it is an admission of failure. Also stated in the same paragraph is the prescription for any successful knowing of God who is truth. "Love knows it," says Augustine. Yet he acknowledged that he was distant from God, estranged. He was without that love which likens one to God and enables one to experience union with him, to see him with the eye of the heart.

For love to be enkindled in the heart of Augustine he had to accept the divinity and leadership of Christ. The Word became flesh to meet persons in their exteriority and to lead them to that interiority where the heart can be enkindled with love for God. Augustine came to realize that knowledge alone would never renew him as an image of the God who is love.

In the *Confessions* Augustine shows a growing awareness of love's importance. When he begins to comment on the fourth gospel we see him realizing love's role in leading from faith to that knowledge that is *sapientia*, where mind and will are united. This wisdom is a practical knowledge, a "doing the truth in charity." It is that living faith which brings understanding. "Faith seeking understanding" is an expression often associated with Augustine, and at times people use it to characterize him as an "intellectual." What is omitted from this picture is his mature position that faith finds understanding only by way of love.

Of course Augustine believes that knowledge has been promised: "And this is eternal life, that they may know thee, the only true God, and Jesus Christ whom thou hast sent" (Jn 17:3). Yet if there is desire for knowledge of God, the motive may be either curiosity or love. But the knowing that is eternal life comes about only through love of God. Such was the love the martyrs had in their desire to know God. And Augustine says that it is not the revolting spectacle that we celebrate on feasts of the martyrs, but their single-hearted love for God, of which there is nothing "more fair if you ask the eyes of the heart."[2]

Understanding, Augustine gradually realized, is the reward of faith, and faith is alive when God and neighbor are loved. This is the will of God as expressed in both the Old and the New Testaments: "Thou shalt love the Lord thy God with thy whole heart, thy whole soul, thy whole mind, and thy neighbor as thyself. And the Lord has said: If any man be willing to do His will, he shall know of the doctrine."[3] This is the evangelical meaning of believing in order to understand. "Not any faith of any kind, but 'faith that works by love'; let this faith be in you . . . and you shall understand that Christ, the Son of God, who is the Word of the Father is not from Himself but is the Son of the Father."[4] So all those who have the faith which works through love will be "worshipers of the Trinity and unity of Father, Son, and Holy Spirit, and one God."[5]

Role of Love

This love which provides understanding enables the believer to see with the eye of the heart. Commenting on St. John's gospel, Augustine firmly teaches that spiritual progress is measured by love:

> . . . seek to grow in the love that is shed abroad in your hearts by the Holy Spirit who is given unto you. . . . For that cannot be loved which is altogether unknown. But when what is known, in however small a measure, is also loved, by that very love one is led on to a better and fuller knowledge. If then you grow in the love which the Holy Spirit spreads abroad in your heart, He will teach you all truth.[6]

And Augustine reminds us that this fullness of truth will not be ours until the time that we see God "face to face." With the Spirit's presence in the soul, however, the pledge of this fullness is ours. This presence roots and grounds the human person in love, bringing the promise: " 'You may be able with all the saints to comprehend what is the length and breadth and height and depth, even to know the love of Christ which surpasses all knowledge, that you may be filled with all the fullness of God.' For in such a way will the Holy Spirit teach you all truth, when He shall shed abroad that love ever more and more largely in your hearts."[7]

By his gift of love the Spirit confers a likeness to Christ and enables persons to become true members of the mystical body, the church whose sacraments, according to Augustine, provide the means of continual growth toward an ever closer union with Christ. The head and members of the total Christ are united invisibly and visibly. Members look to their head for guidance. It is sometimes said that the commandment called "new" by Christ—". . . a new commandment I give unto you, that you should love one another as I have loved you"—is really not new because it was among the commandments given to Moses. But Augustine recognized in the phrase "as I have loved you" the reason for calling this commandment new. First of all, Christ loved his enemies, those who had sinned against him;[8] second, he was the exemplar who was making possible that likeness to God which was a feature of the first creation; third, he offered a new motive in the love of neighbor, his own motive: that God may be all in all.[9]

When this new commandment is obeyed, it renews the image of God where the likeness has been obscured by sin. In this way love transforms human persons into Christians or other Christs. This insight came to Augustine by the recalling of his renewal through *caritas*.[10] To allow love to rule one's life, the Christian, like Augustine, finds that an ascetic and moral life is indispensable. Many approach God, therefore, less by intellectual effort than by moral effort. "He who does the truth comes to the light" (Jn 3:21).

And as the transformation into Christ continues with the increase of love, the likeness brings spiritual beauty. For is not Christ "beauteous, in loveliness surpassing the sons of men?" (Ps 45:2) In loving God a person becomes lovely. "What love must that be that makes the lover beautiful!"[11] He first loved us and enabled us to love. "He loved us who were ungodly, to make us godly; loved us who were unrighteous, to make us righteous; loved us who were sick, to make us whole."[12]

Love purifies the eye of the heart so that one may see God. Augustine teaches that anyone who does not see God is someone who does not love him, and there is no love for him where there is no love for neighbor. "For if he have love, he sees God, for 'love is God': and that eye is becoming more and more cleansed by love, to see that Unchangeable Substance, in the presence of Whom he shall always rejoice, Whom he shall enjoy everlastingly when he joins the angels."[13]

Only the obeying of the second commandment allows one to obey perfectly the first. In doing this the heart is purified for the divine vision.[14] In this life, however, it is a question not of vision but of union with the triune God. It is by Christ that we receive the Holy Spirit of love and thereby know Father, Son and Spirit by way of likeness, by a graced connaturality. One then participates in trinitarian life, the life that beautifies. This is truly personal life, a life of love, self-gift, generating the Son to others, responding to the Father, and, in its infinite and eternal reality of love, being the Holy Spirit, the gift of divine or generous love to humankind, *agape* and *caritas*.

Relating to God

Father, Son, and Spirit—three by being mutually referred to one another, equal, and each within the other. So likewise is the human person a reference to God. Adam was certainly created in original blessing when he was created to the image and likeness of God. But this situation is not preserved except in relation to him by whom this likeness is impressed. Original sin broke the relationship and lost the likeness to God. Persons are only authentic images, that is, true likenesses, when they remember God, understand and love him. If persons do not know themselves as images of God, they lose themselves and become self-alienated.

A true relating to God requires faith and charity—wisdom. The natural presence in all things of God "in whom we live and move and have our being" is the ontological ground for the actual remembering of God. A ground also is our natural creation to the image of God, entailing, as it does, a dynamic tendency toward one's exemplar, God. Even the impious retain the capacity to think of and long for God, a capacity for entering the Trinity's life of love which by creation the divine persons offered to human beings. Perfect likeness is reserved for the afterlife, but now the likeness is ever growing by the grace of *caritas* when the capacity is actuated by the Holy Spirit who purifies the eye of the heart for the eternal vision.

The image in the human person is formed by God the Father, reformed by God the Son, and conformed or clarified by the Holy Spirit who pours charity into the hearts of the faithful. Through the gifts of the Holy Spirit a Christian matures, and through the gift of wisdom can perceive God's presence within the self and in all things.

Thus, Augustine's treatise on the Trinity, completed, as it was, some time after his early discussion of the Trinity in his commentary on the fourth gospel, was intended as an exercise in prayer and hope for all Christians for whom the Trinity was revealed not to satisfy the mind but to awaken affection in the heart. The mind, however, is not belittled. Allusions are made to the importance of reflection upon the Trinity if one is to attain the end of human life by understanding its meaning. In his final chapter on the Trinity, Augustine wrote: "To the remembering, seeing, loving of that supreme Trinity, that one may recall it, contemplate it, and delight in it, the whole of one's life ought to be referred."[15]

It is often said that the Greek fathers emphasize the persons of the Trinity whereas Augustine stressed the unity of their nature. It is notable, however, that Augustine's spiritual doctrine which unites the mysteries of salvation and of sanctification in the doctrine of the "image"—that is, the creation of every person to the image of the Trinity: "let *us* make man to *our* image and likeness" (Gen 1:26)—requires the distinction of persons in the Trinity.

Spiritual Growth

Augustine's teachings on spiritual growth find their unification in this image-doctrine, with the human mind as the source of the image and the human heart as the source of the likeness. The affective aspect of this image-doctrine highlights the centrality of love in Augustine's spirituality. Only in the light of divine revelation is the human person properly understood. For a person is only properly understood as having been created to the image and likeness of God with capacity for friendship with the divine persons and human persons insofar as a human person can participate through grace in the Trinity's self-giving.

Augustine had found in Neoplatonism a theological philosophy. His own Christian Platonism, however, was inspired by the Incarnate Word who revealed God's love for every human being. The Eternal Word or Divine Intelligence (*Nous*) sufficed for Plotinus to appreciate the individual human soul, but it was through the Incarnate Word that Augustine became able to appreciate the dignity and the value of the whole person— body and soul. And this he finally did appreciate, although he never succeeded in explaining the union of body and soul. Platonism was in a certain sense converted when the exemplar of all realities, but especially of the human person, became flesh and dwelt among us and offered friendship to persons of good will. Through good will, the willing of the good, the loving of neighbor, the eye of the heart is gradually purified to see God. "Blessed are the pure of heart for they shall see God" (Mt 5:8). The pure of heart are those who love God and neighbors as themselves, wanting for neighbors what they want for themselves, friendship with God.

Through his exegesis of the fourth gospel, Augustine converted the Platonic doctrine of the subordinate *Nous*, which illuminates human intelligence, to the Christian doctrine of equality with the Father of the Word or Son, who saves the entire human person by becoming incarnate. The love that was only hinted at by Plotinus in some off-guard moments in the Sixth *Ennead*, Augustine discovered in scripture to be explicitly stated, a love that enkindled his own and increased his desire for God and gave him a longing heart. This love was a weight, a *pondus*, a force of gravitation toward the First Principle, a force experienced by the human being as a rational desire for union with God and an affective tendency toward God. This desire is realized through the Spirit's gift of *caritas*. It is a weight in the sense that the truth that love is the supreme value prevails or weighs upon the human consciousness. This *pondus*, an analogy drawn from the physical world, is far removed from deterministic physical forces. Augustine realized that if love is the motive for creation, a free creation, then love is the only proper response for the creature to go to God. And love is always the gift of freedom.

Augustine therefore became a theologian of the heart in teaching that love unifies persons and draws them to their last end. This love is exemplified in Christ. It is defined in the fourth gospel as the very nature of God. It is the central revelation of all scriptures. From whom does the Christian receive the divine love or *caritas* that both likens a person to the Trinity and brings union with God except from God who is love? Likewise, no one can receive existence except from God who is existence (*esse*). God, St. Paul tells us, diffuses love in our hearts by the Holy Spirit and has sent the Holy Spirit into his church to continue the giving of *caritas*, so that there always may be spiritual growth and spiritual perfection.

The love advocated by Augustine was not just any kind of love. It was an ordered love. "He ordered charity in me" (Cant 2:4). In the order of love, God is to be loved above all things, and persons are to be loved as Christ loved them, and all else loved according to God's will. In the last book of the *Confessions* Augustine engages the authority of Paul to propose the "more excellent way" of charity, the "supereminent knowledge of the love of Christ." And so he prayed: "Give Yourself to me, my God, and give Yourself back to me. See, I love, and if my love is too little, I would love more. I cannot measure it so as to know how much my love falls short of what is enough for my life to run to your embraces and never be turned away until it is 'hidden in the hidden place of Thy presence.' "[16]

Conclusion

Two scriptural texts are the source of Augustine's spirituality of the heart, that is, of the role of the heart in the knowledge of God. St. Paul spoke of the "eyes of your heart being enlightened" (Eph 1:18).[17] And Christ said: "Blessed are the pure in heart, for they shall see God" (Mt 5:8).

Now, Augustine often warns his listeners that they should not confuse the eyes of the heart with bodily eyes. Nor does Augustine associate the heart in this phrase with a physiological organ. For him the heart seems to be the inner person, the soul. It is, however, a human soul with the capacity for loving God and human persons by will and feeling. "Return to your heart," Augustine preached; "see there what . . . you can perceive of God, for in it is the image of God . . . recognize its Author."[18] The heart signifies an ardent soul—understanding, desiring, loving.

The eye of the heart is opened through God's incarnation. To see God, the eyes of the heart need to be healed and they need light. "By His birth He made an eye-salve to cleanse the eyes of our heart, and to enable us to see His majesty by means of His humility."[19] What may we see in this humble Christ? "The glory of the only-begotten from the Father, full of grace and truth."[20] Through the incarnation of the divine Son one gains a believing heart. And when faith seeks understanding and works through love of neighbor, it attains understanding. Love provides the light for the soul to see God.

Ever since it was said that the pure in heart will see God, people have probed the meaning of this. Other parts of the gospel illuminate it. In the fourth gospel we learn that faith working through love purifies the heart to see God. Once upon a time Augustine had tried to contemplate directly, and later he taught that the vision of God comes only after death. But in sketching the spirituality of the heart in his commentary on the fourth gospel he realized that even on earth God may be seen with the eyes of the heart by one who has been unified by a single longing for God.

Human hearts, he tells us, have a capacity to lay hold on that which "eye hath not seen, nor ear heard. . . ."[21] For this we can prepare both negatively and positively. Shut the ears of the heart against the wiles of the enemy, and open the eyes of the heart to see God.[22] Then look at the most beautiful things God has made, and let the eye of your heart visualize the beauty of the Word who made them.[23]

The faith and charity needed to purify the eyes of our hearts are God's own gift. "Not our merits but God's mercy purifies the heart that it may see God."[24] And so Augustine asked his congregation to pray for that faith which heals the eye of the heart. Yet even when the eye is healed by faith, there is need of light to see God. This light, as we have seen, comes from loving one's neighbor. One does not see God unless one loves him, and he has said that one cannot truly love him unless one loves one's neighbor. "The love of God comes first in the order of enjoying, but in the order of doing the love of our neighbor comes first."[25] In loving one's neighbor there is light for seeing God.

The motivation for the love of neighbor can arise in the realization of the value God places on each human being. Everyone has been created by God as an act of love; everyone has been offered salvation by Christ through his death on the cross. In creating us, God proclaimed our value. And what has Christ said of our value? "He counted me of some importance, that He was born as a mortal man to make me immortal."[26] "Look for the source of your love of your neighbor—there you will see God."[27] Then give your hearts to the Lord to be filled with love. We are filled with love when, through grace, we participate in the life of the Trinity. We are then risen from the dead and alive in Christ. This resurrection of the soul seeds our hope for the body's resurrection. "They who give you life are the Father and the Son; and the first resurrection is accomplished when you rise to partake of that which you yourself are not, and by partaking become alive. Rise from your death to eternal life."[28] In this way did Augustine encourage his congregation to fill their hearts with love so that they might see God.

By the love the Holy Spirit pours into Christian hearts at baptism we are empowered to grow in the faith that works through love until we spontaneously see God in his images, our neighbors and ourselves. This we do with the eyes of the heart, the heart standing for the human person as a unity of mind, will and affection. Augustine had to accept every part of himself as created and loved by God before he could surrender himself to God. In the surrender of love he was unified. The biblical notion of *cor* as uniting flesh and spirit for union with God inspires Augustine's spirituality of the heart.

NOTES

1. Augustine, *Confessions*, 7.10. J.P. Migne, *Patrologia Latina*, Paris: 32, 659–868; *Corpus Scriptorum Ecclesiasticorum Latinorum*, Vienna; 33, 1–388; crit. ed. M. Skutella, Leipzig: Teubner, 1934.
2. *Homilies on St. John's Gospel, 3.21*. PL 35, 1379–1976; *Corpus Christianorum*, Series Latina, The Hague: Nijhoff 1953–　, 36.
3. *John's Gospel*, 29.6.
4. *John's Gospel*, 29.6.
5. *John's Gospel*, 29.7.
6. *John's Gospel*, 96.5.
7. *John's Gospel*, 96.5.
8. *Homilies on St. John's Epistle*, 9.9. L.PL 35, 1977–2062.
9. *John's Gospel*, 84.3.
10. *Sermons*, 34.6 PL 38, 23–1484; 39, 1493–1736; 46, 817–10004; 47, 1189–1248.
11. *John's Epistle*, 9.9.
12. *John's Epistle*, 9.10.
13. *John's Epistle*, 9.10.
14. *City of God*, 17.7 PL 41, 13–804; CSEL 40, I, 3–660; II, 1–67. crit. ed. E. Dombart and A. Kalb, Leipsig: Teubner, 1928–29. C.C. 47–48 (1955).
15. *The Trinity*, 15.20.39. PL 42, 819–1098.
16. *Conf.* 13.8.
17. *John's Gospel*, 18.10.

18. *John's Gospel*, 18.10.
19. *John's Gospel*, 2.16.
20. *John's Gospel*, 2.16.
21. *John's Gospel*, 1.4.
22. *John's Gospel*, 1.15.
23. *John's Gospel*, 1.7.
24. *John's Gospel*, 2.16.
25. *John's Gospel*, 17.8.
26. *John's Gospel*, 2.15.
27. *John's Gospel*, 17.8.
28. *John's Gospel*, 19.3.

Elizabeth Dreyer

Bonaventure the Franciscan: An Affective Spirituality[1]

One of the challenges of the modern western world, and of contemporary theology and spirituality in particular, is the recovery of our awareness of affectivity.[2] Our interest in this and related areas of "the heart" may reflect the psychic hunger of an over-rationalized culture. Many seek to recover the affective dimensions of a theology too divorced from lived Christian life.[3] Bernard Lonergan analyzes feelings as the cause of our response to value.[4] Karl Rahner speaks of ultimate happiness as acceptance of mystery in love.[5] John Dunne includes affectivity as a central element in his theological method.[6] Today, scholars from a variety of disciplines study symbol and affective channels which give us access to these images.[7]

This renewed interest has led to an awareness of the need for more thorough historical analysis in the area of *affectus*.[8] Increased knowledge and understanding of the tradition can provide necessary information and a more secure foundation for statements about the role of *affectus* in theology and in the Christian life today. Bonaventure is an apt subject for this task. He is a figure who precedes the bifurcation of dogmatic and ascetic or spiritual theology. He clung to the Augustinian, Neoplatonic tradition, sensitive to image and symbol, and at home with feeling. And, perhaps above all, Bonaventure was a Franciscan to the core.

In spite of the differences between Francis and Bonaventure— differences of time, temperament, education—Bonaventure retained a deep reverence for Francis and manifested some of his warm, affective qualities. The appeal of the heart was as strong in some ways in Bonaventure as in Francis, although it is often hidden in the scholastic forms of a university professor. Bonaventure used the newly discovered rational discourse of Aristotle, but at the same time seemed fearful that such an approach would lead to the diminution or loss of the world of the scriptures, with its stories and poetic language that appealed to the heart.

Although Bonaventure's spirituality is clothed in medieval garments, distant and often foreign to modern idiom, I believe that his spirituality can truly be called a spirituality of the heart. It would be a mistake to include in this category only those spiritualities that have the heart itself as a central symbol. On the broad canvas of history, many ideas, images and sentiments have been associated with the heart. While there are numerous methodologies by which one could approach the topic of the heart in Bonaventure, I will be examining Bonaventure's understanding of *affectus*, since affect/feeling are primary elements associated with the heart. In this sense, Bonaventure stands as a precursor to contemporary understandings of the ways of the heart, and knowledge of his work can serve to ground and enhance the practice of the spiritual life today.

In this chapter, I will examine the ways in which *affectus* functions in the spirituality of Bonaventure. Although I will be using the term "spirituality," one could as easily and accurately use the term "theology" since for Bonaventure, theology and what today we call "spirituality" were intimately related.

Affectus is important, in Bonaventure's eyes, to all aspects of the spiritual life—the virtues, the gifts, the beatitudes. But here I will be able to treat only two topics, both of which are central to Bonaventure's portrayal of the spiritual life: (1) the role of *affectus* in Bonaventure's thought on the Holy Spirit; (2) the ways in which *affectus* functions in Bonaventure's spirituality, particularly the way it relates to its mystical contemplative aspects.

1. The Holy Spirit and Affectus

Bonaventure's spirituality is suffused with trinitarian themes. Since the tradition (and Bonaventure) connects the Holy Spirit with affectivity in a distinctive way, I will give more explicit attention to the Spirit, but will keep in mind the broader context of the trinity of persons.

Bonaventure mentions four ways of knowing and naming the divine properties and relations within the Trinity. The first way includes the common and essential properties belonging absolutely to the divine essence, e.g. deity. The second way includes personal and relative properties constituting the divine persons, i.e. their relations and distinctions. The third way includes common properties attributed to one or another of the persons by reason of origin or order. In this way, for instance, goodness is appropriated to the Holy Spirit who is personally and properly Love, uniting Father and Son. The fourth way includes personal properties appropriated to the divine essence as it is referred to an extrinsic effect in creation. That is, this way refers in part to the temporal mission of the Holy Spirit coming to the church at Pentecost, and it is under this fourth category that Bonaventure speaks of the affective qualities of the Holy Spirit.[9]

By virtue of this temporal mission as teacher of truth, the Holy Spirit has a proper role in the constitution of the science and wisdom of theology. As Holy Spirit, this Spirit nurtures in us a life of holiness and makes us spiritual temples of the Trinity. As Gift, the Spirit gives every grace, perfects in us the image of Christ, and completes our conformity to the Trinity. As Love, the Spirit binds the church in faith and charity to the incarnate Word. In general, then, the Holy Spirit's role is to sanctify the church, to give it Christ's grace and to teach it divine truth. It is under this fourth category that Bonaventure speaks of the affective qualities of the Holy Spirit.

In the second article of distinction 10 in Book I of his *Commentary on the Sentences*, Bonaventure asks whether love or charity is something proper to the Holy Spirit. He distinguishes three types of love in God: essential love, by which each person in the Trinity loves individually (*complacentia*); notional love, by which the Father and Son are in harmony in spirating the Holy Spirit (*dilectatio*); and personal love, which is the Holy Spirit because this Spirit who is produced by way of perfect generosity (*liberalitas*) cannot be other than love or delectation.[10] In God, that which proceeds in the harmony of the Father and the Son is "truly and properly love (*amor*)."[11]

Bonaventure also teaches that the Holy Spirit is properly called the bond (*nexus*) or unity of Father and Son because Father and Son communicate in one Spirit. The Spirit is also Love. Therefore, the communication of Father and Son in the Spirit is in one love, which is most properly a bond. The spirit is their mutual love, a unique and "substantified" love. Bonaventure sees this role of bond in a passive sense. For him, the verb "to join together" (*nectere*) can signify passion even in its active form. The Spirit is bond in this passive sense inasmuch as it proceeds from the Father and the Son, receiving from them, not giving something to them. That the Spirit is Love is an effect and not a cause vis-à-vis the Father and Son. In the phrase, "Pater et Filius diligunt se Spiritu Sancto," Bonaventure argues that the verb *diligere* is to be taken in a notional rather than in an essential sense.

In a notional name, there are two elements: (1) the fact of proceeding and (2) the mode of emanation. *Spirare* designates only emanation, while *diligere* further suggests the mode of procession. The latter implies the act of connecting or of being in harmony in spirating, and it is in this sense that Bonaventure understands the connection of Father and Son in love by the Holy Spirit. By spirating the Holy Spirit, the Father and Son are joined in mutual love. The Holy Spirit, then, is seen as a passive bond, a bond forged in and by the loving harmony of Father and Son, a bond which is the product of their common love.

Bonaventure's trinitarian thought relies more heavily on the traditions of Richard of St. Victor and the Pseudo-Dionysius than on that of Augustine. Both Augustine and Richard base their analyses of the Trinity on psychological experience. But Richard's primary orientation is not toward an analysis of human cognitional experience, but rather toward an analysis of the nature of love. He thus chose an element that was marginal in Augustine and made it central to his own trinitarian doctrine. Bonaventure follows Richard, emphasizing the goodness of God, charity, and the nature of love, but he stamps this material with his own distinctive insights and develops them extensively within the overall cohesion of his theology/spirituality.[12]

Bonaventure's theology also reflects a trinitarian character in that he sees theology itself as comprising three forms of knowledge. The first is the science of scripture, the second is the science of faith, and the third is the wisdom of faith, proceeding from the other two forms of knowledge and uniting them by a bond of charity. This third kind of knowledge is important for our purposes, since love is its key element, ordering the whole of theological knowledge to contemplation of God in ecstatic love (RHS 275–76).

This third form of theological knowledge, the wisdom of faith, is a loving contemplation of God. The practical wisdom of theology includes not only a knowledge of God attained through Christian piety or through divine worship in faith, hope, and charity, but also an experiential knowledge of divine goodness which is made known by the Holy Spirit in the gift of wisdom. This gift unites in love the speculative and practical knowledge of theological science and directs it to its proper end which is the good of the Christian life obtained through charity. Its perfection consists in the contemplation of God as God is known by faith and loved for God's own sake in charity (RHS 277, 280).

The role of the Holy Spirit, then, is to unite all forms of theological knowledge in the bond of charity and to order them to the delights of union with God in mystical contemplation. The Holy Spirit operates in the completion or perfection of knowledge and elevates the mind beyond every form of knowledge to experience the hidden mysteries of God in a rapture of ecstatic love. "The perfect state of Christian wisdom is, therefore, a rapture of heart and mind in God by a mystical union of charity. This union, transcending all speculation and understanding, is an experience obtained solely by the grace of the Holy Spirit" (RHS 283), a union that is consummated in the fruits of the Holy Spirit.[13] Let us now turn to the role played by *affectus* in the mystical aspects of Bonaventure's spirituality.

2. Mystical Experience and Affectus

As has been mentioned, Bonaventure's sense of theology is broader than the way many contemporary theologies are understood. He describes theology primarily as a gift of God—a gift of light coming from the Father of lights, but a gift that is not purely intellectual. Theology supposes not just faith in itself, but a faith that is living and active. It encompasses prayer, the exercise of the virtues, and the movement of the soul toward union with God in love.

Bonaventure distinguishes between the wisdom that is theology and the wisdom that is an infused gift of God.[14] The latter is based on a knowledge that comes in an experiential and affective manner. The former is an intellectual wisdom, acquired by effort, the task of which is to understand and reconstruct intellectually the order of the works and the mysteries of God. Theology includes a dynamic synthesis of faith and reason. It is a progressive reintegration of the human person as intelligent being and the whole of the known universe in the unity of God, by love and for love.[15]

Within this broad context, it is possible to come to a fuller understanding of *affectus* in the mystical aspects of Bonaventure's theology which, as we have seen *is* his spirituality, the two being inseparable.[16] It is important to keep in mind that the entire structure of Bonaventure's mystical theology rests on the foundation of grace and the theological virtues. After the soul has been raised to a supernatural level by grace, it is possible for it to move from the simple foundation of faith to the heights of mystical contemplation. Bonaventure seems very conscious of the continuity and the dynamic unity among the various stages of the spiritual ascent (TM 9). Mystical contemplation adds nothing to the light of faith, but rather allows one to penetrate more deeply the truth already accepted on the authority of revelation. Grace is the primordial principle of the deification of the human person. For Bonaventure, the gifts and beatitudes add something to the virtues, but this addition is not foundational. Grace provides the grounding for the entire journey. The graced soul is moved to please God and to be united with God. The activity of grace makes moving through the stages of the spiritual life possible.

In addition to his discussion of grace in general, Bonaventure also emphasizes grace as the specific source of the gifts of the Holy Spirit, the cardinal virtues and the beatitudes—each of which has its special function in the spiritual life. The goal of the virtues is to rectify the soul; of the gifts to make it more supple and receptive to supernatural inspiration; of the beatitudes to bring it to perfection. The practice of the virtues belongs more directly to the active life, while the gifts of the Holy Spirit, especially wisdom (experiential knowledge of the heart), prepare the soul for mystical communications (TM 17).

In his description of the journey into God, Bonaventure employs the traditional theme of the spiritual senses. Smell, touch and taste—senses related to affectivity for Bonaventure—are associated with the higher reaches of the mystical life. (Aquinas departs from this order, placing sight at the pinnacle of the spiritual life.) In the following passage from the *Itinerarium*, we see also that Bonaventure views the "spiritual senses" not as something newly acquired, but rather as a more perfect expression of habits already possessed by the graced soul. The text also highlights the centrality of Christ as the way to contemplation. It is taken from the fourth step of the mystical journey, in which Bonaventure considers the image of God in our natural powers reformed through the gifts of grace. At this stage, the soul has been purified, enlightened and perfected by the three theological virtues.

> The soul, therefore, now believes and hopes in Jesus Christ and loves (*amans*) Him, who is the incarnate, uncreated, and inspired Word—the Way, the Truth, and the Life. When the soul by faith believes in Christ as in the uncreated Word, who is the Word and the brightness of the Father, she recovers her spiritual hearing and sight to view the splendors of the Light. When the soul longs with hope to receive the inspired Word, she recovers, because of her desire and affection (*per desiderium et affectum*), the spiritual sense of smell. When she embraces with love (*Dum caritate complectitur*) the Incarnate Word, inasmuch as she receives delight (*delectationem*) from Him and passes over to Him in ecstatic love (*ut transiens in illud per ecstaticum amorem*), she recovers her sense of taste and touch.[17]

One can see the preponderance of affective language here, even before Bonaventure reaches his discussion of the higher stages of the mystical life in the later chapters of the *Itinerarium*.

Among the actions of preparation for contemplation, prayer and meditation hold an important place in Bonaventure's system. Through prayer, the soul receives the grace which will reform it; through meditation, the soul receives the wisdom that leads to perfection. This meditation which leads to loving wisdom operates at all three stages of the mystical way—the purgative, the illuminative, and the unitive. The way of meditation begins with the prick of conscience and ends with the experience of interior joy. As Bonaventure says, it is practiced in mourning and consummated in love (TM 23). He uses the image "fire of wisdom" to describe that grace in the soul which must be carefully nurtured, set aflame, and finally raised on high.

Prayer, for Bonaventure, is the principle and origin of ecstasy. It is in prayer that the soul asks for the favors of contemplation. It is here that she receives the grace without which the spiritual ascent could not be undertaken. His doctrine is summed up in this phrase from the *Itinerarium:* "Prayer is the mother and origin of every upward striving of the soul."[18] The end of prayer is contemplation, and Bonaventure encourages deliberateness and perseverance in seeking this gift from God. In his description of this act, the language of the heart predominates:

> You should never withdraw your spirit from prayer, but persevere in it until you have penetrated into the place of the wonderful tabernacle, in the house of God, and there, having seen your beloved with the eyes of your heart, and having tasted how the Lord is full of sweetness, and how great is His gentleness, you will throw yourself into His embrace, and cover Him with the most ardent kisses of tender devotion. Then completely estranged from yourself, entirely enraptured in heaven, reformed and transformed in Jesus Christ, you will be powerless to rule over the feelings of your soul.[19]

Along with grace, the virtues, gifts, beatitudes and prayer, Bonaventure also places at the heart of his mystical theology devotion to and imitation of the crucified Christ. Bonaventure's focus on the crucified Christ reflects his Franciscan roots and the important place he gives to affectivity. He devotes an entire chapter of the *De triplici via* and one third of the *Lignum vitae* to this subject, showing how meditation on the mystery of the cross leads the soul to the privilege of the contemplative state.[20] At the beginning of the *Itinerarium*, Bonaventure calls to mind Francis' vision on Alverno of the winged seraph in the form of the Crucified (Prologue 2). The road to peace, which he so ardently sought, "is through nothing else than a most ardent love of the Crucified" (Prologue 3). The final image of the *Itinerarium*—that of the soul falling asleep on the cross with Christ— reveals perhaps more powerfully than any others Bonaventure's sense of the importance of the heart:

> He who turns his full countenance toward this Mercy-Seat and
> with faith, hope, and love, devotion, admiration, joy, apprecia-
> tion, praise and rejoicing, beholds Christ hanging on the Cross,
> such a one celebrates the Pasch, that is, the Passover, with Him
> (7.2).

Bonaventure frequently uses the images of the Song of Songs to help
him speak of love. In his biography of Francis, Bonaventure recounts a
vision Francis had of the crucified: "Francis' 'soul melted' (5.6) at the
sight, and the memory of Christ's passion was so impressed on the innermost recesses of his heart that from that hour, whenever Christ's crucifix-
ion came to his mind, he could scarcely contain his tears and sighs. . . ."[21]
Later in the same text Bonaventure says, "Jesus Christ crucified always
'rested like a bundle of myrrh in the bosom' of Francis' soul (1.12), and he
longed to be totally transformed into him by the fire of ecstatic love" (LM
9.2).

The dénouement, the apogee, the goal of the entire spiritual life is
characterized above all by *affectus:*

> In this passing over, if it is to be perfect, all intellectual activities
> ought to be relinquished and the most profound affection (*apex
> affectus*) transported to God, and transformed into Him (IT 7.4).

Once more, Bonaventure puts forth Francis as the example of perfect
contemplation. It is through Francis' example rather than by his word that
God invites others to this ecstatic, mystical transport. In his biography of
Francis, Bonaventure speaks of the different ways in which he and Francis
came to understand the scripture. "Free from all stain, his genius penetrated the hidden depths of the mysteries, and where the scholarship of the
teacher stands outside, the affection (*affectus*) of the lover entered within"
(LM 11.1). For Francis, the poet and the lover, the way was direct; for
Bonaventure, the scholar and the lover, understanding came with great
labor and study. Bonaventure admits that Francis' way is the superior, but
insists that the goal is the same. I cite Bonaventure's own stirring words in
the final section of the *Itinerarium,* and invite you to consult the Latin in
the footnote to see the extraordinary richness of Bonaventure's affective
language.

> If you wish to know how these things may come about, ask grace,
> not learning; desire, not the understanding; the groaning of
> prayer, not diligence in reading; the Bridegroom, not the
> teacher; God, not man; darkness, not clarity; not light, but the

fire that wholly inflames and carries one into God through trans-
porting unctions and consuming affections. God Himself is this
fire, and His furnace is in Jerusalem; and it is Christ who
enkindles it in the white flame of His most burning Passion.[22]

Bonaventure emphasizes in his spirituality the gratuitousness of the
gift of contemplation, the importance of desire in the soul, and the role of
the affections in the ascent to God.[23] The affections are important in all the
stages of the spiritual life, but they become most predominant at the
higher levels of mystical experience.

Bonaventure uses the language of the heart especially in reference to a
stage he calls "devotion." He describes "devotion" as an affective feeling
toward God and Christ. "Devotion is the sweet affection of love that comes
when one remembers the kindnesses of Christ."[24] And, "devotion is the
holy and humble affection toward God."[25] Devotion consummates the
union of the soul and God. It is a disposition ordained toward God which
raises the soul up to God. When devotion is perfect, it disposes immediately to mystical union.[26] Ecstasy, in effect, has three causes: devotion,
admiration, and joy (IT 4.3: V. 306b).

In the final stage of the unitive way, contemplation, Bonaventure
distinguishes between intellectual contemplation and the contemplation of
wisdom. As we have seen, the gift of wisdom is cognitive in one dimension
and affective in another. The act of science, which is included in the gift of
wisdom, is not the primary act, but rather a preliminary act ordained to
affection. It is this strict subordination of the reason to love in Bonaventure's theology that allows him to attribute the two acts of science and
contemplation to the same habit in the soul (DIC 1825). Both acts are
necessary, but the goal of the cognitive is to lead to that which is higher and
more perfect, namely, the affective. The contemplation of wisdom is, in
the strictest sense, nothing other than love, *affectus*, which causes the soul
to experience God as the divine sweetness.[27] This emphasis on the heart in
Bonaventure's theology is well captured in this summary by Longpré:

> Likewise in the ecstasy of love, the soul embraces God with
> immediacy; but this affective embrace does not take place
> through vision (*per modum visus et intuitus*), but in the manner of
> a tasting, and especially by means of embrace and touch (*per
> modum tactus et amplexus*). . . .[28] She (the soul) tastes the sweet-
> ness to the point of inebriation,[29] the soul becomes inflamed,[30]
> and touches Him in the highest rapture of seraphic love;[31] finally
> the soul is assimilated to Him and becomes one single spirit with
> Him.[32]

In summary, then, we see that Bonaventure's spirituality leads to ecstatic love. The soul is directed in all its activities by the precepts of God, urged to the rapid attainment of perfection by the beatitudes, healed of its wounds by sacramental grace, rectified in its powers by the virtues, and finally recreated in the image of the Trinity by the grace of the Holy Spirit. The soul becomes entirely disposed to this spiritual ascent of which Francis on Mount Alverno is the model. The state of contemplation ends in what is often referred to as a "mystical death," in which love silences all discursive activities. The heart alone remains, beyond intelligence and knowing, beyond imagination and the senses, where "God is all in all."[33]

NOTES

1. A version of this article was first published in *Franciscan Studies*, 42 (1982): 5–20.
2. In fact, the debate about the role of affectivity in the spiritual life is not new in our time and, as might be expected, includes perspectives that guard against any emphasis on affect that might detract from the role of reason. Neither is the discussion limited to western concerns. See Tomas Spidlik, "The Heart in Russian Spirituality," trans. Joseph D. Gauthier, *Orientalia christiana analecta*, 195, 361–374.
3. In response to a talk by Avery Dulles entitled "Revelation and Discovery," Andrew Tallon notes that affective intentionality as access to meaning, so central to the Hebrew Bible, has begun to receive scholarly attention. Questions are being raised about the adequacy of seeing the active, reasoning, logical, verbal agent as primary, and consideration is again being given to the affective, receptive, non-verbal agent-as-patient. He mentions forerunners such as Augustine, Francis, Bonaventure, Pascal and Newman. See *Theology and Discovery: Essays in Honor of Karl Rahner,* ed. William J. Kelly (Milwaukee: Marquette University Press, 1980), 35.
4. *Method in Theology* (New York: Herder and Herder, 1972), 30–39.
5. *Theological Investigations,* V, 38–39.
6. See John Dunne, *The Reasons of the Heart* (New York: Macmillan, 1978); and Jon Nilson, "Doing Theology by Heart: John S. Dunne's Theological Method," *Theological Studies* 48 (1987): 65–86.
7. Some of the important authors include Paul Ricoeur, Victor Turner, John Shea, Morton Kelsey, Antoine Vergote, Joseph Campbell and Mircea Eliade. See also Ira Progoff, *The Symbolic and the Real* (New York: McGraw-Hill, 1963); Carl Jung, *Man and His Symbols* (New York: Dell Publishing, 1964); Mary Douglas, *Natural Symbols* (New

York: Random House, 1970); Robert Doran, *Subject and Psyche: Ricoeur, Jung, and the Search for Foundations* (Washington, D.C.: University Press, 1977).

8. By *affectus*, I mean those things that have to do with the affections, the will—love, passion, feeling, emotion, affectivity. It refers to the language and the images Bonaventure uses to express this dimension of human experience. Some examples include: *diligo, amor, ecstaticum excessum, desideria, ignis, ardens, passio, unctio,* etc.

9. John Quinn, "The Role of the Holy Spirit in St. Bonaventure's Theology," (= RHS) *Franciscan Studies* 33 (1973): 273–74. In Bonaventure, see *1 Sent.* 7.un. 1 (I. 137); and *Breviloquium* 1. 3 (V. 211–212); and 1. 6 (V. 213–214). All references in parentheses refer to the Quarrachi edition of Bonaventure's works.

10. *1 Sent.* 1.2. 1 (I. 201).

11. In this section, I am relying on Walter Principe, "St. Bonaventure's Theology of the Holy Spirit with Reference to the Expression *Pater et Filius diligunt se Spiritu Sancto*," in *S. Bonaventura 1274–1974* (Grottaferrata: Collegio S. Bonaventurae, 1973–74), vol. 4, 255–267.

12. An historical overview of the sources for Bonaventure's trinitarian thought may be found in Zachary Hayes' introduction to Bonaventure's *Disputed Question on the Mystery of the Trinity,* ed. George Marcil (St. Bonaventure, NY: Franciscan Institute, 1979), 13–29.

13. *Collationes in Hexaemeron* 18. 26–31 (V. 418–419).

14. Philotheus Boehner identifies four senses in which Bonaventure uses the term "wisdom": (1) general cognition of things; (2) cognition of eternal things; (3) wisdom proper, or cognition of God according to piety; (4) cognition of God by experience. In Notes and Commentary, *Itinerarium mentis in Deum* (=IT) (Saint Bonaventure, NY: The Franciscan Institute, 1956), 130.

15. See Yves Congar, "Théologie," *Dictionnaire de théologie catholique* 15 (1946), col. 395.

16. I will be relying here on an article by P. Ephrem Longpré, "La théologie mystique de saint Bonaventure" (=TM) in *Archivum Franciscanum Historicum* 14 (1921). See also his article on "Bonaventure" in the *Dictionnaire de Spiritualité* 1 (1937).

17. 4. 3 (V. 306b).

18. *Oratio igitur est mater et origo sursum-actionis,* 1.1 (V. 295a); see also Prologue. 4, and *De triplici via* 2. 1–8 (V. 8–10).

19. *De perfectione vitae ad sorores,* x.x. (V. 119).

20. *De triplici via,* 3.3 (V. 12–14). See also *De perfectione,* 4.2 (V. 120).

21. *Legenda maior,* (=LM) 1.5.

22. "Si autem quaeras, quomodo haec fiant, interroga gratiam, non

doctrinam; desiderium, non intellectum; gemitum orationis, non studium lectionis; sponsum, non magistrum; Deum, non hominem; caliginem, non claritatem; non lucem, sed ignem totaliter inflammantem et in Deum excessivis unctionibus et ardentissimis affectionibus transferentem." 7.6 (V. 313b).

23. This emphasis on affect is corroborated by Hyacinth J. Ennis: "Christian and human love are but a reflection of and a participation in the warmth of the divine giving and receiving. Bonaventure, while not being by any means anti-intellectual, does add a certain primacy to the affective and dynamic in his theology of the Blessed Trinity." In "The Place of Love in the Theological System of St. Bonaventure," *S. Bonaventura*, vol. 4, p. 133.
24. *Sermon 3 de S. Maria Magd.*, (IX. 561a).
25. *Collatio in Joannem*, XII (VI. 587b).
26. Longpré, *Dictionnaire* (=DIC), cols. 1811–12.
27. See *3 Sent.* 35.1.1 ad. 5 (III. 774a).
28. See *3 Sent.* 14. dub. 1 (III. 292a) and 27.2.1 ad 6 (III. 604).
29. See *Soliloquium* 2. 16–19 and 3.13 (VIII. 50–52, 56), and *Collationes in Hexaemeron* 23.30 (V. 449).
30. *Collationes in Hexaemeron*, 22.27 (V. 441).
31. See *3 Sent.* 14. dub. 1 (III 292), and 27.2.1. ad.6 (III. 604).
32. *Dictionnaire*, cols 1829–30. Last citation, see *Collationes* 22.39 (IV. 443).
33. See *Itinerarium* 7.4.6 (V. 312b, 313b), and *Collationes*, 2.29–30 (V. 341).

Walter Principe, C.S.B.

Affectivity and the Heart in Thomas Aquinas' Spirituality

On hearing that Thomas Aquinas was to be studied in a collection of essays on spiritualities of the heart, a friend reacted by exclaiming: "Thomas Aquinas? You've got to be kidding!" Such a reaction might be understandable. Thomas Aquinas, that great intellectual giant? That daring philosopher renowned for his commentaries on Aristotle, for his use of this philosopher and his Arabian commentators? Thomas, that Dominican scholar for whom theology is primarily a speculative science, who taught that the essence of eternal happiness consists in the intellectual vision of God? What has such a person to do with spiritualities of the heart or with affectivity? Does this absorbed thinker, who spent his time at the king's banquet table searching for a convincing argument against the Manichees, even use such words as "heart" or "affect" or "passion" to any extent?

Fortunately, we have Busa's *Concordance* to all Aquinas' writings to help us answer this last question. We can begin with a purely material consideration: Busa lists for "heart" (*cor*) 2,263 texts, for "affection(s)" 440 texts, for "affect" (*affectus*) 1,525 texts. The noun "love" (*amor*) occurs 3,931 times, the verb "to love" (*amare*) 2,512 times; "desire" as a noun is found 1,309 times, as a verb 1,153 times; "to will" (*velle*) is used 7,622 times.[1]

To get a more personal view, let us slip into Thomas' lecture room at Paris or at one of the Italian Dominican houses where he taught. What is the manuscript he is using as the basis of his teaching? It is neither his *Summa theologiae* nor his *Summa contra Gentiles,* the two major systematic works he wrote but rarely if ever actually taught. What he has is a text of sacred scripture. One year it is the gospel according to Matthew, in other

45

years the text of Job or Isaiah or Jeremiah, or a selection of the psalms or some of the letters of Paul. If it is the early 1270's, toward the end of his life, we are treated to his spiritually rich commentary on John, itself showing the fruits of his extensive research for the *Catena aurea*, a "golden chain" of texts he put together from the Greek and Latin fathers to present their commentaries on each section of the four gospels. It is indeed a fact ignored by many students of Aquinas, especially philosophers, that Thomas' regular, ordinary teaching consisted in exposition of scripture, into which he introduced theological discussions although omitting the more technical apparatus of his disputed questions or *summae*, the only works most scholars read.

Since the scriptures are so full of language of the heart and affectivity, it is no surprise that Thomas' commentaries, even though addressed to advanced theological students, are a rich lode that can be endlessly mined for his own language of the heart and affections. Before we consider affectivity in Thomas' theological spirituality more generally, let us hear a few comments from among his many lecture-texts that give prominence to the heart or affectivity.

The psalms are especially rich occasions for such teaching and language, for example, Thomas' commentary on Psalm 38(39):4:

> "My heart glowed within me," that is, the warmth of charity was roused up in my heart, Prov 6: "Can we hide fire in our bosom so that our garments do not burn?" So we cannot hide God's words when our hearts are inflamed with charity, Ps 118(119):140: "Your speech is all afire." Charity is aroused in this way by meditation about divine realities, which is why the psalmist adds: "In my meditation a fire will be kindled." Nothing is loved except what is good and beautiful. . . . And so if you wish to reach spiritual things, your heart must be inflamed with love of God.[2]

On the psalm verse, "Let them exult and rejoice," Thomas comments: "[The psalmist] says that the fruit of the saints is enjoyment because 'delight' expresses 'dilation' of the heart and so signifies that joy is interior, Ps 118(119): 'You have enlarged my heart' " (*In Ps* 34[35]:27 14.276),[3] and he adds: "Exultation expresses joy bursting forth exteriorly from within, and this exultation belongs to the just, Ps. 32(33): 'Exult, you just, in the Lord' " (ibid).[4]

The psalm-verse, "Taste and see that the Lord is sweet," leads him to say: "God is not far from us or outside us but rather within us, Jer 14: 'You are in us, O Lord.' Therefore the experience of God's goodness is called 'taste,' 1 Pet 2: 'If indeed you have tasted how sweet the Lord is' " (*In Ps* 33 (34):9 14.266).

Commenting on Psalm 21(22):15, "My heart has become like melting wax within my bowels," Thomas first says that, typologically, it refers

> not to Christ in himself but to his members: they are indeed the heart of Christ, whom he especially loves, Phil 1: "For I hold you in my heart," followed by "God is my witness how I long for you to be in the bosom of Christ." These were the apostles. . . . Their hearts were like melting wax, first, by a melting that was bad when they fled because of fear . . . and when Peter denied Christ; second, by a good melting, as in the conversion of the disciples: we see this in the case of Peter and Andrew (*In Ps* 21[22]:15 14.221).

Thomas suggests another interpretation of the heart's melting, this time in relation to the properties of love:

> Or we should say that melting is also the fruit of love, Cant 5: "My soul has melted." Before something melts, it is hard and closed in on itself; if it melts, it is poured out and tends away from itself to another. When love comes, a person who was wrapped up in self now tends to another (ibid.).

But if "melting heart" refers to love, then, he says, it may also be applied to Christ:

> This kind of melting can also be explained with reference to Christ as head, for this being melted is from the Holy Spirit and is in the midst of the bosom, that is, in the affections. Or through Christ's heart we can understand sacred scripture, which manifests the heart of Christ. Scripture was closed before Christ's passion because it was obscure, but after his passion it became open because those who now understand it consider and discern how the prophets are to be explained (ibid.).[5]

The Pauline commentaries are also rich in such expressions, for example, Thomas' comment on Phil 1:20:

> *Christ will be glorified in my body . . . . :* We glorify Christ when we spread knowledge of Christ . . . by word and deed, when the greatness of what God has produced shows forth God's greatness.

Justification is such a wondrous effect, but as long as it remains hidden in a person's heart, Christ is not glorified before others but only in that person's heart. But sometimes it bursts forth exteriorly through evident bodily acts: then Christ is truly and properly glorified.[6]

Commenting on Matthew's text in which Christ is presented blessing those who hunger and thirst after justice, Thomas says: "The Lord wants us to pant after that justice in such a way that we will never be, as it were, satiated in this life, just as a miser is never satiated."[7]

Although these and a great number of similar vivid affective expressions are suggested to Thomas by the scripture texts on which he is commenting,[8] it is noteworthy that in his *Commentary on the Sentences, summae,* and *quaestiones disputatae* he also frequently emphasizes affectivity and uses affective terminology. Only a few samplings can be given at this point.

In his *Scriptum super Sententiis* (= *Sent*), this supposedly exaggerated intellectual applies the analogy of love to the Holy Spirit and says:

Knowledge is not perfect unless the will is joined to it. Now a [mental] word is related to love as the intellect is related to the will. Therefore a [mental] word will be imperfect without love. But the Word of God is perfect, and so there is associated with it the One who is perfect Love, the Holy Spirit.[9]

Explaining the name "Spirit" as used properly of the third person, Thomas appeals to our human speech: ". . . We say of two persons who love each other and are in concord that they are one in spirit or that they conspire, just as we also say they are one heart and one soul" (1 *Sent* 10.1.4 1.267).

In the *Summa contra Gentiles* (= *ScGen*) Thomas describes how the *heart* reverences God and how the *soul* is set on fire and drawn to God's goodness:

The consideration [of creatures] leads to admiration of the most high God's power and so gives birth to reverence in human hearts. . . . This consideration inflames human souls to love of divine goodness. . . . If the goodness, beauty, and sweetness of creatures so draws human hearts, then the source of these, God's own goodness, when carefully compared with the rivulets of goodness found in individual creatures, sets human souls on fire and draws them totally to God (2.2).[10]

In the *Summa theologiae* Thomas remarks that "tears burst forth not only when we are sad but also from a certain tenderness of affect, especially when we consider some delightful thing that is mixed with something sad" (1–2.82.4 ad 3).[11]

Thomas points out the rejection of God's precepts as well as the serious sin that results "when a person's heart is not fixed in God" (1–2.109.8c). Thus the miser's "heart is not softened by mercy so that he might help those in misery from his riches" (2–2.118.8c), whereas at times "someone's heart is moved by the Holy Spirit to believe and love God and repent over sins" (3.66.11c). This would have been the case with Paul, "because suddenly, although he was advancing in sin, his heart was perfectly moved by God through his hearing and learning and coming [to Christ], and therefore he suddenly acquired grace" (1–2.112.2 ad 2).

The Meaning of "Heart" in Thomas Aquinas

Because there are over two thousand texts in which Thomas speaks of the heart, it is impossible to summarize all the nuances he gives to the term. At times, to be sure, he speaks of the bodily organ, but more often he gives "heart" a spiritual interpretation. He himself knows the many divergent ways in which the fathers used the term "heart," and he gives several examples from them in his explanation of the precept to love God (2–2.44.5c). In this text his own views about the precept to love God "with one's whole heart and whole mind and whole soul and whole strength" include a clear statement about the heart:

> We must consider that love is an act of the will, *which is here signified by "heart"*: for just as the bodily heart is the principle of all bodily movements, so also the will, *especially as it intends the ultimate end, the object of charity*, is the principle of all spiritual movements.

The heart thus understood becomes for Thomas the driving force of the other acts and powers:

> Acts moved by the will [= heart] have three principles, namely, the intellect, which is signified by "mind," the lower appetitive power, signified by "soul," and the interior executive power, signified by "fortitude" or "power" or "strength." Therefore we are commanded to bring our whole intention to bear on God, which is "with all our heart," to subject our intellect to God, which is "with our whole mind," to regulate our appetite accord-

ing to God, which is "with our whole soul," and to obey God by
our exterior activity, which is to love God "with our whole fortitude or power or strength."

Although in this text the heart is linked with the will, in other cases,
including a number already quoted, Thomas sees the heart as part of the
sensitive or emotional aspect of human nature.

Affectivity in Aquinas' Theological Spirituality[12]

Turning from these concrete examples of Aquinas' teaching and language concerning affectivity and the heart to his more general theological
principles, we shall examine a few of many points where his teaching on
affectivity and love are keys to his spirituality.

First, it should be emphasized that the foundation for everything
Aquinas says about human affectivity, including the will's activity, is the
eternally dynamic and ever-present procession of the Holy Spirit from the
Father and Son through love. For, Thomas maintains, when the Holy
Spirit proceeds from the Father and Son as the "formal effect" of their
love, the Father and Son love not only the divine goodness and each other,
but also each human person and indeed all creatures, "by the Holy Spirit,"
who is Love. Each human person is therefore involved as a true if secondary object of the Father's and Son's active dynamic mutual love by the
Holy Spirit (1.37.2c & ad 3m).

According to this teaching, then, at each moment of our existence we
are being known, freely chosen to exist, and loved into existence within the
Father's and Son's eternal ecstatic breathing forth of the Holy Spirit of
Love. Moreover, each of us who responds to the call of grace receives the
Son and Holy Spirit, *sent* to us in "invisible missions." And since the
Father "comes" with the Son and Spirit when they are sent, the three
divine persons dwell in us in order to be possessed and enjoyed as objects
of our grace-infused knowledge and love. Our minds are thereby conformed to the Son, who is the mental Word of the Father, and our affective
powers are conformed to their Love, the Holy Spirit; thereby we are
drawn to the Father, the first source of all missions, sendings, and graces
of indwelling. For Thomas Aquinas, then, Christian spirituality is trinitarian in character, and its affective, loving aspects result from our being
caught up into and being conformed with the personal going-forth and
return of the divine person who is Love.[13]

Here, it should be noted, Thomas makes it abundantly clear that the
knowing and the conformity of our minds to the divine persons in such
missions and indwelling take place only when affective love is involved. He

makes this point in answer to an argument that he presents in detail but then rejects. The argument begins by accepting Thomas' own position that an [invisible] mission or sending of a divine person takes place only by reason of grace. But, the argument continues, the Son, who proceeds as the *intellectual* Word in God, should not be sent invisibly since the gifts pertaining to the *intellect* can be had without the grace that is charity (1 Cor 13:2 is quoted). To this reasoning Thomas replies in one of his most sublimely spiritual statements. He first speaks of the conformity to the Holy Spirit through charity in the mission of the Holy Spirit:

> The soul is conformed to God through grace. Hence in order that some divine person be sent to someone through grace the recipient must be made like the divine person who is sent through some gift of grace. Because the Holy Spirit is Love, the soul is made like the Holy Spirit through the gift of charity. Hence the sending or mission of the Holy Spirit is by way of charity.

With this established, he now applies the doctrine to the case of the Son as intellectual Word:

> Now the Son is the Word—not any word of any kind, but the Word breathing forth Love (*Verbum spirans Amorem*): hence Augustine says . . . : "The Word we mean to speak of is Knowledge with Love." Therefore the Son is not sent [to us] in any and every kind of knowledge we acquire but [only] in that kind of intellectual instruction whereby we burst forth with affections of love, as is said . . . in Ps 38(39):4: "In my meditation a fire is enkindled" (1.43.5 ad 2).[14]

When Thomas uses traditional scriptural and patristic language to speak of the human person as the image of God, especially of the trinitarian God, he again relates the graced knowledge and love of the human person to the trinitarian life.

> . . . The divine image of the Trinity ought to be found in the soul according as it best arrives, so far as is possible, at representing the likeness of the divine persons. Now the divine persons are distinguished according to the processions of the Word from the Speaker and of Love connecting them. . . . Therefore the image of the Trinity will be found first and chiefly in our mind by reason of its acts, that is, in so far as, by thinking, we form a

word interiorly from the knowledge we have and from this burst
forth into love (*in amorem prorumpimus*) (1.93.7c).

When we are thus constantly being loved into existence within the
very divine trinitarian love and fashioned through graced knowledge and
love into images of the Trinity, we are so constituted in our very being and
powers, Thomas teaches, that we have not only a natural capacity for such
a divine-like (supernatural) existence and life but also a necessary drive
implanted within us by God. Therefore, whether consciously or not, we
are always seeking God as our only true beatitude, our only ultimate good
or end. The gift of existence given us, within and by God's knowledge and
love, implants in us an affective thirst to see and enjoy God perfectly, a
thirst that can never be satisfied by any creaturely good. This inborn
thirst, derived from knowledge, is the root source of human free choice, an
essential component of any spirituality. Affectivity is at the center of all
human striving for beatitude (1.12.1, 59.3; 1–2.2.8, 3.8, 13.6).

This doctrine leads us to Thomas' doctrine of human beatitude or
perfect happiness. Aquinas' position is often misunderstood because he
holds that the *essence* of beatitude consists in the intellectual grasp of God's
essence in the beatific vision (1–2.3.4, 8). Others who disagree with
Thomas locate the essence of beatitude in perfect love of God. To understand Thomas on this point, we must be aware that for him the *essence* of
this or any act is not the whole reality. For Aquinas, the integrity or full
perfection of beatitude necessarily "requires" an accompanying overflow
from vision of God into blissful delight, love, and joy such that nothing
other than God's infinite goodness could ever attract the human heart (1–
2.4.1, 5.4, 11.3). And if the essential act of beatitude is for him the
intellectual vision of God, this act of vision itself is a great *good* that human
persons seek and attain through love: then, on reaching this vision, the
object of their affective longing and desire, they experience its perfect
completion in affective bliss (1–2.3.4; 1.12.1).

Related to this question, and fundamental to Thomas' spirituality, is
his position concerning the relative nobility of the human intellect and
will. Something similar to what has been seen about beatitude operates
here. Taken in themselves and absolutely, Thomas teaches, the intellect is
a higher and nobler power than the will. This, he says, is because the
object of the intellect is the very notion (*ratio*) of the good that the will
seeks, and the notion of that good is simpler and more absolute than the
good itself sought by the will. Here one sees Thomas' intellectualism to the
fore. But he then goes on to develop a theme that is crucial to his spirituality. If, Aquinas says, we look at the intellect and will as relating to the
objects they seek, the will can be nobler than the intellect. This is the case

when what the will seeks is nobler in being than what the intellect knows. Why is this so? Because knowing draws a thing into the mind by a likeness of the thing, whereas willing or loving goes out to a thing in its real existence. Thomas' own explanation is clear:

> . . . The action of the intellect consists in this, that the notion (*ratio*) of the thing that is known is in the one knowing, whereas the act of the will gets its perfection by the will's inclining to the thing itself as it exists in itself. . . . When therefore the thing in which good is found is nobler than the soul itself in which its notion is understood, then, in comparison with such a thing, the will is higher than the intellect. But when the thing in which good is found is lower than the soul, then, in comparison with such a thing, the intellect is higher than the will. Hence love of God is better than knowledge, but conversely knowledge of bodily things is better than love for them (1.82.3c; cf. *Ver* 22.11c).[15]

Here Thomas' existentialism leads him to a doctrine often ignored by philosophers who examine his views only about human powers in themselves, neglecting what he says about their role within the dynamic spiritual development of the human person. In our spiritual development, he holds, the relation between ourselves as a willing, loving subject and the object of our willing and loving is basic to personal spiritual growth. The good we seek and love affects our very personal being and goodness. If it is God who is loved, we become better; if we love any creature inordinately, whether ourselves or other persons or material things, we become debased and defective in personal goodness. As Thomas puts it:

> The love of a fitting good makes the lover more perfect and better, but love for a good that is unfitting for the lover wounds the lover and makes the lover worse. Hence we are especially perfected and made better through love of God, but are wounded and made worse through love of sin . . . (1–2.28.5c).

This is because love for an object "formally effects a union" with the beloved "because love itself is such a union or bond" with the beloved in its existential reality and therefore in its quality of goodness or evil (1–2.28.1c). Or, as Thomas says most forcefully, through the theo-logical (God-centered) virtue of charity in our will we achieve "a certain conformity to our end [God]" and are ordered to "a certain spiritual union, by which we are in a certain way transformed into [our supernatural] end [God]" (1–2.62.3c).[16]

Some of Thomas' richest teachings on affectivity occur within his long discussion of the human emotions or passions (1–2.22–48), in which he gives absolute primacy to love as the source and root of every other emotion (25.2) and in which his philosophico-theological analyses include a phenomenology of human love and friendship ("in the love of friendship the lover is in the beloved in so far as the lover considers the friend's good or evil as his or her own and the will of the friend as her or his own": 28.2c). He speaks of love as leading to union, to mutual "inhesion" or interpenetration of lovers when their love is truly friendship and not mere self-seeking; he describes love as ecstatic and zealous, as in some sense wounding the lovers, and as the cause of all that lovers do, including all the other emotions they experience or express (28.1–6).

When Thomas Aquinas studies the emotions or passions, he integrates them into moral-spiritual development in a way superior to the view of many whose spirituality is primarily volitional or affective, but who often maintain that for spiritual progress the will must suppress the emotions and put them to sleep, a view that, put into practice, can lead to repression and psychological disturbance.[17]

Thomas, on the contrary, views the emotions or passions as sharing in the goodness of a morally good act because they share in the order of our reason and our will by being moderated through reason (1–2.24.1 & 3); they are "by nature able to obey reason" (3.15.2 ad 1). Indeed they add to the goodness (or evil) of an act, so that

> just as it is better for someone both to will the good and to do it by an external act, so it also belongs to perfect moral good that we be moved toward the good not only through our will but also through our sensitive appetite, according to the saying of Ps 83(84):3: "My heart and my flesh have rejoiced in the living God": taking "heart" to mean the intellective appetite and "flesh" to mean the sensitive appetite (1–2.24.3).

For Aquinas the ordering of the emotions or passions is indeed brought about by what he calls "the impression of reason" on the appetites (1–2.60.1). But this is no external act of the intellect and will, tyrannically restricting the spontaneity of the emotions. Rather, Aquinas sees the right ordering of the emotions under the impress of reason as flowing immediately from virtues such as moderation (*temperantia*), courage (*fortitudo*), great-heartedness (*magnanimitas*), and meekness (*mansuetudo*); these, he holds, reside not in the will (that is, not on the intellectual level exterior to the emotions) but in the very seat of these emotions, the sense appetites or sense-seeking powers (1–2.60.4c).

In this view the whole affective emotional side of human existence can be given spontaneous full play to the extent that these virtues, which order them from within, have been cultivated through a discipline guided by reason and aided by God's grace. This was preeminently the case with Christ, who had full, strong, human passions or emotions rightly ordered from within because his virtues of moderation, courage, and meekness were so perfect in their intensity (3.15.2c). Because Aquinas sees the human person as so much a one spiritual-sentient-corporal being, he strongly champions the emotions in spirituality. Therefore he opposes any Stoic, Manichean, or Platonic debasement of the body and bodily emotions (1–2.24.2–3). In this sense he is also a champion of human affectivity, especially of passionate love, which he always speaks of as the prime moving force among the emotions.

In the higher reaches of the mind (beginning with faith), affectivity and love are also crucial to Thomas' spirituality. If for him the act of faith is an assent of the intellect to God as First Truth (2–2.1.1), the intellect can bring forth this assent only insofar as it is moved by the will, itself being moved by God's gracious intervention. The mysteries of God so surpass the grasp of the created human mind that it cannot grasp their evidence or intelligibility and so cannot assent to them as it does to truths that are accessible to its level of being; it is the sweet—or sometimes upsetting—movement of affective assent to God's gift that impels the person to the risk of faith and the gift of self to the Ultimate Mystery experienced as gracious (2–2.2.1 ad 3m, 2.2, 2.9; 2–2.4.1–3). Commenting on Romans 10:10, Thomas says:

> [Paul] expressly says: "By believing from the heart," that is, from the will. For if we lack such will, we can do other things belonging to external worship of God, but we cannot believe unless we will to do so. For the believer's intellect is brought to assent to the truth [of faith] not by necessary reasoning (as is the intellect of someone knowing in a scientific way) but by the will. And therefore [because] justification resides in the will, to know does not belong to our being justified, but believing does; thus Gen 15:6 says: "Abraham believed God and it was credited to him as justice."
>
> But after we are justified through faith, our faith must work through love so that we may reach salvation. Hence Paul adds: "by confessing with your lips you are saved," that is, you attain eternal salvation; thus Is 51:8 says: "My salvation will be forever."[18]

Among the theo-logical or God-centered virtues of faith, hope, and charity, charity is the greatest virtue because "the love of charity is about that which is already possessed [i.e. God]: for the beloved is in a certain way in the lover and the lover is also drawn through affection to union with the beloved, which is why 1 John says: 'They who abide in love abide in God and God in them' " (1–2.66.6c). In a striking analogy Thomas, viewing charity as love based on sharing spiritual life with God, concludes: "Therefore it is clear that charity is *a kind of friendship* between a human person and God" (2–2.23.1c & ad 1).

This existential union of the lover with God as the beloved, a union loftier in this life than the mind's grasp of God, is for Thomas the source of a special type of knowledge unattainable by ordinary human study or experience. Aquinas sometimes calls this a "knowledge by compassion" or "by connaturality." That is, by existential union through love, one "feels with" or is "co-natured with" the beloved. "This kind of compassion or connaturality toward divine things," he says, "comes about through charity, which unites us to God, according to 1 Cor 6:17: 'Those who adhere to God are one spirit [with God]' " (2–2.45.2). Love unites the lover existentially with God, and this begets an experience, a "sweet knowledge" that Thomas equates with wisdom (1.43.5 ad 2), a wisdom quite different from the wisdom a scholar acquires through study. The simplest person, without theological training but deeply united with God by love, is able to judge wisely about spiritual and moral matters (1.1.6 ad 3; 2–2.45.2).

At its loftiest, this knowledge derived from love and affectivity, from living within love, is a contemplative grasp of God, an infused wisdom:

> Uncreated Wisdom . . . unites herself to us first of all through the gift of charity, and as a result of this reveals mysteries to us, the knowledge of which is infused wisdom. Therefore infused wisdom, which is a gift, is the effect rather than the cause of charity (2–2.45.6 ad 2).[19]

Indeed, it is a mystical experience of an indwelling person of the Trinity: "When the Holy Spirit is sent to us invisibly, grace pours into our minds from the fullness of divine love; through this effect of grace we receive an experiential knowledge of that divine person . . ." (1 *Sent* 16.1.2c 1.373). Thus the contemplative life that Aquinas praises so highly is not only the theologian's speculative inquiry into the mysteries of God but also, and even more, that contemplation which is caused by love, which seeks greater love of God, and which is riveted on God in love. Of it Thomas says:

> The contemplative life consists principally in contemplation of God under the impetus of divine love; hence there is delight in the contemplative life both by reason of [the act of] contemplating and by reason of divine love itself. . . . In each respect the delight of contemplation surpasses every human delight (2–2.180.7c).

Thomas holds that, in order to live one's spiritual life on the high and demanding level of Christian faith, hope, and love, a person needs guidance and constant activation by the Holy Spirit, who is personal Love in the Trinity. The Spirit's presence and gifts bring it about that the person "is disposed to be promptly guidable by divine inspiration." Adding a theme from Aristotle, Thomas says that those so guided "are moved through a divine instinct" and "need not take counsel from human reason; rather, they follow an interior instinct because they are moved by a better principle than human reason," that is, by the Holy Spirit (1–2.68.1c; cf.2c). Elsewhere Aquinas says that the new law instituted by Christ is "chiefly . . . the very grace of the Holy Spirit given interiorly" and "bestowed on Christ's faithful"; instruction in faith, commands about what is to be done, indeed even the letter of scripture are secondary and are meant to serve this chief aspect of the new law, the grace of the Holy Spirit (1–2.106.1, 2).

This reference to the new law given the Christian community reminds us that Thomas' spirituality is not only individual and personal but also communitarian and ecclesial. In our concrete history of salvation, the spirituality of the new law relates us to Christ, our way to the Father, the head of the mystical body, and the giver, with the Father, of the Holy Spirit, who produces the fruits of love and an inspired guidance loftier than that given by reason or intellect.[20]

This Christic and ecclesial view brings us back to the theme of the heart we saw at the beginning in texts of Aquinas. When Thomas examines the role of Christ as head of the church, he says that the head has a clear preeminence in relation to the body's exterior members, whereas "the heart has a certain hidden influence." From this he concludes: "With respect to the visible nature by which . . . Christ himself is set before and above other humans, he is compared to the head. But the Holy Spirit, who invisibly gives life to the Church and unites it, is compared to the heart" (3.8.1 ad 3).

Thomas regards the Holy Spirit not only as the one who confers the gifts of life and unity on the members of Christ, but as, personally, the very unity of the church: "The uncreated Holy Spirit is numerically the same in the head and in the members, and in some way comes down from the head to the members not divided but one" (3 *Sent* 13.2.1 ad 2 3.408).[21] Again:

"In the Church there is a certain continuity [between Christ as head and his members] by reason of the Holy Spirit, who, numerically one and the same, fills and unites the whole Church" (*Ver* 29.4c). According to this comparison, the Holy Spirit is the loving heart from which flows that affective love which for Thomas is so central to the spiritual life of individuals and of the whole church.

Summary and Conclusion

We have seen, then, the crucial place Thomas gives to affectivity and the heart not only in his language but also in some of his most fundamental theological insights, which in some cases are uniquely his own. For him knowledge is imperfect without love, and consideration of creatures should inflame our hearts and souls with love and admiration of God: in us, as in the trinitarian life, our mental word should breathe forth love. The heart, especially as signifying the will, is the driving force of our other powers and acts. The Holy Spirit, who is Love in the trinitarian life and in the eternal act creating each of us, is also the strongest source of affective human love in our spiritual growth, warming our knowledge with the fire of love, conforming us to the Spirit, perfecting the image of God in us, leading us to that love of God which for wayfarers is better than any knowledge because it unites us existentially to God, the infinite Good. God puts in us an affective thirst to see God, a vision that overflows in blissful joy. Thomas also welcomes the affective life of the emotions and passions as part and parcel of human spiritual growth, as forces that should be developed and fostered for the contribution they can make to the integrity of truly human activity. Faith in the ineffable God would be impossible without the will's affective guidance, leading us to risk our personal assent to God even though we lack compelling intellectual evidence for such an assent. Growth in love of God, seen as friendship with God, begets the gift of infused wisdom, a gift of the Holy Spirit that produces a loving experiential knowledge of God surpassing studied knowledge; the Spirit intervenes with other gifts to guide the Christian to live according to the new law of the gospel. Indeed, the Holy Spirit, who is the heart of the mystical body, Christ being the head, is the source of the life and unity of that body, the Christian community or church, and this not only by vivifying and uniting the members by the gifts and virtues, but even more by being one identical person dwelling in all the members.

In concluding, however, it would be well to recall that if our study has stressed the affective aspects of Thomas' spirituality, Aquinas nevertheless speaks of the Holy Spirit as the Love that is breathed forth by the *Word*— *VERBUM spirans Amorem*. For Thomas, that is, love and affectivity in our spiritual life should always be guided by the knowledge and wisdom associated with the Word. This includes stages of growth in which, as we have seen, love and affectivity, first flowing from ordinary knowledge and from faith, beget a higher type of knowing than that of intellect, reasoning, and even the study of theology. The strong emotional and willed love that Thomas recognizes as integral to the spiritual life is for him not a tempestuous, unbridled enthusiasm but a love that flows from human sharing in divine knowledge and wisdom. His spirituality is a spirituality of the Word as well as a spirituality of the Holy Spirit of Love. For Thomas, loving friendship with God should result from the mind's eager pursuit of wisdom. Thus he says:

> The study of wisdom is very sublime because through it we especially reach a likeness to God, who *made all things in wisdom* [Ps 103(104):24]. So, because love is caused by likeness, the study of wisdom especially joins us with God in friendship, which is why Wis 7:14 says that wisdom *is an infinite treasure for human beings; those who use it become sharers in friendship with God* (*ScGen* 1.2).

If, then, we remain aware of all that is implied by Thomas' speaking of "the Word breathing forth Love," and if, at the same time, we recognize the integral role in spirituality that Thomas assigns to affectivity and the heart in relation to the Holy Spirit, we may conclude as follows: since for Thomas Aquinas the Holy Spirit is the life-giving and unifying *heart* of the church in all its members, we may (borrowing his typical cautionary qualifier) characterize his spirituality as, "in a certain way," a "spirituality of the heart."

NOTES

1. See Roberto Busa, ed., *Index thomisticus: Sancti Thomae Aquinatis operum omnium indices et concordantiae*, sectio 2: *Concordantia prima*, 23 vols. (Stuttgart, 1974–1975), under each word.
2. *Postilla super psalmos* (= *In Ps*), 38(39):4; Parma edition (1863, rpt. New York: Musurgia, 1949) 14.296. Here and elsewhere the Vulgate numbering of the psalm, used by Aquinas, is given first, with the Hebrew numbering in parentheses. All translations are our own.
3. In this text Thomas sees *laetitia* as expressing *latitudo* of the heart; we have tried to indicate this play on words by translating them as "delight" and "dilation" respectively.

4. Cf. also *De veritate* (= *Ver*), q. 26, a. 4 ad 5: ". . . according as the intensity of interior joy breaks forth into certain exterior signs, and in this way there is exultation. . . ."

5. As will be seen below, Thomas sees Christ as head of the mystical body and the Holy Spirit as its heart. The manifestation of Christ's heart through scripture, opened for understanding after the passion, may be an allusion to the opening of Christ's side by a lance as he hung on the cross.

6. *In Phil* 1, lect. 3, no. 31; in R. Cai, ed., *S. Thomae Aquinatis super epistolas S. Pauli lectura*, 2 vols. (Turin, 1953) II, 96.

7. *In Matt* 5:6; ed. Parma (1860, rpt. New York: Musurgia, 1949) 7.52.

8. Other rich sources of affective language are Thomas' sermons, prayers, and the Office of Corpus Christi composed by him. For example, praying to God the Father, he asks "that you will deign to bring me, a sinner, to that ineffable banquet where you with your Son and Holy Spirit are for your saints true light, full satiety, eternal joy, complete pleasure, and perfect happiness" (*Oratio post communionem;* ed. R. M. Spiazzi, *Opuscula theologica* 2 (Turin-Rome: Marietti, 1954, rpt. 1972), p. 288.

    Speaking of the eucharist, he exclaims: "Oh precious banquet so worthy of admiration, so saving, so full of every sweetness! What could be more precious than this banquet in which there is set before us to be eaten not (as once in the Law) the flesh of calves and goats but Christ, our true God? What is more admirable than this sacrament?" (*Officium de festo Corporis Christi*, lect. 2; ed. cit. 2, 277).

    Preaching on love of God and neighbor, he says that, in order to fulfill the precept of love of God, we must "first remember God's benefits because everything we have—our soul, our body, exterior goods—we have from God, and so we must serve God in everything and love God with a perfect heart. For we would be terribly ungrateful if we should reflect on what we have received from someone and still not love that person. . . ." Again, "we should consider God's excellence, for God is greater than our heart. . . . Hence, even if we serve God with our whole heart and with all our powers, we would not be doing enough, for as Sirach 43:30 says: 'When you glorify the Lord as much as you can, the Lord will still surpass your abilities. . . . When you bless the Lord, exalt the Lord as much as you can: the Lord is greater than all praise' " (*In duo praecepta caritatis . . . expositio: De dilectione Dei;* ed. cit., 2, nos. 1161–62, p. 249).

9. 1 *Sent* 1.1.sc 2; ed. P. Mandonnet (Paris: Lethielleux, 1929) 1.262.

10. One of my students, Michael Arges, who called this text to my atten-

tion, suggested perceptively that the whole chapter corresponds in Thomas to Bonaventure's *Itinerarium mentis in Deum*.

11. Although, as we have indicated, Thomas' spirituality is richly developed in his commentaries on scripture as well as in his sermons, prayers, and the Office of Corpus Christi composed by him, in what follows we shall quote mainly from the *Summa theologiae*.

    Unless otherwise indicated, all references will be to this work as follows: *Prima pars* = 1; *prima pars secundae partis* = 1–2; *secunda pars secundae partis* = 2–2; *tertia pars* = 3. These are followed by the numbers for the question and then the article; "sc" = sed contra; "c" = the main response; "ad 1" = the reply to the first argument.

12. For the notion of "theological spirituality" see our essay, "Toward Defining Spirituality," *SR: Studies in Religion/Sciences Religieuses* 12 (1983) 127–41, and, for an introduction to Aquinas' theological spirituality, our study, *Thomas Aquinas' Spirituality*, The Étienne Gilson Series, 7 (Toronto: Pontifical Institute of Mediaeval Studies, 1984). Our suggestion for a definition of spirituality is "Life in the Holy Spirit as brothers and sisters of Jesus and daughters and sons of the Father": this expressly links spirituality with the Holy Spirit and views it as trinitarian in character.

    Among many studies see the following: M.-D. Chenu, *St. Thomas d'Aquin et la théologie*, Maîtres spirituels, 17 (Paris: Seuil, 1959); Alvaro Huerga, *Santo Tomás de Aquino, teólogo de la vida cristiana* (Madrid: Fundación Universitaria Española, 1974); Yves Congar, "Saint Thomas, Maître de vie spirituelle," *Seminarium* 29 (1977) 994–1007. Related to our theme are J. Aumann, "Thomistic Evaluation of Love and Charity," *Angelicum* 53 (1978) 534–56, and Mary Ann Fatula, "The Holy Spirit and human actualization through love: the contribution of Aquinas," *Theology Digest* 32 (1985) 217–24.

    On the rich, often affective, spirituality of Thomas' sermons see Jean-Pierre Torrell, "La pratique pastorale d'un théologien: Thomas d'Aquin prédicateur," *Revue thomiste* 82 (1982) 213–45.

13. For these themes see 1.38.1–2 (the Holy Spirit as "gift"); 1.43.3–5 ("invisible missions" of the Son and Spirit; the Father's indwelling), and 1 *Sent* 14–15 (1.315–65: the Spirit as gift; missions of the Son and Spirit; the Spirit's gift of love and the Son's gift of wisdom as manifesting the Father, "who is the Ultimate to whom we return" [1.15.4.1 1 350]).

14. The same doctrine is developed in an earlier lengthier text (1 *Sent* 15.1 ad 3 1 350–51), in which Thomas says: "We possess a likeness of the Word only when we have the kind of knowledge that issues in love, a

love joining us to what we know by reason of fittingness (*convenientia*). And so we do not have the Son dwelling in us unless we receive that kind of knowledge, which we can have only through the grace that makes us pleasing to God" (351).

15. In 2–2.27.4c Thomas applies the same principles to conclude that in this life, although *knowledge* of God is mediated through knowledge of *creatures*, our *love* of God tends first to *God* and then to others: "and according to this charity loves God immediately, but other things mediately through God." To an argument that since knowledge of God is mediated, so must love of God be mediated, Thomas replies: "Because love of God is something greater than knowledge of God, *especially in our wayfarers' state*, [love of God] presupposes [knowledge of God]." The remark we have emphasized undoubtedly means to leave open the question of final beatitude, but in any case we are mainly concerned here with Thomas' teaching on life in the Spirit in our wayfarers' state, where for him love of God is greater than knowledge of God.

16. As F. Russell Hittinger puts it in a penetrating study of this question, according to Thomas,

> when we are related to things whose existence is inferior to our own, it is the intellect that shepherds the community, and ennobles that union. When we are related to that which is existentially superior to ourselves, it is the heart that follows the lead of God, who mysteriously ennobles our very being. The existential structure of beings guides Thomistic ethics.

See his article, "When It is More Excellent to Love than to Know: The Other Side of Thomistic 'Realism'," *Proceedings of the American Catholic Philosophical Association* 57 (1983) 171–79; the quotation is from pp. 177–78.

17. A clinical psychiatrist, Conrad W. Baers, in his "Christian Anthropology of Thomas Aquinas," *The Priest* 30/10 (October 1974) 29–33, brings out the harm done to mental health by such spiritualities and the psychological and medical soundness of Thomas' views on the passions and emotions.

18. *In Rom* 10, lect. 2, no. 831; in R. Cai, ed., *S. Thomae Aquinatis super epistolas S. Pauli lectura*, 2 vols. (Turin, 1953) I, 154.

19. Cf. ibid., ad 3m: ". . . To contemplate divine things belongs to wisdom in so far as it is a gift [of the Holy Spirit]".

20. Although in the *Summa theologiae* Thomas reserves his study of Christ

to the *tertia pars*, he holds that in our concrete sinful human history Christ is the only way to the Father for all. Therefore everything he says about life in the Spirit in the earlier sections must be reread and understood as communicated and lived in and with Christ, our Savior. The prologue to the *tertia pars*, speaking of our situation, indicates this:

> Our Savior, the Lord Jesus Christ . . . when 'saving his people from their sins,' showed us in himself the way of truth through which we can arrive at the bliss of immortal life. Hence to complete our entire theological work . . . we must consider him who is the Savior of all and the benefits he has bestowed on the human race.

On this see our article, "Aquinas' Spirituality" (above, n. 12), pp. 25–26, in which stress is laid on the value of Thomas' scriptural commentaries for seeing Christ's indispensable role in every facet of our life in the Spirit.

21. Cf. 3 *Sent* 13.2.2.sol.2; ed. M. F. Moos (Paris, 1933), p. 412: "The Holy Spirit, one in number, fills all [the members]," and *In Joan.* 1, lect. 10, 1, no. 202; in R. Cai, ed., *S. Thomae Aquinatis super Evangelium S. Ioannis lectura*, 5th ed. (Turin, 1952), p. 40: ". . . One and the same Holy Spirit, who is in Christ, fills all those who are to be sanctified."

Suzanne Noffke, O.P.

Catherine of Siena: The Responsive Heart

Introduction

Catherine of Siena, one of only two women to bear the title "doctor of the church," and that quite belatedly (in 1970 she and Teresa of Avila were so named), was a central figure in the church and society of her lifetime, 1347 to 1380. Because of her reputation for holiness, her influence among those who believed in her was profound. Disciples as varied as theologians, writers, and simple women and men, religious and lay, and clients from senators to queens to popes, looked to her for counsel—whether or not they would always accept it.

From her adolescence until her death at the age of thirty-three, without the benefit of any formal schooling but with a keen and searching mind, she developed for herself and for all who would listen a synthesis of what we would today call theological reflection on the ways of God with humankind and with the individual human spirit.

Letters began to become for Catherine a favored vehicle of communication, preaching, and direction perhaps as early as 1370. We possess today three hundred eighty-two of these letters. Between Advent of 1377 and October of 1378, in the midst of intense ministerial activity and personal stress, she composed the book which would later be called *The Dialogue* (because she cast it as a conversation between God and herself). This was her closest attempt at presenting her thought in any organized fashion. And during the last three and a half years of her life, secretaries and friends recorded twenty-six of her spontaneous prayers while she spoke in ecstasy.[1]

It is clear from her works that Catherine absorbed much from the Christian tradition as she gleaned it from preachers, books, and friends. One can isolate instances of obvious influence from sources such as Augustine, Gregory the Great, Bernard, Thomas Aquinas, Domenico Cavalca, and others. Yet her writing is not speculative or systematic or analytical, in spite of the Dominican scholastic atmosphere in which she moved. Her intent is practical and pastoral, her tone personal and warm, her method not conceptual argumentation but passionate exhortation wrapped in a weaving of images which she continually develops and integrates, one with the other, as she goes. Her love and knowledge of scripture, particularly of John and Paul, are everywhere evident.

Catherine's synthesis is, in the end, so tightly woven into the fabric of her images that it is difficult if not impossible to separate its elements into a neat analysis. Different commentators have argued even for different central theses in the saint's thought and spirituality, and each argument has some validity, since her themes, as it were, dance around each other.[2] I would, however, articulate the pivot of her thought as follows: God is truth/love—truth that is love and love that is truth—revealed in Jesus Christ and discovered in knowledge of oneself in God and of God in oneself. And the reality that stands as symbol at the heart of this dynamic IS the heart: the heart of Jesus as revelation of the heart of God, and the human heart as drawn to respond to that heart of divinity-engrafted-into-humanity.

Il cuore, "the heart," for Catherine does not have the precision of her very Augustinian use of the trinity of memory/understanding/will. It consorts rather with two other terms which seem to grapple more with the integrity of the human spirit: affetto, which, though usually translated as "affection," is very close to "will" and carries the sense of movement, impulse, toward doing, the will reaching for what memory and understanding hold out as good; and mente, which, though often translated as "mind," has more the sense of the human spirit as a whole entity. The heart emerges as the physical reality it is, but more as the seat of all human (and, analogously, Godly) response. So we find expressions such as "heart and spirit" (mente), "heart and affection" (affetto), "cold heart," "hard heart," "lift up your heart." It is in the heart that good or evil thoughts (pensieri, cogitazioni) reside, from the heart that good or evil designs come, within the heart that God dwells. If, in Augustinian and later scholastic terms, truth resides in the understanding (intellect) and love in the will, the heart is where truth and love meet and become one. Or, negatively, if the love in the heart is untrue, selfish and self-centered, it is in fact a cloud over faith, understanding's window onto the light of truth.[3]

Thus charity, which can only be true love springing from God, is the only source of life for the human heart, the only means by which the human heart can in this life "see and experience" God, embrace the truth/love that God is by following in the footsteps of Jesus (*P*19 170–175).[4] So the story of Catherine's spirituality is ultimately the story of charity; hers is indeed a "spirituality of the heart."

The Heart of Jesus as Revelation of the Heart of God

Before we can begin to discuss any aspect of the mystery of Jesus in Catherine's spirituality, we must review very briefly her trinitarian language, the most basic of it inherited from Augustine. The attribution of power to the Father, wisdom to the Word, and love/mercy to the Holy Spirit is a constant point of gravitation for her thought. And the highest analogue to the Trinity thus understood is the human trinity of memory (:Father), understanding (:Word), and will (:Holy Spirit). Catherine's concrete images for the persons of the Trinity, and their implications for the present study, will find their place within these frameworks.

Catherine insists again and again that one can never speak of any person of the Trinity without speaking at least implicitly of the others, since God is indivisible. This is nowhere more true than when we speak of the mystery of Jesus. Thus: "In Christ crucified we find the Father and share in his power; we find the wisdom of God's only-begotten Son, which enlightens our understanding; we see and experience the mercy of the Holy Spirit by discovering the affectionate love with which Christ gave us the benefit of his passion" (*LT*158, to Nino da Pisa).[5] Always as we discuss the mystery of Christ the Trinity will be present, and we shall have to revert often especially to the intimate bond in Catherine's thought between the incarnate Word and the Spirit.

For Catherine the most basic truth of our relationship with God is that God created us "out of a boundless love" and "for love," that we might be made holy in God and share eternally in the divine goodness. But because the human heart has been alienated from God's love by sin, this truth could never be realized except through the mystery of redemption. This is why we can discover the truth of God's love (and therefore the reality of who we are) only in the crucified Christ. And for Catherine the locus of that discovery is the open side of the crucified, for there, in his heart, we see just how boundlessly we are loved.

But why, Catherine asks in the *Dialogue*, did Christ want his heart to be pierced when he was already dead? "There were plenty of reasons," he said, "but I shall tell you one of the chief. My longing for humankind was infinite, but the actual deed of bearing pain and torment was finite and could never show all the love I had. This was why I wanted you to see the secret of my heart, wanted to show it to you opened up, so that you would see that I loved you more than finite suffering could show" (*D*75 138).[6]

"The secret of his heart," "*il segreto del cuore*": it is the inmost heart, "secret" in the sense that it had been hidden until it was revealed when his side was pierced.[7] The open heart of the crucified is thus a revelation: a revelation of love alternately described by Catherine as Christ's love and, because they are inseparable, God's love. And it is an invitation, as love always is: an invitation to contemplate, to be consumed, to bathe, to hide, to drink, to rest. The foundation for this, often explicitly cited by Catherine (from the Vulgate, freely), is in John 1:32: "If I am lifted up high, I will draw everything to myself." For "the human heart is always drawn by love." (*D*26 65) "And it was to draw the soul's affection to high things, and to bring the mind's eye to gaze into the fire, that your eternal Word wanted to be lifted up high" (*P*19 172).

We are invited first to gaze, to contemplate the mystery revealed in the open heart of the crucified. Always Catherine stresses, when she speaks of the object of that contemplation, that in that heart we will find "the God-man," "*Dio-e-uomo*," that is, the whole mystery of the incarnation of the Word, the whole mystery of God's dealing with humankind, the whole mystery of creation, redemption, and salvation. This is to find self-knowledge and knowledge of God, to discover who we are in God and who God is to us. And this is to "discover hearty love, for all that Christ does in us he does, as this shows, with that sort of hearty love" (*LT*158).

The mystery we gaze upon in the heart of Christ is often described as fire: "you will discover fire" (*LT*158),[8] "for then [in the passion] the fire hidden under our ashes began to show itself completely and generously by splitting open his most holy body on the wood of the cross" (*P*19 172). We are invited over and over, especially in Catherine's letters, to plunge ourselves into this fire and there be consumed, made one with the fire—which is none other than God's charity, God's Spirit. The passion of Jesus is in fact, for Catherine, as intimately the work of the Holy Spirit as is the incarnation itself, "for there is no blood without fire" (*LT*80, to Master Giovanni Terzo).

Thus we enter into the mystery of the blood of Christ, which so penetrates all of Catherine's writings. She opens every letter with: "I Caterina . . . am writing to you in his precious blood." And "there is no blood without fire." Every attribute of the Spirit is attributed also to the blood, and so the blood is charity, mercy, generosity, compassion, liberation, "because the blood was shed out of love" (*LT*158). It is the Holy Spirit who taps the cask of Jesus' body to set his blood flowing for us.[9]

Oh boundless love, charity! I am not surprised that in your blood
I find the power of compassion, for I see that it was out of divine
compassion, not because you owed it to us, that you shed your
blood. And you took vengeance on the cruelest of cruelties, the
cruelty we inflicted on ourselves when by sin we made ourselves
worthy of death (*LT*210, to Matteo Cenni).[10]

As fire of charity, the blood consumes its opposite, sin, which is
ultimately selfish love, a dampness that keeps the wood of our being from
becoming wholly one with the fire (*LT*80, *D*66 125). And so Catherine sees
it also as a cleansing bath in which she is continually exhorting her disciples to immerse themselves. When she comments on the flow of blood and
water from Jesus' heart pierced by the lance of Longinus (Jn 19:34), she
sees in the water the cleansing of sacramental baptism and in the blood the
cleansing of martyrdom ("baptism of desire") and of sacramental confession (*D*75 138–139).

Perhaps one of the richest clusters of imagery in Catherine's writings
centers around the invitation to drink from the open side of Christ. Her
love for this mystery is certainly rooted in her own experience very early in
her public ministry when, to force herself to remain with the cantankerous
Andrea whom she was nursing, she pressed her mouth to the woman's
cancerous breast, and on another occasion drank the fetid water with
which she had washed the sore. In response, the following night she felt
herself physically drawn by Jesus to drink from the wound in his side.[11]

Whenever Catherine speaks of drinking from the side of Christ, from
his heart, there is a clear assumption of willingness to let go of all selfish
love, to "become so sated and drunk that we no longer see ourselves," no
longer see anything "but the blood that was shed with such blazing love"
(*LT*75). How vividly she writes to Bartolomeo Dominici, who has complained to her of his reticence to preach to those to whom he has been sent:

Do as a heavy drinker does who loses himself and can no longer
see himself. If he really likes the wine he drinks even more, till
his stomach becomes so warmed by the wine that he can no
longer hold it, and out it comes! Truly, son, here is the table on
which we find this wine: I mean the pierced side of God's Son.
This is the blood that warms, that drives out all chill, clears the
voice of the one who drinks it, and gladdens heart and soul. For
this blood is shed with the fire of divine charity. It so warms us
that out *we* come from our very selves—and from that point on,
we cannot see ourselves selfishly, but only for God, and we see
God for God, and we see our neighbors for God. And when we

have drunk enough, out it comes over the heads of our sisters and brothers (*LDT*6).

Here the encounter with the open side of Christ, with "the secret of his heart" (the second stair on Catherine's three-staired bridge of the crucified, of charity), becomes one with "the kiss of peace" (the third and highest stair).[12] Here Catherine's mystical experience fairly sings in her images. Charity is the mother at whose breast the soul drinks in the milk of divine goodness that makes everything bitter become sweet. And this mother charity is at once the Holy Spirit and the crucified Christ. "Such a soul [wholly surrendered to God's love] has the Holy Spirit as a mother who nurses her at the breast of divine charity. The Holy Spirit has set her free, releasing her, as her lord, from the slavery of selfish love" (*D*141 292).

She receives the fruit of spiritual calm, a union of the emotions with my gentle divine nature in which she tastes milk, just as an infant when quieted rests on its mother's breast, takes her nipple, and drinks her milk through her flesh. This is how the soul who has reached this final stage rests on the breast of my divine charity and takes into the mouth of her holy desire the flesh of Christ crucified (*D*96 179).[13] Christ acted like a wet-nurse who is nursing a baby. When the baby is sick she takes the medicine for it because the baby is tiny and weak and wouldn't be able to tolerate the bitterness since it drinks nothing but milk. Oh dearest love, Jesus! You are the wet-nurse who took the bitter medicine. . . . You took the bitterness so that we receive health (*LT*260, to the prisoners in Siena).

This breast of charity is, then, the heart of Christ crucified, she emphasizes again and again, and to drink there we too must be open to the love that crucifies, the love that will go to any length for our neighbors' good:

I long to see you always feeding and nursing at the breast of the gentle mother, charity, for I am convinced no one can have life without the milk this glorious mother gives us. She is so sweet and mild to souls who taste her that in her everything bitter becomes sweet and every heavy burden light. This doesn't surprise me, because when we live in this charity and love we are living in God. So says St. John: "God is charity, and when we live in charity we are living in God, and God in us" [1 Jn 4:16]. . . .

And just as a baby draws milk through its mother's breast, so souls in love with God draw God to themselves through Christ crucified. . . . Let your heart and soul burst with the heat of love [as you drink] at this breast of charity through the flesh of Christ crucified (LDT59, to Monna Bartolomea).

We cannot, in fact, nourish others unless we first nourish our own soul on true solid virtues [the only evidence we have to offer, says Catherine, that charity is alive in us], and we cannot do this unless we cling to the breast of divine charity and from that breast draw the milk of divine sweetness. . . . Therefore we must cling to the breast of Christ crucified, in whom is the mother, charity. And through his flesh we shall draw the milk that nourishes our soul, charity's offspring, the virtues. . . . And we cannot be nourished on this milk without suffering (LT86, to the abbess of Santa Maria degli Scalzi).

In other words, we are back to Catherine's experience with Andrea: we cannot drink from the heart of Christ unless we are willing also to drink from the wounds of our neighbors! And when we do, we ourselves become sources of that same nourishment for others, "having within ourselves the sweet mother charity" (LT356, to three Neapolitan women).[14]

The open side of Christ is also for Catherine a cavern of refuge and rest. From the beginning of our life with God it is a place of refuge from the temptation to selfish love, a haven in which to learn what true love is,[15] the "cell" in which we find knowledge of self and of God (LT36, to certain novices at Monteoliveto).[16] And in the end it is a place of intimacy, rest, and peace, our home, the place where we belong.[17]

The Human Heart Responds

It is in the heart, as was said above, that truth and love meet and embrace, or refuse to embrace. Here Catherine's image of the eye becomes pertinent. Understanding is our spiritual eye, and its pupil (the opening that lets in the light of truth) is faith. Self-centeredness is a cloud that covers this pupil and distorts reality, so that truth appears to be falsehood and falsehood, truth; virtue appears repulsive and sin desirable. The heart, however, cannot help responding in love to whatever understanding presents as good, and so, in proportion to our determination to hold on to or let go of self-centeredness, our love will embrace falsehood or truth.

If, then, we are honestly trying to let go of self-centeredness (the first of Catherine's three stairs, the feet of affection (D26 54) we will look into the open heart of Christ crucified and there see the truth of God's love for us, the truth that God, loving us unspeakably much, "created us for the glory and praise of his name, so that we might be made holy in him and might share in his eternal beauty" (*LT*102, to Raymond of Capua). And since we cannot help loving what our understanding tells us is true, we will begin to love this truth of God. Now "two opposing loves cannot live together" in our heart, and so we will necessarily begin to be stripped of our self-centeredness and "clothed in God's love." And as this process intensifies, "when the devil finds the heart ablaze in the fire of divine charity, he doesn't come around much—just as a fly avoids a boiling pot" (*LT*287).

But how are we to know just how true or false, how self-centered or God-centered, our love is? Our human emotions, Catherine says, reflected in our tears, will tell us—for "all tears come from the heart; nor is there any other bodily member that can satisfy the heart as the eyes can" (*D*88 161).[18]

As long as we hold on to our self-centeredness, the tears we shed, and all our other emotions as well, are essentially lifeless, since they are spent only on our own selfish interests and on false values. But once we even begin honestly to let go of that self-centeredness there is room for truth to start to make its inroads. Of course, elements of selfishness linger for a long time in our response, because we do not grow into perfect truth and love all at once. So our first life-giving tears are still mostly for ourselves; they are tears of sorrow for sin, but only because sin means punishment for us. And the responses of our heart to other people are the same: we respond out of fear of God's wrath. As we begin to discover, however, that God is merciful, our tears become tears of hope springing from the beginnings of self-knowledge and knowledge of God's goodness. But these tears and all of our emotional responses at this stage are still tinged with a subtle "spiritual selfishness," and if from one source or another we are deprived of the *consolation* that often comes with loving God or others, our tears turn to tears of "tender self-pity."

Only to the extent that we have let go of even this "spiritual selfishness" can we respond with the sort of love we find in the heart of Jesus. This is that blessed juncture at which our gazing into the open heart of the crucified is transformed into the "kiss of peace."

But how are we who are so natively selfish ever to arrive at such a juncture at all? We cannot, in fact, except through honest desire. "I who am infinite God," says the Father to Catherine in the *Dialogue*, "want you to serve me with what is infinite, and you have nothing infinite except your soul's affection and desire." It is the mouth of our desire that presses to the breast of Christ crucified to drink and thus kisses the very wellspring of the fire of true love, of charity. Catherine emphasizes that it is to his *flesh,* his humanity, that we so join ourselves. "In other words, [the soul] follows his teaching and his footsteps because she has learned . . . that she could not follow me, the Father. For no pain can befall me, the eternal Father, but it can befall my beloved Son, the gentle loving Word. And you cannot walk without pain, but must achieve proven virtue [the offspring and proof of charity] through suffering. So the soul rests on the breast of Christ crucified who *is* my love, and so drinks the milk of virtue."

It is at the "table of the cross" that we must eat, and our food must be the souls of our neighbors, in that same sense that Christ's food was to do the will of God who had sent him, which will was the accomplishment of our salvation. And for this there is no way around the cross.

In the summer of 1370, Catherine herself had prayed, "Create a clean heart in me, O God," to which Christ responded by mystically removing her own heart and several days later replacing it with another, saying, "See, dearest daughter, a few days ago I took your heart from you; now, in the same way, I give you my own heart. For the future, it is by it that you must live." Later she would say of it, "While this fire is burning in me it . . . brings . . . a boundless love for my neighbor, so that I would readily undergo death itself with joy and gladness for my neighbor's sake" (*LCS* 174–176).

In the *Dialogue* and in her letters she speaks of the human heart as a lamp, a vessel, which must be filled with the blood of Christ:

> The heart really is a lamp. Like a lamp, it should be narrow at the bottom and wide at the top. I mean your desire and affection should be restricted where the world is concerned, while your heart's affection in Christ crucified should be expansive, loving him and holding on to him with a true and holy determination. Then you will fill this lamp at the open side of Christ crucified. There you will find the fire of divine charity shown you in Christ's wounds, and his open side reveals to you the secret of his heart, that what he has given and done for us he had done in simple love (*LT*112, to Countess Bandecca Salimbeni).[19]

God in the *Dialogue* speaks also of the vessel of our heart being "filled with the sea that is my very self, the most high eternal Godhead." And, being filled with the sea, it overflows in charity, "and so she weeps with those who weep and rejoices with those who rejoice" (*D*89 164). It is the same response of which Catherine wrote to Bartolomeo Dominici, when she spoke of the wine, the blood, so warming us "that out it comes over the heads of our sisters and brothers" (*LDT*6). And in her own desperate love for a broken church she would pray near the end of her life: "I have nothing to give but what you have given me. Take my heart, then, and squeeze it out over this bride's face" (*LT*371, to Raymond of Capua).[20]

So the tears that we shed, and our blood, which is the very blood of Jesus when we love with the love of the crucified, become a river in which others can be cleansed and refreshed. Over and over in her letters Catherine assures her correspondents that she is shedding such tears for them— "with blood and sweat." And she urges her disciples to do the same. These tears and blood and sweat, in fact, are so one with the fire of charity that they *are* "tears of fire," whether accompanied by physical tears or not. "In this fire the Holy Spirit weeps in my presence for them and for their neighbors. I mean that my divine charity sets ablaze with its flame the soul who offers me her restless longing without any physical tears. These, I tell you, are tears of fire, and this is how the Holy Spirit weeps."

Such is the love of the crucified to which the human heart is called:

> You must love [others] with the same pure love with which I love you. But you cannot do this for me because I love you without being loved by you, even before you existed. . . . [Y]ou cannot repay me. But you must give this love to other people, loving them without being loved by them. You must love them without any concern for your own spiritual or material profit, but only for the glory and praise of my name, because I love them (*D*88 165).

A Case in Point: Friendship, Heart and Heart in God's Heart

Catherine speaks often of loving others "with a special love." This is the love of friendship, the love which wants to share secrets (*D*60 115). She so loves her family, disciples, and close friends, and her love is evident in her letters to them, where each is treated so uniquely that it is obvious Catherine knows them intimately and respects their individuality. And it is evident in her recorded prayers, where she often remembers particularly those God has given her to "love with a special love, with a special concern." She asks God to punish her for their sins, "for I am the cause of them" (*P*11 94). In no way does she want her own sins to be an obstacle to those God has put on her shoulders. "I give them back to you, since I am weak and inadequate" (*P*14 123). She prays that they may have the gift of compassion and the "compassionate cruelty" of the cross (*P*15 134). "Join and engraft them into yourself," she begs, "so that they may bring forth the fruit of life (*P*17 152). Set their hearts so afire that they may be coals . . . alight and ablaze with charity for you and for their neighbors" (*P18* 163). And in her last recorded prayer: "I offer and commend to you my children, whom I so love, for they are my soul. . . . Give, O give to us, eternal Father, your gentle benediction" (*P26* 226).

The gift of this sort of "special love" for another can be a "holy trick" on God's part, we are told in chapters 64 and 302 of the *Dialogue*. For if it is less than a union of hearts in God, we will sooner or later be forced to face our imperfection when the relationship falls short of our more selfish expectations. The "collision" may come through a necessary separation, or through any supposed slight. Perhaps we suspect that our friend loves or keeps company with someone else more than with us, or loves us less than we love him or her. Any distress we feel is a sure signal, the Father says to Catherine, that that "special love" and all our loves need re-examination. It is a "holy trick" because such re-examination will lead us to love not only our special friend but everyone else more perfectly.

And Catherine is quick to point it out to her disciples when she suspects their love for her or for anyone else is less than this ideal requires. She and Biancina Salimbeni know each other well, for Catherine has been Biancina's guest during her rather lengthy stay at Rocca d'Orcia, and so the latter will probably recognize without having to be told what the reference is when Catherine writes at length about loving only in God. "We are constantly clinging," she chides. "God cuts one branch out from under us and we grab on to another" (*LT*111).

And in another letter she tells Melina Barbani, a new and somewhat infatuated disciple in Lucca, that God wants no human friendship getting between us and God. Our love should be "so clean and free that we love no one, nothing, spiritually or temporally, apart from God." If we do, it will interfere with our being united with Christ and transformed in him. "God asks us to give ourselves freely, as he did . . . getting rid of any medium, anything that gets in between—except divine charity, which is a sweet and glorious medium that doesn't separate but unites."

She goes on to develop the first of two wonderful images of the sort of union of hearts she is thinking of. A mason, she writes, gathers many stones and joins them with mortar, and so they become both "stones" and "wall." The medium, the mortar, God has used to join us is the blood of Christ, and so we become most perfectly one with each other by becoming one in God. So, she concludes, "If you still want poor wretched me as intermediary," go to the cross. "There you will find the Lamb and me, and there you can graze and fulfill your desires" (*LDT*58).

The second image is found in the *Dialogue* as well as in a number of her letters. Friendship, the Father tells her, "is just like a vessel that you fill at the fountain. If you take it out of the fountain to drink, the vessel is soon empty. But if you hold your vessel in the fountain while you drink, it will not get empty. Indeed, it will always be full" (D64 121). And from numerous other references we know that the fountain is the heart of Christ, and the love that we drink in perfect friendship is his blood, the fire of charity, the Holy Spirit of God.

Such friendship is not just for the two friends nor only for this life but extends in its effects to all the world and on into eternity. For the blessed "know a special kind of sharing with those whom they loved most closely with a special love in the world, a love through which they grew in grace and virtue. . . . [T]hey have not lost that love; no, they still love and share with each other even more closely and fully, adding their love to the good of all. For I would not have you think this special good they have is only for themselves" (D41 83). In a letter to her own dearest friend, Raymond of Capua, Catherine writes, "Pray . . . that you and I together may drown ourselves in the blood of the humble Lamb, which will make us strong and faithful" (LT344).

The kind of love to which these "special loves" of ours introduce us so "expands our heart" that we become as concerned about others' well-being as we are about our own. We want to help wherever and however we can; we are just to all, great or small, rich or poor; we refuse to judge anyone unfairly but always assume the best intentions under even the most apparent wrongdoing; we are grateful and appreciative, merciful even to the seemingly undeserving; we are peace-loving and faithful. Our heart becomes so large, in fact, that we have "room for the whole world" (LT263, to Monna Montagna) in it, and "every place is our place; every time is our time" (LT349, to several public officials of Rome). It is indeed a precious gift within the heart of Christ.[21]

Conclusion

The heart of Christ is for Catherine, then, the revelation of the very heart of God, with the entire mystery of God's unspeakable love for humankind in general and for every person in particular. The divine-human reality of that heart draws our heart to respond in such a way that it transforms us little by little, even through "holy tricks," into Christ, so that we come finally to love with his own love. And in the end we are drawn in peace into the very self of God in eternity, there to experience the fullness of every love with which we have been gifted on earth.

NOTES

1. Catherine's letters have gone through several editions in Italian, the most complete recent edition being that of Niccolò Tommaseo, revised by Piero Misciattelli in six volumes, *Le lettere di S. Caterina da Siena*, Siena: Giuntini & Bentivoglio, 1913–1922). The first volume of the only truly critical edition was published by Eugenio Dupré Theseider, *Epistolario di S. Caterina da Siena*, Roma: Istituto storico italiano per il Medio Evo, 1940); the work is presently being continued by Antonio Volpato under the same auspices. A forthcoming English translation of her letters, based on the latest critical work on the texts, is currently in process. The first volume of *The Letters of Catherine of Siena*, edited by the present author, has been published (1988) by Medieval and Renaissance Texts and Studies, Binghamton, and the remaining three volumes are projected to be published over the next four to five years. In the meantime, a total of one hundred five letters are available in English in Vida Scudder's *Selected Letters of Catherine Benincasa: Saint Catherine of Siena as Seen in Her Letters* (London: J.M. Dent & Sons, Ltd., and New York: E.P. Dutton, 1927) and Kenelm Foster and Mary John Ronayne's *I Catherine: Selected Writings of Catherine of Siena* (London: Collins, 1980). *The Dialogue* (=D) is available in translation by Suzanne Noffke, O.P. (New York: Paulist Press, 1980), based on the critical edition by Giuliana Cavallini, *Il Dialogo* (Roma: Edizioni Cateriniani, 1968). G. Cavallini also published the critical edition of *Le Orazioni* (Roma: Edizioni Cateriniani, 1978), available in English as *The Prayers of Catherine of Siena* (=P), translated by S. Noffke (New York: Paulist Press, 1983).

   More complete bibliographies can be found in my translations as well as in my article "Catherine of Siena" in *The Encyclopedia of Religion* (New York: Macmillan, 1987). The most complete Catherinian bibliographies available, with good coverage of all major languages, are those published by Edizioni Cateriniani in Rome under the title *Bibliografia analitica di S. Caterina da Siena: 1901–1950* by Lina Zanini; . . . *1951–1975* by Zanini, edited by M.C. Paterna; 1975 to present in process.

2. Scholars whose works are especially significant here include (in roughly chronological order): Jacques Leclerq, Giulio Bertoni, Robert Fawtier, Francesco Valli, Giovanni Getto, Arrigo Levasti, Alvaro Grion, Tito Centi, Innocenzo Colosio, Giacinto D'Urso, Giuliana Cavallini, Gabriella Anodal, Adriana Odasso Cartotti, Kenelm Foster. Only the last of these, unfortunately, wrote in English. A recent work which is the nearest approximation yet in English to a synthesis of the

major themes of Catherine's spirituality is Mary Ann Fatula's *The Way of Catherine of Siena* (Wilmington: Michael Glazier, 1987).

3. So, for example, in *LT*287, to Brother Niccolò di Nanni di Ser Vanni of Monteoliveto, and to Don Pietro di Giovanni di Viva, Carthusian monk at Maggiano near Siena: "One cannot attain true love unless one's heart and affection are stripped of selfish self-love. Such selfish love and softness toward one's selfish sensual passion robs one of the life of grace and obscures the light of understanding; it is in fact a cloud put over [that eye's] pupil, the light of most holy faith." (All translations from the letters are mine. "*L*" = Letter; "T" indicates the Tommaseo numbering, whereas "DT" will indicate the new and more accurately chronological numbering, where it exists, of Dupré Theseider.)

4. *P*19, pp. 170–175. (All references to Catherine's prayers are thus indicated, the numbering and page reference being that of the Noffke translation.)

5. See also, for illustration of this inseparability of the Trinity, *P*10, pp. 78–79, and *D*110, p. 206, for just a few examples.

6. Translation corrected from published version. All references to the *Dialogue* give first the chapter number, which is consistent in all editions, and then the page number in the Noffke translation. Cf. also *LT*55, to Don Guglielmo, Prior General of the Carthusians.

7. Catherine may have borrowed the idea from St. Bernard, *In Cantico sermo LXI:* "The secret of his heart is revealed through the wounding of his body,"

8. Also *LT*75, to the Monastery of San Gaggio in Florence and to the Abbess and nuns of the Monastery in Monte Sansavino; and in many other places as well.

9. *LT*136, to Angelo da Ricasoli: "His humanity is the cask that enclosed the divine nature, and the cellarer, the fire and hand that is the Holy Spirit, tapped that cask on the wood of the most holy cross."

10. Cf. also *P*19, p. 172.

11. *The Life of Catherine of Siena* (=*LCS*) by Raymond of Capua, translation by Conleth Kearns (Wilmington: Michael Glazier, 1980), pp. 148–157.

12. Cf. *D*26, pp. 64–65, and 75–76, pp. 137–141.

13. Translation corrected from published text.

14. I have changed the text from second person to first here for the sake of continuity with the present context.

15. Cf. *D*124, p. 239, and *LT*47, to Pietro di Giovanni Venture of Siena, as well as many other letters in which she urges her disciples to hide themselves in the open side of Christ crucified for safety.

16. Here Catherine's "spirituality of the heart" becomes linked with all that she has to say about this inner "cell of self-knowledge and of the knowledge of God," which would bear a lengthy treatment in itself.
17. Cf. LT262, to Monna Tora, daughter of Pietro Gambacorti of Pisa; D124, p. 239; LT36, T47, DT31.
18. D88, p. 161. All that follows on tears and emotion is based on D88–96, pp. 161–182, unless otherwise noted.
19. Catherine may have borrowed the image of the lamp from Giovanni Colombini, who uses it in his Letter I, but not in the detail Catherine gives it. There is also a comparison of virginity to the lamp, narrow and closed below and open and lighted above, in Girolamo da Siena, Soccorso de' poveri, p. 49; he may have borrowed it from Catherine.
20. Though labeled by Tommaseo as having been written to Pope Urban VI, this letter, judging from internal evidence, must have been an appendix to T373, to Raymond of Capua.
21. We could go on yet to discuss the presence of the heart of Christ in the world through the church, the wine cellar from which the blood is dispensed by Christ's vicar, the pope. The latter is, in fact, spoken of as "the mother who nurses us at the breasts of divine charity" (LT270, to Pope Gregory XI), as "the dear Christ on earth," as Catherine often so intimately calls him.

Jared Wicks, S.J.

Martin Luther:
The Heart Clinging to the Word

Annually reformation scholars and theological libraries around the world receive copies of the *Lutherjahrbuch,* with essays, book reviews, and an extensive bibliography of works on Martin Luther. The cover of each volume bears a sketch of the coat of arms Luther chose for himself in 1530. The reformer stipulated that a golden ring should encircle a field of blue. The petals of a white rose open on the field, and in the center of the rose stands a human heart. On the heart, a black cross is embossed.

Luther explained how his chosen emblem gave compendious expression to his theology.

> There is first to be a black cross upon the heart, but with the heart having its natural color. Thus I would remind myself that faith in the Crucified saves us. For if one believes from the heart, he becomes righteous. Being a black cross, it mortifies and means to bring pain, yet it leaves the heart still its own color, not ruining our nature. Thus the cross does not kill, but keeps alive. *Iustus enim ex fide vivet, sed fide Crucifixi.* Such a heart should stand in the center of a white rose, to show that faith gives joy, consolation, and peace. . . . The rose is in a field of heavenly blue, to show that our joy in the Spirit and in faith is a beginning of heavenly happiness to come, which we already have by laying hold of it in hope, although it is not yet manifest.[1]

Martin Luther did understand himself as a teacher of the true meaning of faith in Jesus Christ. On the one hand, he set forth the "theology of the cross," for in Christ Crucified the wisdom of God has paradoxically made itself known. The message, however, conveys to the believer a consoling grace of certainty and conviction about God's mercy and loving-kindness. The fretful heart finds peace and assurance in the word God has spoken through his crucified Son.

Luther's concern over fixing the mystery of Christ upon the believing heart became explicit at times in his preaching. On December 27, 1533, he explained the responses of Mary and the shepherds of Bethlehem to the coming of Christ.[2] Although the shepherds came to see the new-born baby and later told others about the marvelous events, few in fact came to genuine faith. This reveals the inconstancy of the human heart, so liable to forget if God does not supply new signs and wonders. But Mary kept the words in her heart, meditating and pondering the significance of what had happened. Mary became deeply convinced that this child of hers was the Savior.

> Just so our Lord God wants us to cradle his word diligently in our hearts and so impress it that it becomes second nature. As in the Canticle, "Fix me on your heart like a seal" and indelible character. The word is not to sit lightly on the heart, like a swan on water. . . . She said, "I want God's word so impressed on my heart that it is a mark no one can remove, like a natural growth no one can uproot." Such was the heart of Mary, where the words remained as she absorbed them. And whoever so retains the word has in fact the true "character" of Christ which they allow no one to take away.[3]

An earlier exposition of the same passage was more specific on the nature of faith and more positive on the shepherds. Divinely-given faith is one that ascribes little importance to the speaker serving as God's intermediary. Such faith is lasting:

> Godly faith clings to the word, which is God himself; it believes, trusts, and honors the word not on account of the one who has spoken it, but feels that here is such a certainty of truth that nobody can ever tear it away.[4]

The shepherds attended only to what was said, not being overly fascinated with the angelic messengers. And Mary was not disturbed by the low estate of the shepherds as she fixed the words themselves in her heart.

The word itself, as you disregard the person, must satisfy the heart, must embrace and capture the believer so that he, like one who is imprisoned in it, feels how true and right it is, even if all the world, all angels, all the princes of hell, had a different message.[5]

Luther had not always been so clear and precise about how the believing heart clings to God's word of grace and thereby finds the work of Christ operative in itself. Luther's accounts of both the content and the mediation of salvation show development. His autobiographical flashbacks, which recur with some frequency after 1531, stress that he had moved ahead in spurts, under providential guidance, in his understanding of God and of saving faith. There were breakthroughs and liberating discoveries.[6] These reminiscences are notoriously hard to correlate with the actual contents of Luther's extant early works and letters, but his works show clearly enough that his teaching underwent development.

In the present context, concerning the heart and the word, we will present three distinct emphases that successively came to the fore in Luther's theological work. There was early emphasis on the heart confronted by Christ's call to conversion and lifelong purification. But beginning in 1518, Luther sounded a new accent as he laid great emphasis on how the heart is given a consoling gift mediated by Christ's sacramental word of forgiveness and life. However, the older Luther could teach with yet another emphasis as he also called hearts to be obediently submissive to the words and signs we encounter in the dispensation willed by God and instituted by his Son's own decisions. In Luther's work, earlier themes do not disappear from the doctrinal and spiritual field, but they remain in later phases, being however repositioned around new emphases called forth by the interaction of personal insight with defensive and clarifying responses by Luther to the views of his adversaries.

"Poenitentiam Agite" (Mt 4:17)

No action taken by Martin Luther is better known than his protest, under date of October 31, 1517, over the way Johann Tetzel, O.P. was promoting the indulgences offered by the popes to those who would contribute to the building fund for the new St. Peter's.[7] Less well known is the tight connection between Luther's 1517 protest and the doctrine of sin and repentance he had been working out since he began his career as scripture professor in Wittenberg University in 1513. By late 1517, Luther had given lectures on the psalter (1513–15), Romans (1515–16), Galatians (1516–17), and the early chapters of Hebrews (1517). He had also published an edition of the vernacular mystical treatise, *A German Theology* (December 1516), and had brought out his own first independent work, an exposition of the seven penitential psalms (spring 1517).[8]

Then, in October 1517 Luther addressed himself, by mail, to the archbishop of Mainz and Magdeburg, the prelate who had given Tetzel his commission to proclaim the abundant graces of the St. Peter's indulgence. Luther sent Archbishop Albrecht a letter of thoughtful admonition, a list of ninety-five propositions for theological debate, and a short treatise on indulgences which set forth a better grounded view of sin and repentance than was implied in Tetzel's campaign.[9]

Both the spirit and the sense of Luther's alternative proposal are captured well in the opening theses:

1. When our Lord and teacher Jesus Christ said, "Repent (*Poenitentiam agite*)," he meant that the whole life of believers should be one of repentance.

2. This text cannot be taken as referring to sacramental penance. . . .

3. Nor does it refer solely to interior repentance, for this is nothing unless it produce outward mortifications of the flesh.

4. Therefore such penance continues as long as hatred of self (which is genuine interior repentance) remains, namely until one enters the kingdom of heaven.[10]

Following this forceful assertion of the normative character of the penitential life, Luther's theses offer some ninety statements on sin and its punishment, on remission of punishment here and in purgatory, on ecclesial aids conferred by use of the keys, and on rightly regulated preaching in this area. The concluding theses indicate the basic motif of proper preaching.

94. Christians should be exhorted to concentrate on following Christ their Head in penances and enduring death and hell.

95. So they seek to enter heaven more through many tribulations than by trusting in any present security of peace.[11]

Thus, Jesus' evangelical call for *metanoia* and his own example of patient suffering should shape the message of the Christian preacher even on an indulgence campaign.

Luther's treatise gave the rationale underlying the demanding message of the theses. Central in the treatise is the doctrinal distinction between a commutation of the satisfactory works imposed in confession and the interior cleansing of concupiscence, a malady of the human heart, by God's healing grace. Since indulgences do not directly contribute to the latter, the preacher must take care not to mislead people into thinking that after gaining a plenary indulgence they are exempted from the penitential life. Characteristically, Luther's emphasis is less upon the exertions of lifelong mortification than upon God's work by grace in the affective center of the person. Contrasting with the extrinsic "grace" of an indulgence, there is God's inner transformation of the heart's aspirations.

> Infused grace is an interior illumination of the mind and a kindling of the will. This is an eternal illumination into the soul like rays of the sun, and it does not become inactive after a plenary indulgence. This grace is necessary for the extirpation of concupiscence, until it is completely rooted out. This process is complete when a person is so filled with disgust for this life that he sighs longingly for God and finally breaks free from the body out of desire for God.[12]

Whatever might be worked out for understanding purgatorial cleansing after death, the consequence for Christians in this life is ongoing concern over the sinful roots lodged deep in the human spirit. There is a "root sin" to be dealt with, which is both the legacy from the time of our origins and the residue of sinful acts.

> You must still make efforts to advance and take care not to grow lethargic and snore away thinking you are purified and thus secure. Then you must diligently crucify your members and mortify the source of sin, that is, your concupiscence.[13]

This penitential dedication was for Luther the source of a typical form of prayer, a yearning for God's healing grace.

> Therefore, we must be quite earnest is preventing indulgences, that is, satisfactions, from becoming a cause of security, laziness, and neglect of interior grace. Instead, we must be diligent to fully cure the infection of our nature and thirst to come to God out of

love for him, hatred of this life, and disgust with ourselves. That is, we must incessantly seek God's healing grace.[14]

Further elucidation and grounding for Luther's 1517 views of repentance can be found in abundance in his treatment of sin and purification of heart in the corpus of his early biblical lectures. A fundamental conviction had emerged from Psalm 51. Luther's exegetical comments *On This Basic Penitential Text* (ca. 1514) emphasized the paradoxical identity which obtains between being righteous before God and making a heartfelt confession of sin: *"Iustus enim primo est accusator sui et . . . iudex sui."*[15] This holds because those who judge themselves are thereby agreeing with the truth of God's own fundamental word about humankind. God's light appeared in his Son's coming to save sinners (1 Tim 1:15).[16] When God lays scourges and crosses upon us, he shows we have sinned and deserve punishment.[17] In commenting on Romans in 1515, especially on the citation of Psalm 51:4 in Romans 3:4, Luther spoke at length on how justifying faith involves taking to heart God's revelation of my own sinfulness.[18] The key to faith's genuine expression, in Luther's earliest extant lectures, is a heartfelt, *"Tibi peccavi."*

Luther was convinced that the Christian enters upon the way of conversion through submitting to God's words of judgment and thereby accepting a wholly new self-assessment.[19] This rests, of course, not upon the prescriptions of the law, against which we offend, but on the endemic root-sin we have inherited and further solidified by our choices. Confession of sin signals the start of a process of purification of heart lasting to the end. Romans 3:10 says laconically, "None is righteous." For Luther this means that we are always underway in a penitential project and bound to beg for God's healing.

> Those therefore who are truly righteous not only yearn for and implore the grace of God because they see that they have an evil will and so by this are sinful before God, but as well because they see that they can never fully grasp how deep is the evil of their will and how far it extends. They thus always believe that they are sinners, as if the depth of their evil will were infinite. Thus they humble themselves, thus they plead, thus they yearn, until at last they are perfectly healed—which takes place in death.[20]

Luther therefore had good reason to publish an exposition of the penitential psalms in 1516 and to become critical of the easily misunderstood "graces" of the indulgences offered in 1517. For him, the whole of the Christian life is subsumed under the heart's yearning for God's interior work of renewal.

> The whole life of the new people, the faithful people, the spiritual people, is nothing else but prayer, seeking and begging by the yearning of the heart, the voice of the mouth, and the labor of the body, always seeking and striving to be made righteous, even to the hour of death. They never stand still, are never in possession, and never in any work put an end to the acquiring of righteousness, but they always await it as something still dwelling beyond them, and always live as people who still exist in sin.[21]

Close in time to his intervention of October 1517 on indulgences, Luther spoke on Zacchaeus' change of heart as exemplifying the proper response to Jesus' call for repentance.

> Interior repentance is true contrition, true confession, and true spiritual satisfaction. Then penitents really and utterly displease themselves in all they do. They turn efficaciously to God in genuine admission of their guilt and they confess to God from the heart. Then their self-hatred gnaws at them interiorly and leads to self-imposed punishment. Thus they make satisfaction to God. Truly repentant persons desire that, if it were possible, all creation would see and hate their sin, and they are ready to be trampled on by all. They do not seek indulgences for the remission of punishments, but instead the actual bearing of punishments.[22]

Luther's earliest teaching, we see, was centered on the change of heart occurring in repentance. Such a personal shift of outlook rests on confession of sin before God and issues in the dedicated quest of purification under God's healing grace. The young Luther thus deserves to be ranked among the great Christian exponents of penitential and purificatory spirituality.

Fides Sacramenti

In the wake of the indulgence controversy of 1517–18, Luther became greatly concerned with explaining the sacraments. Soon he was saying less about doing penance and much more about the certain and assuring gifts of forgiveness and grace conferred as the sacramental effect. Luther would have the Christian make the transition from self-accusing faith to a faith made assured by laying hold of God's gift. Central now is the well-known "fiducial" faith, an act and attitude of wholehearted trust which, though, has its solid basis in the sacramental word.[23]

It could be that this shift of emphasis in Luther's teaching was the consequence of a dramatic insight. Luther did claim that his life changed when he suddenly realized that "the righteousness of God" (Rom 1:17) is a quality of divine mercy and generous giving. It is difficult to pinpoint when this breakthrough took place, but it may well have brought with it a new understanding of faith, because right in Romans 1:17 Luther would find in his Vulgate Paul's brief citation from the Old Testament, "*Iustus enim ex fide vivit*" ("For the righteous person lives by faith," from Habakkuk 2:4).[24]

But, however the new emphasis arose, Luther's accounts in 1518–19 of sacramental reception make frequent appeal to an axiom which Luther says is very well known and often cited in theology. While commenting on Hebrews 5:1, Luther stressed the need that belief be focused on the actual efficacy of a sacrament, and gave as his warrant the "*vulgatissimum et probatissimum dictum, 'Non sacramentum sed fides sacramenti iustificat.'* "[25] By this widely known saying, with its nearly axiomatic truth, Luther shows that his new instruction on the sacraments and justification by fiducial faith is not a dangerous innovation. Rather, the theological community should recognize here a consequence of a widely accepted principle. Luther holds that *fides sacramenti*, faith *in* the sacrament, should be central in Christian existence, for by it the believing heart lays hold of God's gift present with its power to renew human hearts. The sacrament expresses and makes present an efficacious promise of Jesus himself.[26]

In 1520, Luther explained Jesus' words of eucharistic institution as his testamentary promise of grace, which we encounter in every celebration of the Lord's supper. Worthy participation is by faith in the sacramental promise, and this transforms the heart. Faith grasps Jesus' gift of himself, in his body broken and his blood shed for the forgiveness of our sins. Here faith receives an immense benefit.

> Hard upon this faith there follows spontaneously a most sweet affection of the heart, by which the human spirit is enlarged and enriched (in charity granted by the Holy Spirit in the midst of faith in Christ). Thereby one is swept toward Christ, who left this testament in his graciousness and bounty, and one becomes a completely new and different person. . . . How can one help loving so great a benefactor, who offers, promises, and confers the riches of this eternal inheritance to one who is unworthy and actually merits much different treatment![27]

Thus Luther instructed Christians to cut through the complexities of traditional sacramental doctrine, for example, the ingenious subdivisions of benefits or "fruits" of the mass for body and soul. The one benefit attached to Christ's supper is the forgiveness of sins, the grace expressed in the word of institution over the cup of his blood. His purpose was to give our lives a new existential basis,

> so that the human heart, clinging to these words by faith, should gain strength in everything good against sin, death, and hell. His word and work were not intended to help us in a temporal way, but in a spiritual and eternal way. . . . A person should receive the sacrament . . . and not doubt that in him there takes place the intent and content of those same words of Christ, namely, that Christ's body is given for him and that his blood is shed for him, and that he is an heir of the New Testament, that is, of God's grace and favor for eternal life.[28]

Luther's new configuration of doctrinal and spiritual themes had first focused attention on sacramental penance where the words of absolution are a paradigmatic mediation of salvation. He could even say that our trust rests on what comes from the mouth of the confessor.[29] Troubled hearts are helped by the church's ministry of consolation and encouragement, centered on the sacramental word as Christ's effective address.

> Our salvation therefore lies in the word, but not really in the word, for Christ is joined to the word. There must be no tottering here. A sacrament is a rock grounded in Christ.[30]

Other texts from 1518 had begun working out how this new insight into faith and the word had consequences for the proper reception of holy communion. Christ purifies and pacifies the troubled heart by his blood shed for us, but this gift is mediated by a word of Christ which we are to believe, "This is the blood shed for you and for many for the forgiveness of sins."[31]

With such a basic insight into the present gift of salvation, Luther felt well equipped to turn to the broader public of literate Germans in numerous short works on fundamental aspects of the Christian's relationship to God. The year 1519 saw eight such pastoral instructions appear, explaining the Our Father, meditation on Christ's passion, married life, petitionary prayer, preparation for death, and the sacraments of penance, baptism, and holy communion.[32] Each work was quickly and repeatedly reprinted

both in Wittenberg and in other cities such as Leipzig, Augsburg, Nuremberg, and Basel.

Typical of these works was Luther's high recommendation of the
power of the sacraments in overcoming the assaults on the heart by our
spiritual enemies in the struggle preceding death.

> We must earnestly, diligently, and highly esteem the holy sacra-
> ments, hold them in honor, freely and cheerfully rely on them,
> and so balance them against sin, death, and hell that they will
> outweigh these by far. We must occupy ourselves much more
> with the sacraments and their virtues than with our sins.[33]

In the sacraments God gives the heart a sure sign of his grace in
Christ, in an expression that does not deceive. God's own word resounds in
absolution; the holy body of Christ is a gift of "communion," not only with
Christ but as well with his angels and saints as helpers in my suffering.[34]
Faith lays hold of these gifts offered.

> In the sacraments we find God's Word—which reveals and prom-
> ises Christ to us with all his blessings and which he himself is—
> against sin, death, and hell. . . . The right use of the sacraments
> involves nothing more than believing that all will be as the sacra-
> ments promise and pledge through God's Word.[35]

Luther's insistence on clinging to the sacramental word of grace did not
fade away in the years after 1518–20. Later it was second nature for him to
refer to sacramental reception as the privileged case of faith in God's saving
word. In 1532, explaining Psalm 51:10 ("To my hearing you will give joy and
gladness"), Luther expressed a basic tenet of his reformation.

> We attribute everything to hearing or to the Word or to faith in
> the Word—these are all the same—and not to our works. Yes, in
> the use of the sacraments and in confession we teach people to
> look mainly at the Word . . . so that the chief part of the whole
> action might be the voice itself of God and the hearing itself.[36]

> So turn your eyes far away from your contrition, and with your
> whole heart pay attention to the voice of the brother absolving
> you. And do not doubt that this voice of the brother in the
> Sacrament or in absolution is divinely spoken by the Father, Son,
> and Holy Spirit Himself, so that you completely depend on what
> you hear, not on what you think.[37]

Luther's last great lecture-course, on Genesis, from 1535 to 1545, was laced with brief references to the sacraments, especially as the Christian analogues to God's promises to the patriarchs and their responses of faith.[38] But a new accent had appeared in the late 1520s, when Luther was defending Christ's bodily gift of himself in the Lord's supper against the spiritualism of Zwingli and his Swiss colleagues.

The Heart Submissive to God's Ordinances

A well-studied phase of Luther's theological career is his spirited defense of objective sacramental mediation and the presence of Christ's body and blood in the eucharistic elements.[39] These concerns loomed large from 1525 into 1530 as Luther debated with his former colleague Karlstadt and with the Swiss reformers, Zwingli and Oecolampadius. In our context we will note only one aspect of Luther's extensive argumentation in these years, an aspect which does bring out a theme previously latent in his doctrine of the believing heart and God's word of grace.

Luther had to confront the Swiss application of John 6:63 ("The Spirit gives life; the flesh is of no avail") to the gift offered in holy communion. Zwingli had concluded that this text leaves only a spiritual "eating," a rememorative act of devotion that is little more than faith in Christ's redemptive death. Luther's response did grant that "spirit" and "flesh" are basic anthropological categories, applicable to the whole person as believer or unbeliever. However, in the supper, Christ's body is not "flesh" in the sense of the controverted text, but a gift which in fact avails in a grand and glorious manner. Receiving communion rightly, according to Luther, is to eat Christ's body physically *while* believing in one's heart in the redemptive gift of Christ. The gift however is not one that leads to escape from the body.

> The heart knows well what the mouth eats, for it grasps the words and eats spiritually what the mouth eats physically. But since the mouth is the heart's member, it also must live in eternity because of the heart, which lives eternally through the Word, because here it also eats physically the same eternal food which its heart eats spiritually at the same time.[40]

Thus, in binding together mouth and heart, Luther connected the eucharistic presence of Christ's body with a quite holistic view of salvation.

But a yet more fundamental religious issue was at stake in the debate with these adversaries. The Swiss were asking what need or use there was for a bodily presence of Christ over and above his spiritual and effective presence in the gospel and the message formulated in the words of institution. But this kind of questioning, in Luther's estimation, revealed a proud heart. To ask why, in this manner, is equivalently to lay down limits that one wants to say Christ should not transgress.

> A faithful, God-fearing heart does this: it asks first whether it is God's Word. When it hears that it is, it smothers with hands and feet the question why it is useful or necessary. For it says with fear and humiliation, "My dear God, I am blind; truly I know not what is useful or necessary for me, nor do I wish to know, but I believe and trust that thou dost know best and dost intend the best in thy divine goodness and wisdom. I am satisfied and happy to hear thy simple Word and perceive thy will."[41]

In the Marburg Colloquy of 1529, Luther drew a sharp line between himself and those Protestants who were questioning God's own sacramental ordinances.

> I am not inquiring whether or not it is necessary; that has not been entrusted to us. In that case I could neither be baptized nor believe in Christ. Christ gives himself to us in many ways: first, in preaching; second, in baptism; third, in brotherly consolation; fourth, in the sacrament, as often as the body of Christ is eaten, because he himself commands us to do so. If he should command me to eat dung, I would do it. The servant should not inquire about the will of his lord. We ought to close our eyes.[42]

Still, the Lord's supper is not simply a matter of blind obedience to divine decrees. The Swiss adversaries were claiming that their view safeguarded the transcendent glory of the divine Savior, by denying that anyone handles and carries about the body of Christ. But Luther countered with his own account of the true glory of Christ, who treats humankind with marvelous mercy.

> It is a glory and praise of his inexpressible grace and mercy that he concerns himself so profoundly with us poor sinners and shows us such gracious love and goodness, not content to be everywhere in and around, above and beside us, but even giving us his own body as nourishment, in order that with such a pledge he may assure and promise us that our body too shall live forever, because it partakes here on earth of an everlasting and living food.[43]

Thus, the great debate of the late 1520s was much more than a reactionary phase in Luther's career as a Christian teacher. Deep truths emerged about God's redemptive intention, which embraces even our bodily existence, and about how that intention has concretized itself in Christ and his economy of grace. There is need, though, of hearts submissive to God's chosen ways or ordinances, if the grandeur of his saving dispensation is to break forth before the eyes of faith.

Thus we can mark out three different prevailing emphases in Luther's spiritual teaching. He moved from forming repentant hearts to an insistence on how the heart should cling to the liberating and consoling word of Christ encountered in the sacraments. But then, when a more radical spiritualism emerged as part of the Protestant movement, Luther responded with an emphatic case for a more humble submission of heart before the full range of God's gifts, even when it is not clear how God's manner of giving fits with my idea of what is needful or appropriate.

Still, these three repeated emphases are not the whole story. In addition to these spiritual themes that are recurrently present in the different periods of Luther's work, we find as well some particular teachings that broke forth only momentarily in Luther's works. We will conclude this essay by relating just two of these. First, Luther did offer at least one account of the meaning of the term "heart." And then, in a gem of spiritual instruction, he led the believing heart toward an encounter with the heart of God himself.

The Believing Heart and God's Own Heart

Psalm 51 expresses an aspiration Luther felt was the immediate consequence of receiving God's justifying grace of forgiveness: "Create a clean heart in me, O God." The commentary of 1538, based on lectures of 1532, tells how one favored with a right relationship to God here begs to be maintained and strengthened in certainty about God's mercy and in dedication to doing his will. All this takes place by the Spirit's creative work in the heart—a consideration that leads Luther to clarify the term "heart."

> Just as such a clean heart is not by our powers but by divine creation, so we cannot ourselves preserve this creation against the devil. We see how often we are polluted by sudden troubles and sadness. Hence this prayer and preservation of a clean heart ought never to stop. . . . The word "heart" in German is almost the same as what the Hebrew calls "spirit." What in Latin we call

"mind, intellect, will, affections"—almost all this the Germans render as "heart."[44]

The heart then is the cognitive and affective center of the person, where faith and righteousness come to be implanted through the word in which God both reveals and effects the person's new relationship to himself. A heart submissive to God and clinging to his chosen words of grace then yearns for ongoing confirmation, healing, and renewal. Such are in fact the basic structures of the Christian spirituality taught by Martin Luther. But there is more. Luther was, among all else, an insightful teacher of prayer, especially of meditative prayer on the fundamental truths and realities of revelation.[45] A Christian should go in spirit regularly to Christ on his cross, there to be impressed ever again with the costly manner in which God realized his dispensation of mercy, forgiveness, and new life.

Luther's 1519 instruction on meditating on our Lord's passion leads up to the recommendation to cast off all reliance on self-achieved goodness and to cling instead to the scripture verses on the redemptive value of Jesus' suffering, such as Isaiah 53:6, "He has laid on him the iniquity of us all," and 1 Peter 2:24 and 2 Corinthians 5:21. One casts one's own sin, guilt, and anxiety upon the Redeemer. Prayer, however, does not simply dwell upon texts, but becomes a more active and alert perception of the personal basis of redemption. Our last citation of Luther will be long enough to afford vivid contact with this articulate and profound exponent of a spirituality of the heart—that is, of Christ's heart and the heart of the Father.

> You can spur yourself on. First, no longer envisaging Christ's suffering in itself (for this has done its work and frightened you), you should pass through to see his friendly heart and how this heart full of love for you impels him to bear with pain your bad conscience and sin. Your heart will be thereby sweetened and the confident assurance of your faith strengthened. Then go on to rise through the heart of Christ to the heart of God to see that Christ would not have shown his love for you, had not God in his eternal love wanted this. For Christ in his love for you is obedient. Thus you will come to the divine, fatherly heart and, as Christ says, be drawn to the Father through him. Then you will grasp the saying of Christ, "God so loved the world that he gave his own son" (John 3:16). To know God rightly is to lay hold, not of his power or wisdom (which are terrifying), but of his kind-

ness and love. Then faith and assurance can stand steadfast and one is truly reborn in God.[46]

Martin Luther thus directed the believing Christian heart not just to a consoling and saving word of God. Such a word should dominate the foreground of the heart's concerns as it clings submissively to the promise of forgiveness and life in Christ. But Luther also led the heart further into the background and wellspring of the word, where the heart encounters in all amazement the loving heart of our God.

NOTES

1. Letter of July 8, 1530, from Castle Coburg, to Lazarus Spengler of Nuremberg. Translated from *Luthers Werke: Kritische Gesamtausgabe. Briefwechsel* (Weimar, 1930ff) (hereafter, WABr) 5, 445, but following variant readings given in WABr 13, 155.
2. *Luthers Werke: Kritische Gesamtausgabe* (Weimar, 1883ff) (hereafter, WA) 37, 245–248.
3. WA 37, 246, citing Cant 8:6. But Luther improvised the citation expressing Mary's heartfelt desire. The reference to "character" offers Luther's alternative to the traditional doctrine of the permanent, indelible effect of baptism, confirmation and ordination.
4. From Luther's *Church Postil* of 1522 on the liturgical readings of the Christmas season, WA 10/1/1, 130, in translation from *Luther's Works. The American Edition* (St. Louis & Philadelphia, 1955–86) (hereafter, LW) 52, 33.
5. Ibid.
6. Examples of Luther reminiscing over his own development: LW 54, 193f, 309, 442f (from his Table Talk); LW 12, 313f, 370 (from 1532 lectures on Ps 51, published in revised form in 1538); LW 5, 157f & 7, 251f (from lectures on Genesis in 1542 and 1543); and LW 34, 327–338 (Preface of 1545 to vol. 1 of Luther's Latin works).
7. On Luther's intervention: Erwin Iserloh, *The Theses Were Not Posted* (Boston, 1968). This work shows that Luther's own accounts make it very unlikely that any public or semi-public protest, such as a public posting of theses, occurred at any of Wittenberg's church doors in autumn 1517.
8. The doctrine and spirituality taught in these works is the subject of my *Man Yearning for Grace* (Washington, 1968 & Wiesbaden, 1969).
9. Letter: WABr 1, 110–112; LW 48, 45–49. Ninety-Five Theses: WA 1, 233–238; LW 31, 25–33. *The Treatise:* WABr 12, 5–9, translated in

Man Yearning for Grace, 241–261 (with commentary) and in "Luther's Treatise on Indulgences," *Theological Studies* 28 (1967) 481–518.

10. My translation from WA 1, 233.

11. WA 1, 238.

12. WABr 12, 6; *Man Yearning for Grace*, 244, and *Theological Studies* 28 (1967) 497.

13. WABr 12, 8; *Man Yearning*, 255, and *Theological Studies* 28 (1967) 510.

14. WABr 12, 9; *Man Yearning*, 260f, and *Theological Studies* 28 (1967) 517.

15. In free translation: "The righteous person is marked first of all by self-accusation and self-judgment." From WA 3, 288 and LW 10, 236, that is, the *Dictata super Psalterium* of 1513–15. Michael Baylor sees here a key to Luther's originality in understanding conscience. *Action and Conviction. Conscience in Late Scholasticism and the Young Luther* (Leiden, 1977), 212–224.

16. WA 3, 290; LW 10, 239.

17. WA 3, 292; LW 10, 242.

18. WA 56, 214–234; LW 25, 199–219.

19. WA 56, 233; LW 25, 217.

20. WA 56, 235; translation adapted from LW 25, 220f.

21. WA 56, 264; translation adapted from LW 25, 251f. Although the sense of sinful need dominates self-understanding, Luther did hold that God's gift is effective in the human heart. See, for example, the 1517 *Disputation against Scholastic Theology* (WA 1, 224–228; LW 31, 9–16), in the counterpointed theses 55, 67, 75, 84, 89, on the influence of grace, which thesis 55 describes as always a *"vivus, mobilis, et operosus spiritus"* (WA 1, 227). Luther's 1536 *Disputation Concerning Justification* contains a vivid account of the ongoing cure of endemic sinfulness (WA 39/1, 112–114; LW 34, 181–183). Luther had a solid doctrine of the Spirit's transforming work in the heart.

22. My translation of WA 1, 99, from Luther's sermon of May 30, 1517. On the dating: N. Floerken, "Ein Beitrag zur Datierung von Luthers 'Sermo de indulgentiis pridie Dedicationis,' " *Zeitschrift für Theologie und Kirche* 82 (1971), 344–350.

23. I treated Luther's transition in *"Fides sacramenti—Fides specialis:* Luther's Development in 1518," *Gregorianum* 65 (1984), 53–87. The best book-length treatment of Luther's teaching on the sacraments is the rarely cited work of Wolfgang Schwab, *Entwicklung und Gestalt der Sakramententheologie bei Martin Luther* (Frankfurt/M. & Bern, 1977).

24. Luther often spoke of his breakthrough to a new understanding of *iustitia Dei* in the autobiographical passages listed in n. 6, above. Some

interpreters do place this breakthrough in early 1518 and relate it to Luther's new approach to the sacraments, e.g. Ernst Bizer, *Fides ex auditu* (Neukirchen, 3rd ed., 1966); Oswald Bayer, *Promissio* (Goettingen, 1971); Martin Brecht, *Martin Luther. His Road to Reformation, 1483–1521* (Philadelphia, 1985), 221–237. Citations of *"Iustus ex fide vivit"* did occur in 1518 at the end of disputation theses on absolution (WA 1, 633) and at the beginning of Luther's defense against Cardinal Cajetan's objection to the new doctrine (WA 2, 13; LW 31, 270).

25. WA 57/3, 170. Luther defended himself against an early attack by Johann Eck with an appeal to the axiom as *"dictum illud communissimum"* (WA 1, 286). Other citations of the *dictum:* WA 1, 324, 544, 631; WA 2, 15, 715.

26. *Fides sacramenti* is a case of an objective genitive, with the sacrament's principal word being that which one believes with all trust.

27. *De captivitate Babylonica* (1520), WA 5, 515f. This passage follows Luther's assertion of the correlation of God's promise and a dependent, trusting faith: "Ubi enim est verbum promittentis Dei, ibi necessaria est fides acceptantis hominis, ut clarum sit initium salutis nostrae esse fidem, quae pendeat in verbo promittentis Dei" (514). See the whole passage: LW 36, 38–44.

28. "Sermon on Worthy Reception of the Sacrament" (1521), WA 7, 695f; LW 42, 175 (cited).

29. *"ut . . . in ore sacerdotis collocetur fiducia nostra."* WA 4, 657, from a sermon at the first mass of a newly ordained priest in spring 1518.

30. WA 4, 658.

31. From Luther's comment on Hebrews 9:14. WA 57/3, 207f; LW 29, 208f.

32. Original texts in WA 2; translations in LW, vols. 35, 42, and 44. These works were recently studied by Ursula Stock in *Die Bedeutung der Sakramente in Luthers Sermonen von 1519* (Leiden, 1982).

33. WA 2, 686; LW 42, 100 (cited).

34. WA 2, 692f; LW 42, 110f.

35. WA 2, 695; LW 42, 111 (cited).

36. WA 40/2, 411; LW 12, 369f (cited with adaptations).

37. WA 40/2, 412; LW 12, 370 (cited with adaptations).

38. This even began in comments on Genesis 1:2, with an admonition to hold to the God who envelops himself in baptism and absolution (LW 1, 11) and continued down to Judah's blessing in Gen 49:11f (LW 8, 270f).

39. Mark Edwards inserts this controversy into the broader context of Luther's polemics against other adherents of the Reformation. *Luther and the False Brethren* (Stanford, Cal., 1975), 82–111.

40. WA 23, 181; LW 37, 87 (cited).
41. WA 23, 247f. LW 37, 127 (cited).
42. WA 30/3, 116; LW 38, 19 (cited). In his treatise, *The Keys* (1530), Luther insists on the divinely instituted means of forgiveness as what Christ commanded us to do in the church. This is Luther's basic framework for understanding Matthew 16:19 and 18:18. See LW 40, 364–369 and 372–376. The divine ordinances should free people from the plague of uncertainty, as Luther explained in 1542, commenting on Genesis 26:9 (LW 5, 42–50, especially 45).
43. WA 23, 155–157; LW 37, 71 (cited).
44. WA 40/2, 424f; LW 12, 379 (cited).
45. This has been systematically set forth by Martin Nicol in *Meditation bei Luther* (Göttingen, 1984).
46. WA 2, 140f. See the larger context of this passage in LW 42, 12–14.

Harvey D. Egan, S.J.

Ignatius of Loyola: Mystic at the Heart of the Trinity, Mystic at the Heart of Jesus Christ

Introductory Remarks

St. Ignatius of Loyola is commonly depicted in the following way. He began his "worldly" career as a courtier, a gentleman, and a soldier. After a profound religious conversion, he became a wandering pilgrim for the sake of Christ and attained heroic sanctity. For apostolic purposes, "to help souls," he decided to study and to become a priest. He gathered together a group of companions in Christ, founded a renowned religious family, established colleges, universities, and charitable institutions, and always kept his hand in directly pastoral activity. He directed a vast missionary network, and undertook sensitive diplomatic appointments. Moreover, he authored the highly influential *Spiritual Exercises*, the Jesuit *Constitutions*, and thousands of letters that demonstrate his far-reaching sociopolitical involvement.

Yet, as Evelyn Underhill points out, "the concrete nature of St. Ignatius' work, and especially its later developments, has blinded historians to the fact that he was a true mystic."[1] But to overlook Ignatius' mysticism is to overlook his heart and soul. Ignatius of Loyola was an incomparable mystic whose mystical and apostolic gifts were really two sides of the same coin. Ignatius was apostolic because he was one of the greatest mystics the church has ever seen. His apostolic successes are the mystical expressions, the sacramental embodiment, of his radical mysticism. Ignatius' decisive influence in world and church history flows from his mystical love of God and neighbor. In other words, his mysticism remains the definitive horizon within which everything said about him must be considered.

Because Ignatius attained the fullness of Christian life, the perfection of the life of faith, hope, and love, he was a mystic, and vice versa. The triune God purified, illuminated, and transformed Ignatius. The Trinity bestowed upon him full participation in its life, especially through Ignatius' radical imitation of Christ's life, death, and resurrection. The triune God called Ignatius to the very depths of his spirit and beyond all narcissistic introversion to share fully in the divine life. Ignatius courageously risked everything and surrendered totally to the Trinity. And the more deeply God united Ignatius to the inner-trinitarian life, the more deeply God united him to others in loving service to the entire world. What began in his very depths compelled Ignatius to communicate it to all dimensions of human existence.

Thus, Ignatius experienced not only the mysticism of everyday life. That is, his mysticism is more than the courageous living of the banality and grayness of daily life in often humdrum Christian love. He was also, and primarily, a mystic in the strictest sense. He experienced, therefore, the radical intensification and the full-flowering of Christian spirituality. Under God's palpable initiative and direction, he fell explicitly in love with God. At times abruptly, at times gradually, through God's special activity he realized that God is in love with us, and therefore we are all at least secretly in love with God and with each other. God's seizure of the very root of his being gave rise to an immense longing. He was allowed no peace until he was irrevocably purified by, illuminated by, united to, and transformed into God's very own life.

It is widely—but erroneously—presumed that since the spirituality of the heart of Jesus was so integral to the spirituality of the Society of Jesus, it must surely have come through Ignatius. But one can search the entire corpus of Ignatius' writings without finding one explicit reference to the heart of Jesus. Therefore, this article will focus upon St. Ignatius *at* the "heart" of the Trinity and *at* the "heart" of Jesus Christ which this author contends is the cornerstone of Ignatius' mysticism and spirituality.

This means that Ignatius mystically experienced not only "God" and Jesus Christ. He also had a mystical relationship with the Father as Father, the Son as Son, and the Holy Spirit as Holy Spirit. In addition, not only did he grasp mystically the mutual indwelling of the three divine persons; he also penetrated mystically to the Trinity's very "heart," that is, to the Trinity's essential unity "prior" to the distinction between Father, Son, and Holy Spirit. On most occasions, Ignatius experienced the Father as the heart of the inner-trinitarian life, that is, the Father as the source of the other divine persons. But in addition to this Greek-like trinitarian mysticism, Ignatius sometimes experienced the divine "being" or "essence" as the source, or heart, of the Father, Son, and Holy Spirit.[2] On these occasions his trinitarian mysticism is more in keeping with the theological tradition stemming from Augustine. Furthermore, through his trinitarian mysticism, he likewise penetrated to the "heart" of the hypostatic union, to the mystery of Jesus' divine-human identity.

Because Ignatius grasped mystically the differentiated unity of the inner-trinitarian life itself and of Jesus' divine-human life, he is a mystic *at* the heart of the Trinity and *at* the heart of Jesus Christ. Perhaps because of this, one can say that his mysticism and spirituality is, broadly speaking, also one of the human heart.

For example, his *Spiritual Exercises* attempt to make the exercitant aware of his or her primordial unity. These *Exercises* implicitly view the human person as a differentiated unity, as a unified plurality whose integrity has been damaged by sin and inordinate attachments. In short, by plunging the exercitant into the heart of the Trinity by way of contemplations on the life, death, and resurrection of Jesus Christ, Ignatius expected to heal the human heart, that is, to render the person integral.

But most commentators agree that Ignatius' mysticism is first and foremost trinitarian.[3] This author contends, too, that Ignatius' personal experiences with and of the Trinity are perhaps the most profound of any mystic in the entire Christian tradition. The way he expressed and formulated his exceptionally fertile trinitarian mysticism is often astonishingly unique. Ignatius was indeed a mystic at the heart of the Trinity.

Profound mystical experiences of the Trinity punctuated Ignatius' entire life.[4] His early companions attest that the saint received the most profound illuminations on all matters of the faith, but especially on the Trinity, and spoke often with those closest to him about the Trinity and about his great desire to write a book on the Trinity.[5] Although these trinitarian mystical experiences occurred during his early conversions, they were especially frequent during his mature years.[6] Constantly in communication with the triune God, Ignatius received gifts from each of the divine persons corresponding to that person's nature.[7] That is, he experienced not only "God" or the "Trinity," but more specifically the Father as Father, the Son as Son, and the Holy Spirit as Holy Spirit. Moreover, Ignatius penetrated not only to the Trinity's mutual indwelling but also to the "heart" of the Trinity, that is, to the source or origin of the divine persons.

Ignatius' trinitarian experiences enabled him to find the Trinity in all things and all things in the Trinity. He saw mystically how the entire world came from the Trinity and was destined for the Trinity (*Auto*, no. 29).[8] So profound were Ignatius' trinitarian experiences that even if no scriptures had existed to teach him, this mysticism rendered him willing to die for "these matters of faith" (*Auto*, no. 29).

The Trinity and the *Spiritual Diary*

In 1555, only a year before Ignatius' death, Fr. Luis Goncalves da Câmara, the Jesuit to whom Ignatius narrated his *Autobiography*, stated that Ignatius had shown him a "rather large packet of writings" (*Auto*, no. 100). It contained information about Ignatius' experiences of the Trinity, Christ, and Our Lady—experiences that confirmed points found in the *Constitutions*. Ignatius refused to allow Father da Câmara to see these papers, however, because of their personal nature.

The *Spiritual Diary*, as it is now called, consists of only two small surviving notebooks from this "packet."[9] Interspersed among Ignatius' deliberations on a minor aspect of Jesuit poverty is an astonishing record of his mystical intimacy with the triune God.[10] One finds remarks about mystical tears, trinitarian visions and illuminations, various kinds of locutions, profound mystical consolations, mystical touches, mystical repose, mystical joys, and consolations without previous cause. In fact, these two notebooks "belong together with the most beautiful and most noble pages that Christian mystics have set down on paper."[11]

The *Spiritual Diary* is perhaps the most remarkable mystical document on trinitarian mysticism ever written in any language.[12] Ignatius mentions the Trinity explicitly 170 times, and nearly every page refers to Ignatius' prayers to and experiences of the "Most Holy Trinity," the "Divine Majesty," the triune "God," "the very Being or Essence of the Most Holy Trinity," the "Three Divine Persons," the "Father," the "Son," and the "Holy Spirit."

Moreover, since most entries begin by telling us which mass Ignatius said that day, we know that of the 116 masses named, thirty masses of the Trinity were said. Whether preparing for mass, during mass, after mass, or throughout the day, Ignatius enjoyed inexpressible intimacy with the Trinity and a host of accompanying secondary mystical phenomena. Even the thought of being unworthy to invoke the name of the Most Holy Trinity brought Ignatius intense interior devotion (*SD*, no. 64).

Ignatius frequently used the word "devotion" (*devoción*) with respect to the Trinity.[13] Especially in connection with the mass Ignatius experienced "devotion," "much devotion," "fresh devotion," "plenty of devotion," "warm devotion," and "greater devotion." On occasion, this devotion was so warm and ardent that it brought sweetness and a light "mingled with color (bright light)" (*SD*, no. 117). Even a warm room on a cold night moved him to devotion to the Most Holy Trinity.[14]

Moreover, his mystical devotion, or "ease in finding God" (*Auto*, no. 99), was often directed toward and terminated in the Trinity or a person of the Trinity. He had little difficulty attaining devotion, although he says explicitly that he still had to prepare for it and that it was not always given.

Ignatius spoke frequently of his intense love for the Most Holy Trinity.[15] Deep sobbing, mystical tears, and spiritual visitations that drew him totally into the trinitarian life (*SD*, no. 108) often accompanied this love.[16] He likewise experienced "very deep inner touches . . . and great and excessive love" (*SD*, no. 107) that terminated in the divine Trinity. So intense was his mystical love for the Trinity that it produced great pressure in his chest (*SD*, no. 51). Often Ignatius only had to remember the Trinity to be totally drawn to its love (*SD*, no. 110). And it should be noted that physical phenomena often accompanied Ignatius' mystical experiences.

The *Spiritual Exercises* speak of a "consolation without previous cause."[17] They state that "it belongs to God alone to give consolation to the soul without previous cause, for it belongs to the Creator to enter into the soul, to leave it, and to act upon it, drawing it wholly to the love of His Divine Majesty" (*Ex*, no. 330). Moreover, "there is no deception in it" (*Ex*, no. 336), because only God can give this type of consolation.

The *Spiritual Diary* attests that Ignatius frequently received trinitarian visitations, or consolations without previous cause. In this way, Ignatius experienced a God-given consolation that was irrefutable proof of the Trinity's presence and that drew him wholly to it.

Mystical insights, illuminations, understandings, intellectual lights, and spiritual memories about the Trinity permeate the *Diary*. For example, uncertain about how to proceed in the matter of poverty, Ignatius "felt much devotion with many intellectual lights and spiritual memories of the Most Holy Trinity . . . while vesting, with lights about the Trinity" (*SD*, no. 51).

Two things should be noted. First, Ignatius possessed a mystical memory. That is, simply remembering earlier graces brought about still more. Or else these graces stayed with him throughout the day so that he could easily find the Trinity in all things (*SD*, no. 55). Second, these trinitarian intellectual lights gave him consolation and confidence in the matter of the "election," that is, the decision concerning the degree of poverty of the Society's churches.

These trinitarian lights, spiritual illuminations, and understandings were so profound that he knew that he "could never learn so much by hard study . . . [I] felt and understood . . . more than if I had studied all my life" (*SD*, no. 52). Furthermore, these experiences often guided Ignatius in selecting the person to whom he would pray, "more by feeling and seeing than by understanding" (SD, no. 54).

On occasion, mystical graces drew Ignatius' understanding to "behold the Most Holy Trinity, as if seeing, although not as distinctly as formerly, Three Persons" (SD, no. 87).[18] On other occassions, the visions seem less profound, that is, he had no "distinct vision of the Three Persons, but a simple advertence to or representation of the Most Holy Trinity" (SD, no. 101). Finally, he experienced vision-like understandings of the Trinity that lasted for some time (SD, no. 140).

One must also appreciate Ignatius' visions of the divine indwelling, that is, the "circumincession" or "perichoresis" of the three persons. For example, in praying to the Father, Ignatius realized that "He was a Person of the Most Holy Trinity . . . [and] . . . was moved to love the whole Trinity all the more since the other Persons were present in Him essentially" (SD, no. 63). It seems that Ignatius experienced first the three divine persons individually and then moved to the unity of their mutual indwelling. From this he mystically grasped that he could rejoice in any of the divine persons, since his consolations somehow came from all three.

In this way Ignatius untied the trinitarian "knot" that had puzzled him from his days at Manresa. At Manresa he had prayed to each divine person individually and, not knowing why, added a fourth prayer to the Holy Trinity (Auto, no. 28). He claimed that saying four prayers to the Trinity—there being only three persons—"appeared to him to be a matter of little importance and gave him no difficulty" (Auto, no. 28). Yet, he clearly remembered this trinitarian difficulty some thirty years later when dictating his Autobiography to Father da Câmara.

Ignatius' trinitarian mysticism moved not only from the divine persons to their mutual indwelling. It also proceeded from their circumincession to the divine essence itself, that is, to the Trinity's heart. For example, occasionally Ignatius could not feel or clearly see the persons, but had "visitations" that ended in the "Name and Essence of the Most Holy Trinity" (SD, no. 110). He also felt or saw "very clearly, the very Being or Essence of God . . . the Being of the Most Holy Trinity" (SD, no. 121). On one occasion, a mystical vision revealed to him how the three persons "proceeded or exited from the Divine Essence . . ." (SD, no. 123). Or he simply saw this same being in spherical form, or had visions of the divine essence, the divine being, and the being of the Most Holy Trinity.[19]

Ignatius saw the divine persons not only as individuals, not only in the mystery of their mutual indwelling, but also in the very unity of the divine being. Furthermore, he experienced this unity as radically associated with the person of the Father.

His mysticism, therefore, fully grasped the powerful trinitarian ten-

sion that exists between the personal fullness of the three divine persons
and their eternal unity in the divine essence. Hence, Ignatius could pray in
a way that recalled something of the Manresa "knot" he untied: "Eternal
Father, confirm me; Eternal Son, confirm me; Eternal Holy Spirit, confirm me; Holy Trinity, confirm me; my only God, confirm me" (SD, no.
48).

A Mysticism of the Father and of the Divine Essence

Ignatius mystically experienced the Father as Father. For example, at
La Storta the Father uttered the words that transformed Ignatius' heart: "I
shall be favorable to you [plural] at Rome."[20] Moreover, when the eternal
Father and his cross-bearing Son appeared to Ignatius at La Storta, it is
again the Father who says to Christ, "I want you to take this man as your
servant." And Christ replied to Ignatius, "I want you [Ignatius] to serve us
[Father and Christ]." The explicitly Father-centered aspect of Ignatian
mysticism cannot be denied.

The *Spiritual Diary* attests clearly to the importance of the eternal
Father in Ignatius' mysticism. Ignatius prayed to the Father for the Spirit
of the Father and the Son to discern, decide, and be confirmed on a matter
of Jesuit poverty (SD, no. 15). When he made the oblation to the eternal
Father after resolving to have no revenue, he received mystical favors of
devotion, graces, tears, and sobbings (SD, no. 16). Yet, preparing to say
mass, he felt powerfully drawn to say, "Eternal Father, confirm me. . . .
Eternal Father, will You not confirm me?" (SD, no. 48).

Again, getting ready to say mass, but not knowing which one to say,
the thought came to him that "the Father was revealing Himself more to
me and was drawing me to His mercies, feeling that He was more favorable
and ready to grant what I desired" (SD no. 32). This mystical grace
blossomed into great confidence in the Father and mystical tears.

The eternal Father also stirred Ignatius in a variety of ways. For
example, the Father drew Ignatius to himself so powerfully that the saint's
hair stood on end (SD, no. 8). In allowing Ignatius to feel and to see him,
the Father often caused Ignatius to experience delectable bodily warmth
(SD, nos. 8, 30). Some consolations terminated decisively in the Father
alone (SD, no. 129). Moreover, the Father often indicated to Ignatius
which mediator to use to pray to him (SD, no. 30). The mere saying of the
Father's name brought Ignatius great devotion, tears, and interior sweetness (SD, no. 28).

Often the Father permitted himself to be found through Christ. In
fact, Ignatius mystically felt that he had access to the Father through
Christ (SD, no. 8), who both presented and accompanied his prayers to the

Father (*SD*, no. 77). It is the Father "Who set in order the affairs of the Son" (*SD*, no. 33) and bestowed delightful spiritual lights.

In one lovely passage, Ignatius states that Jesus attracted all his love and devotion. Nonetheless, "I could not apply myself to the other Persons, except to the First Person as being the Father of such a Son. . . . How He is the Father, how He is the Son!" (*SD*, no. 73).

The Father is prominent even in Ignatius' mystical penetration of the divine circumincession, perichoresis, or mutual indwelling. For example, by mystical vision and understanding, he grasped how the second and third persons are in the Father (*SD*, no. 89). Moreover, he experienced "an increase of intense love for the Being of the Most Holy Trinity, without seeing or distinguishing the Persons, except that *they proceed from the Father*, as I said" (*SD*, no. 121, my emphasis).

He also "felt something towards the Father, as though feeling *the other Persons in Him*" (*SD*, no. 95, my emphasis). During an experience of the Father as a person of the Most Holy Trinity, Ignatius was moved to "love the whole Trinity all the more since the other Persons were *present in Him essentially*" (*SD*, no. 63, my emphasis). When he prayed to the other persons he experienced the same thing, namely, that the two persons are present in the Father essentially (*SD*, no. 63). Thus, Ignatius mystically grasped how the Son and the Spirit are first and foremost in the Father.

Furthermore, Ignatius' mysticism discloses an intimate relationship between the Father and the divine essence. For example, he saw "in a certain way the Being of the Father, that is first the Being and then the Father—my devotion terminating first in the Essence and then in the Father . . ." (*SD*, nos. 142–143). He received a "partial revelation of the Being of the Father . . . and likewise of the Being of the Most Holy Trinity" (*SD*, no. 153). Hence, although Ignatius experienced the distinction between the Father and the divine essence, nonetheless it is the Father who seemingly has the most intimate relationship with it. He never speaks of the Son or the Spirit in this fashion.

This intimate relationship between the Father and the Trinity's being also revealed itself in a "vision of the Divine Essence several times ending in the Father, in a circular figure . . ." (*SD*, no. 172). Moreover, visions of the divine essence in circular form occurred "several times," "as before," and so on (*SD*, nos. 174, 180). The Father likewise seemed to close the circle, that is, "I also had a vision at different times of the Divine Essence, sometimes terminating in the Father, in the form of a circle" (*SD*, no. 183).

Ignatius mystically experienced the emphasis by the Greek fathers that there is one God because there is one eternal Father. But he also experienced the Augustinian Trinity, that is, he saw that "the Father on the one hand, the Son on the other, and the Holy Spirit on the other, *proceeded or exited from the Divine Essence . . ." (SD,* no. 123, my emphasis). And Ignatius "felt and saw . . . very clearly, the very Being or Essence of God . . . and *from this Essence the Father seemed to go forth or derive" (SD,* no. 121, my emphasis).

A Mysticism of the Eternal Son

The *Diary* witnesses clearly to Ignatius' mystical experiences of the eternal Son, the second person of the Trinity. He prayed to the eternal Son to confirm him, "Eternal Son, confirm me. . . . Eternal Son, will you not confirm me?" (*SD,* nos. 48, 53). In his prayer to the Son, Ignatius experienced how the Son is present essentially in the Father (*SD,* no. 63). In fact, even his Father-centered mysticism contains a Son-directed aspect because the Father, for Ignatius, is the Father of *this* Son.

Not only did Ignatius mystically see the Son proceeding from the Father (*SD,* no. 121); he also saw the Son proceeding or exiting from the divine essence (*SD,* no. 123). These Son-centered experiences brought him mystical understanding, certitude, consolations terminating in the Son in a "detached way," tears of reverent surrender and loving humility terminating in the Son, and an ever greater love of the Trinity.[21]

Often referring to Jesus Christ as the Son who intercedes with the Father,[22] or the Son whose affairs the Father sets in order (*SD,* no. 33), Ignatius said twenty masses of the name of Jesus during the relatively brief election period. During this time, he mystically "felt or saw" that "Jesus Christ Himself presented the orations that were addressed to the Father, or that he accompanied those I was saying to the Father" (*SD,* no. 77). In fact, prayer to the Father seemed to be Jesus' "duty" (*SD,* no. 84).

However, Jesus began to guide Ignatius somewhat differently during the process of discernment, election, and confirmation. Because Jesus had sent "the Apostles to preach in poverty . . ." (*SD,* no. 15) and was now the Society's head, Ignatius grasped mystically that this Jesus was the "greater argument to proceed in total poverty than all the other reasons" (*SD,* no. 65). These thoughts consoled him so deeply that he expected his decision to remain firm even in times of temptation and trial.

A La Storta-like experience also occurred: "I thought, in some way, that the appearance or the felt presence of Jesus was the work of the Most Holy Trinity" (*SD,* no. 67). The trinitarian gift of the felt presence of Jesus poor seemed to confirm his decision and ended the election process. All that mattered now for Ignatius was "to carry so deeply the name of Jesus" (*SD,* no. 68).

The Father had engraved Jesus' name on Ignatius' heart at La Storta.

This experience now emerged as a mystical "representation" of Jesus' name that brought "much love," "confirmation," and an "increased will to follow Him" (*SD*, no. 71).[23] And these experiences also gave birth to Ignatius' radical mysticism of the name of Jesus. One might speculate that his mysticism of the name of Jesus grounded the later Jesuit devotion to the heart of Jesus.

Ignatius had desired initially that the Trinity confirm him. Now he "felt that it was given to me through Jesus, when He showed Himself to me and gave me such interior strength and certainty of such confirmation, without any fear of the future" (*SD*, no. 73).

Ignatius' felt visions of Jesus continued, bringing with them love, devotion, and tears. So strong was this love that he thought nothing could separate him from Christ, nor cause any doubt about the confirmation he had received. The experience of Jesus communicating himself gave Ignatius the courage to go on with the election.[24]

Ignatius' trinitarian and Jesus-centered mysticism now took yet another turn. By continued prayer to Jesus and a variety of Jesus-directed mystical experiences, Ignatius eventually began to pray to Jesus with the sole purpose of having Jesus make him "conform to the will of the Most Holy Trinity, in the way He thought best" (*SD*, no. 80). Ignatius also realized that self-seeking had crept into his approach to the Trinity, especially in the matter of the election. He learned not to ask Jesus for confirmation, but only that Jesus "do His best service in the presence of the Most Holy Trinity, etc., and by the most suitable manner . . ." (*SD*, no. 82). In this way, Ignatius indirectly received infused "indifference." That is, his passionate love for Christ led him to the mystical realization that only God's will matters, that everything else must be grasped only in relation to it. This became Ignatius' true consolation and confirmation.

Ignatius likewise began to receive three types of visions that show still other aspects of his trinitarian and Jesus-centered mysticism. In the first kind, both the Trinity and Jesus appeared to Ignatius. They mystically taught him that it is Jesus who presents Ignatius to the Trinity and who is the means of union with the Trinity, "in order that this intellectual vision [of the Trinity] be communicated . . ." (*SD*, no. 83).[25] In fact, Ignatius "felt or more properly saw . . . the Most Holy Trinity and Jesus, presenting me, or placing me, or being the means of union with the Most Holy Trinity" (*SD*, no. 83). Thus Jesus became, explicitly and mystically, Ignatius' means of loving union with the Trinity. At La Storta, the Father placed Ignatius with his Son. Now it is Jesus who placed Ignatius with the Trinity. At La Storta, Ignatius mystically experienced Jesus from a trinitarian perspective. Now he experiences the Trinity from Jesus' perspective.

These visions infused Ignatius with respectful surrender and loving reverence. Through Jesus, the Trinity brought Ignatius to grasp mystically the mystery of the ever-greater God who must be worshiped for God's own sake. And "the same loving humility should be directed later to all creatures, for this is to the honor of God our Lord" (*SD*, no. 179). This means that God can be found in all things, when all things are used only insofar as they fulfill the purpose of life: the praise, reverence, and service of God (*Ex*, no. 23). Ignatius' mysticism of respectful surrender and loving reverence moved his focal point from himself to God. He saw the trinitarian God and all God's creatures from a trinitarian perspective, not from his own.[26]

The second type of visions revealed "Jesus at the feet of the Most Holy Trinity" (*SD*, no. 88) and brought Ignatius tears, devotion, consolations, and confirmation. Now he experienced himself continuing the election process under Jesus' "shadow" and guidance,[27] which increased, rather than decreased, his trinitarian graces, especially graces of loving reverence.[28] In addition, consolations and visions that terminated in Jesus and in the Trinity intensified notably.[29]

Ignatius likewise realized mystically that Jesus was life itself, and he proclaimed that he would rather "die with Him than live with another . . ." (*SD*, no. 95). These mystical experiences also sensitized Ignatius to the devil's power to stymie the election process. The clarity given through these experiences enabled Ignatius to conclude the election process successfully.

In the third kind of vision, Ignatius grasped Jesus' divinity by way of his humanity. Both the *Autobiography* and the *Diary* attest that Ignatius often saw Jesus as white light with an undifferentiated body. In one entry, however, Ignatius states: "I thought in spirit I had just seen Jesus, that is, white; i.e., His humanity, and at this other time I felt it in my soul in another way, namely, not His humanity alone, but *being all my God*, etc. . . ." (*SD*, no. 87, my emphasis). Ignatius had mystically experienced, grasped, and explicated the mystery of Jesus' twofold sonship. The Ignatian Christ is always the Son of the Virgin Mary according to the flesh and the Son of the eternal Father.[30] This is a mysticism at the "heart" of Jesus.

A Mysticism of the Holy Spirit

References to the Holy Spirit abound in Ignatius' *Spiritual Diary*, attesting to the Holy Spirit's explicit presence in his mystical life. Of the 116 explicitly named masses in the *Spiritual Diary*, for example, he said nine of the Holy Spirit.

On numerous occasions he prayed to the Holy Spirit, whom he saw or felt in a dense brightness.[31] Mystical experiences of the Holy Spirit produced mystical tears and intense consolations. More importantly, these experiences rendered Ignatius firm and satisfied with the decision, or election, concerning the Society's poverty.[32] This is the context for understanding Ignatius' plea to the Father that he mediate with the Spirit and place the Spirit in him. For only the Father's Spirit could inspire him to discern the particular point on poverty (SD, no. 36). Ignatius prayed to the Spirit, "Holy Spirit, confirm me. . . . Holy Spirit, will you not confirm me" (SD, nos. 48, 53).

On several unforeseeable occasions, the Holy Spirit drew Ignatius to himself in powerful "visitations" (SD, nos. 99, 140, 162). He sensed mystically, in fact, when he should pray to the Spirit and when consolations and movements "terminated" in this divine person (SD, nos. 54, 162). From time to time, Ignatius mystically saw how the Holy Spirit proceeds from the divine essence (SD, nos. 123, 125), and how the Spirit is in the Father essentially (SD, nos. 63, 89).

Thus it is obvious why Ignatius related to Nadal and Laynez, two of his first companions, that some of the most important gifts of his life were bestowed by the Holy Spirit. Toward the end of his life, contemplating the Holy Spirit was the most frequent grace he experienced.[33]

Concluding Summary

Ignatius gives a lovely summary of his trinitarian and christocentric mysticism, a mysticism at the heart of the Trinity and at the heart of Jesus Christ, in his short explanation of the sign of the cross. He writes:

> When we make the holy Sign of the Cross, we place our fingers first on the head; and this is to signify God our Father, who proceeds from no one. When we touch our breast, this signifies the Son, our Lord, who proceeds from the Father and who descended into the womb of the Blessed Virgin Mary. When we place our fingers on both shoulders, this signifies the Holy Spirit, who proceeds from the Father and the Son. And when we fold our hands together again, this symbolizes that the Three Persons are one single substance. And finally, when we seal our lips with the Sign of the Cross, this means that in Jesus, our Saviour and Redeemer, dwells the Father, the Son, and Holy Spirit, one single God, our Creator and Lord—and that the divinity was never separated from the body of Jesus, not even at His death.[34]

To sum up: we have seen how Ignatius penetrated to the very heart of the inner-trinitarian life. He experienced each of the three divine persons, their mutual indwelling, the Father's proximity to the divine essence, and the Trinity's very being. In short, he untied the trinitarian "knot" that mystified him for years. He was a mystic at the heart of the Trinity.

We have seen, too, that Ignatius' mystical experiences moved easily from Jesus in his humanity to Jesus as Son, the second person in the Trinity. Ignatius mystically grasped in and through Christ's humanity that Jesus was "all" his God. But Ignatius could also begin with experiences of the eternal Son and proceed to experience Jesus "at the foot of the Trinity." Ignatius thereby untied the christological perichoresis of the human and divine natures in the person of Jesus Christ.[35] In and through his trinitarian mysticism, therefore, Ignatius likewise penetrated to Christ's heart, that is, to the inmost core of Christ's personal reality. Ignatius is a mystic at the heart of both the Trinity and Jesus Christ.

NOTES

1. *Mysticism* (New York: E.P. Dutton, 1961), p. 468. For example, *The Oxford Dictionary of the Christian Church* (ed. F.L. Cross. Second revised edition by F.L. Cross and E.A. Livingston [Oxford: Oxford University Press, 1983], p. 690) says that "Ignatius' paramount endeavours had been the reform of the Church from within, principally by education and the more frequent use of the Sacraments, and the preaching of the Gospel to the newly discovered pagan world," but merely mentions in passing that he was a mystic. William James (*The Varieties of Religious Experience* [New York: The New American Library, 1958], p. 317, my emphasis), the father of American pragmatism, writes that "St. Ignatius was mystic, *but* his mysticism made him assuredly one of the most powerfully practical human engines that ever lived." The *Encyclopedia Americana* ("Loyola, Saint Ignatius of," volume 17, p. 815) comments: "but above all it is as a leader of men that Ignatius is outstanding." Many commentators on Ignatius' *Spiritual Exercises* miss their genuinely mystical foundation when they contend that the *Exercises* teach only highly discursive, image-bound, and somewhat mechanical methods of prayer, suitable only for beginners, and an actual barrier to deeper, more mystical levels of prayer. One example of contemporary caricatures of the so-called Ignatian method of prayer is Paul Sauve's *Petals of Prayer* (Locust Valley, N.Y., 1974), pp. 40–46. For an example of one author who severely criticizes the *Exercises* for their alleged anti-mystical orientation, see Al-

dous Huxley's *Grey Eminence* (New York: Harper, 1941), pp. 94–97, 101–102. Victorino Osende, *Pathways of Love* (St. Louis: Herder, 1958) pp. 83–88, is more nuanced than Huxley, but still not insightful enough into the mystical dimension of the *Spiritual Exercises.*

2. Of course, what one makes of or how one reconciles theologically these two different mysticisms of the heart of the Trinity is beyond the scope of this article.

3. See Adolf Haas, S.J., "The Mysticism of St. Ignatius according to his *Spiritual Diary," Ignatius of Loyola. His Personality and Spiritual Heritage*, ed. Friedrich Wulf, S. J. (St. Louis: Institute of Jesuit Sources, 1977), pp. 164–199. Henceforth abbreviated as "The Mysticism of St. Ignatius"; Harvey D. Egan, S. J., *The Spiritual Exercises and the Ignatian Mystical Horizon* (St. Louis: Institute of Jesuit Sources, 1976), pp. 112–131. Henceforth referred to as *Ignatian Mystical Horizon*. Simon Decloux, *Commentaries on the* Letters *and* Spiritual Diary *of St. Ignatius of Loyola* (Rome: Centrum Ignatianum Spiritualitatis, 1982), pp. 80–123; Hugo Rahner, S.J., *The Vision of St. Ignatius in the Chapel of La Storta*, tr. Robert O. Brennan, S. J. (Rome: Centrum Ignatianum Spiritualitatis, 1979), pp. 69–132. Henceforth referred to as *Vision of La Storta;* Joseph de Guibert, S.J., *The Jesuits: Their Spiritual Doctrine and Practice*, tr. William J. Young, S. J. (St. Louis: Institute of Jesuit Sources, 1972), pp. 50–52. Henceforth referred to as *Jesuits*.

   In view of contemporary trinitarian timidity and the "Unitarianism" that pervades much of Christian theology and spirituality, my article wants to stress the importance of Ignatius' trinitarian mysticism for contemporary Christian spirituality. As Karl Rahner says, "one might almost dare to affirm that if the doctrine of the Trinity were to be erased as false, most religious literature could be preserved almost unchanged throughout the process." See "Remarks on the Dogmatic Treatise 'De Trinitate,' " *Theological Investigations* IV, tr. Kevin Smyth (Baltimore: Helicon, 1966), p. 79.

4. See my *Ignatius Loyola the Mystic* (Wilmington, Delaware: Michael Glazier, 1987), especially chapter three, "A Trinitarian Mysticism."

5. *Fontes narrativi de S. Ignatio de Loyola et de Societatis Iesu initiis.* Vol. I, ed. D. Fernandez Zapico, C. de Dalmases, P. Leturia (Rome, 1943), p. 82. Henceforth referred to as *FN* I.

6. *Monumenta Nadalis* (letters and instructions of Ignatius' companion, Jeronimo Nadal), vol. V, p. 162. Henceforth abbreviated as *MNad* followed by the volume number.

7. *MNad* IV, p. 645.

8. *A Pilgrim's Journey. The Autobiography of Ignatius of Loyola.* Intro.,

tr., and commentary by Joseph N. Tylenda, S.J. (Wilmington, Delaware: Michael Glazier, 1985). Henceforth abbreviated as *Auto*, followed by the appropriate marginal number.

9. The first notebook is a diary covering the period from February 2 to March 12, 1544. During this time, Ignatius was deliberating on the degree of poverty to be observed by the churches of the Society. The second notebook covers the period from March 13, 1544, to February 27, 1545. It contains much shorter entries, many algebraic symbols, abbreviations, and cryptic notations. It is unknown what happened to the rest of the "rather large packet of writings." See Antonio T. de Nicolas, *Powers of Imagining. Ignatius of Loyola. A Philosophical Hermeneutic of Imagining through the Collected Works of Ignatius of Loyola with a Translation of these Works* (Albany: S.U.N.Y. Press, 1986). De Nicolas has translated Ignatius' *Spiritual Exercises, Spiritual Diary, Autobiography,* and some of his letters. Be careful of the typos. References to the *Spiritual Diary* will be taken from de Nicolas' translation, and abbreviated as *SD*, followed by the appropriate marginal number. For clarity, I have eliminated the brackets, parentheses, italics, and the like found in the text. Also, references to the *Spiritual Exercises* will be abbreviated as *Ex.*, followed by the appropriate marginal number.

10. It must be emphasized that Ignatius made these entries on the Trinity in the *Diary* when he was writing the *Constitutions* and deciding issues of Jesuit poverty. Hence, Ignatius experienced the Trinity in the context of the "election," that is, seeking and finding God's will. Ignatius' *Spiritual Exercises* call the decision to be made about a way of life or about the reform of one's life the "election." See *Ex.*, nos. 169–189. His ineffable trinitarian experiences are bound inextricably to his fervent desire to be *confirmed* in the matter of the election. Hence, his *Diary* reveals nothing about contemplation for its own sake. "Holy idleness" and "spousal" union are totally absent. Rather, Ignatius' trinitarian mysticism is one of discernment, election, and confirmation.

11. Alfred Feder, *Aus dem Geistlichem Tagebuch des heiligen Ignatius* (Regensburg, 1922), p. 1. Quoted by Adolf Haas, S.J., "The Mysticism of St. Ignatius," pp. 164–165.

12. No less an authority than Joseph de Guibert, S.J. (*St. Ignace mystique d'après son Journal Spirituel* [Toulouse, 1938], p. 35, quoted by Haas, p. 169) says: "I believe it will be difficult to find a mystical development of this mystery of spirituality which is more perfect than that which is revealed in the *Spiritual Diary* we are studying here."

13. See *SD*, nos. 6, 51, 104, 106, 107, 113, 117, 118, 137, 139, 140, 144.

14. During the "fourth week" of the *Spiritual Exercises*, that is, when the

exercitant is contemplating Christ's resurrection, Ignatius recommends taking advantage of a winter's fire, among other things, to promote joy in the Lord (*Ex*, no. 229).

15. See *SD*, nos. 51, 101, 105–110, 112, 115, 121, 122, 129, 130, 162.

16. In Ignatius' letter of September 20, 1548, to Francis Borgia (*Letters of St. Ignatius of Loyola*, selected and tr. William J. Young, S.J. [Chicago: Loyola University Press, 1958], pp. 180–181), he forbids Borgia to shed even one drop of blood for his penances. He recommends instead that Borgia seek especially the gift of tears that flow from a "loving consideration of the three Divine Persons" (p. 181).

17. For a discussion of this type of consolation, see my *Ignatian Mystical Horizon*, pp. 31–65, 140–141. Also see Jules J. Toner, S.J., *A Commentary on Saint Ignatius' Rules for the Discernment of Spirits* (St. Louis: Institute of Jesuit Sources, 1982), pp. 216–222, 243–256, 291–313.

18. For a similar experience, see *SD*, no. 112.

19. See *SD*, nos. 123, 125, 136, 143, 153, 172, 174, 180, 183.

20. On this important experience, see Hugo Rahner, S.J., *The Vision of St. Ignatius in the Chapel of La Storta*, tr. Robert O. Brennan, S.J. (Rome: Centrum Ignatianum Spiritualitatis, 1979).

21. See *SD*, nos. 122, 125, 129, 156, 159, 162.

22. See *SD*, nos. 4, 8, 23, 27, 46, 47.

23. The Ignatian mystical connection between visions, confirmation, and transformation also shows itself here.

24. See *SD*, nos. 75–76.

25. See also *SD*, nos. 85–87.

26. See *Ex*, nos. 3, 38.

27. See *SD*, nos. 95, 98, 101, 113.

28. See *SD*, nos. 138, 103, 112, 162.

29. See *SD*, nos. 98, 103, 137, 138, 140.

30. When the *Diary* speaks of "Jesus," this usually refers to the God-*man* and *incarnate* Savior. The designation "Son" refers to the second person of the Trinity. On this point, see Joseph de Guibert, S.J., "Mystique ignatienne," *RAM* 19 (1938), p. 114, n. 3.

31. See *SD*, nos. 14, 18, 169.

32. See *SD*, nos. 14, 18.

33. See *MNad* IV, p. 645 and *FN* I, p. 138. Also see K. Truhlar, "La découverte de Dieu chez saint Ignace de Loyola pendant les dernières années de sa vie," *RAM* 24 (1948), pp. 313–337.

34. *Monumenta Historica Societatis Jesu. S. Ignatii Epistolae* XII, ed. V. Augusti, F. Cervos, D. Restrepo (Madrid, 1911), p. 667. Quoted by Adolf Haas, "The Mysticism of St. Ignatius," pp. 185–186.

35. Hugo Rahner, S.J. (*Ignatius the Theologian*, tr. Michael Barry [Lon-

don and New York: Herder and Herder, 1968], p. 15) speaks of a mystically experienced *communicatio idiomatum,* or "communication of properties." Because of the hypostatic union, the properties of both the human and the divine nature must be predicated of the one person Jesus Christ. For an excellent introduction to Ignatius' christology, see his *Ignatius the Theologian,* pp. 53–135.

Margaret Brennan, I.H.M.

Teresa of Avila: ". . . Undaunted Daughter of Desire"

In the Preface of his book *Habits of the Heart*, Robert Bellah makes reference to a phrase of Alexis de Tocqueville which inspired the title of what was to become a best seller. In 1830, this French social philosopher used the term "habits of the heart" to describe the mores which he felt formed the American character. The phrase, for Tocqueville, included those fundamental moral views of Americans that had both shaped and determined a value system.[1]

My point of reference in introducing a chapter on Teresa of Avila with this expression of Tocqueville is to suggest that this woman, whose spirituality challenged the societal mores and value systems of Castilian Spain, was one who called into question long-standing "habits of the heart."

The spiritual genius of Teresa, however, was not one that came to fruition through a process of social analysis or academic research. Rather, it emerged from an experience of God that rose as from a spring of water deep within the center of her soul and overflowed from "brim-filled bowls of fierce desire."[2] Great desires were for Teresa the hallmark of courageous souls who are resolved to do great things for God. Indeed, the fostering of such intense longing was to become for her a "habit of the heart"—that is, an acquired behavior pattern regularly followed until it had become almost involuntary.

If desire is an expression of the heart's longing that is translated into action and the ability to face obstacles with firmness and without fear, then Teresa can be said to have a spirituality of the heart. She expresses herself

114

convincingly in this regard: "I have never seen any such person (that is, one with great desires) hanging back on this road, nor any soul that, under the guise of humility, acted like a coward, go as far in many years as the courageous soul can in a few" (*Life* 13, 2).

The purpose of this essay is to reflect on this woman whose experience of God in prayer not only encouraged countless others to undertake the interior journey, but also moved outward as a critique to societal and cultural structures that militated against the full human and spiritual liberation and integration of women and men in sixteenth century Spain. Such a reflection may be able to shed some light on the struggles of our own time. Hopefully, too, it can provoke the realization that for us too the experience of God can become the most powerful means of challenging the dualisms and cultural fetishes that take shape in unjust structures and systems within society and the church.

Historical Background

Teresa de Ahumada, born in Avila (1515), was to live her entire life in Castile, the center of Spain which had become the largest empire the world had ever seen. At the same time, it was also a kingdom which arrogantly assumed a posture of pride and superiority. Isolated from the rest of Europe by the Pyrenees mountains, it took advantage of its insularity to build up an ideology of social relationships that had become the very soul of the nation's marginalizing and excluding all those who were not "pure-blooded Spaniards." To have mixed blood was to be "inferior." In militantly Catholic Spain it meant having an "inferior faith" as well.

The "honor" attached to the social phenomena of "true hidalgoism," i.e. men of honor and "pure blood," touched women in a different way than men. For them it had meant originally a kind of sexual decorum. For men, in particular, it meant having "untainted blood." Teofanes Egido's study of this period points out that "a loss of 'honor' in the first sense might be forgiven, but there was no possibility, at least in theory, of repairing the breach of 'honor' in the second sense."[3] Yet the fact that only those of "untainted blood" were allowed entrance into most religious orders meant that there was a social significance attached to such a vocation whose members, including women, were considered part of the existing "aristocracy" possessing illustrious lineages even if they were not wealthy.

The situation of women in sixteenth century Spain, apart from the social situation of "hidalgoism," also reflected the cultural and anthropological view of women that prevailed in European society. In general women were thought to be biologically and intellectually inferior to men. Perhaps this was even more prevalent in Spain where the works of Aristotle had been the subject of study and reflection particularly through Moslem philosophers.[4] The teaching of Aristotle regarding women as symbolizing the lower realm of body or matter as opposed to the transcendent mind which is more naturally symbolized by men is well stated in his *Politics*.[5] Carried over into church teaching, this anthropology led to the view that women were not capable of spiritual equality with men and that their capacities in this regard would not be realized fully in this life. Indeed their very salvation depended on their willingness to be directed by male power in both church and in society.[6]

Reading Teresa's works on prayer against the tapestry of this background, indeed seeing them as woven into it, allows us to comprehend how prophetic was the experience of God to which she remained faithfully committed and which in turn became a radical critique of the society in which she lived. Her steadfastness and courage inspired her to propose a doctrine of prayer which challenged the prevalent scholastic teaching as well as societal mores. In the words of Segundo Galilea, "St. Teresa undertook the reform of Carmel precisely in order to make the religious life a sign of liberation from all the idols of her time, as a counterculture and a counter-current to the spirit of the world."[7]

Teresa's Teaching on Prayer

When Teresa at the age of twenty left her father's house in secret to enter the Incarnation on November 2, 1535, she became part of a convent of nuns housing about two hundred persons. This included not only the religious but their servants and sometimes their relatives as well. Kieran Kavanaugh, one of Teresa's most dedicated researchers, points out that contrary to most opinions, this convent was actually more austere than lax. As was customary in most religious houses of the time, the prayer life centered around a solemn recitation of the Divine Office in Latin accompanied by minute rubrics and intricate ceremonies. No time for mental prayer was prescribed or promoted, nor was any instruction on meditation given to the novices.[8]

Teresa's acquaintance with mental prayer came some time later when she was introduced to Osuna's *Third Alphabet*, a book given to her by an uncle when she was on the way to her sister's home while waiting to undergo a cure for the illness (and perhaps breakdown) that overcame her two years after her religious profession. Osuna, a Franciscan, was a member of the "alumbrados," and as such a promoter of recollection as a means of developing an interior life and union with God. On her return to the Incarnation some months after recuperating from the illness which nearly resulted in her death and was to forever impair her health, Teresa writes of experiencing a period of eighteen years in which the practice of prayer was filled with difficulties. "Very often, for some years, I was more anxious that the hour I had determined to spend in prayer be over than I was to remain there . . . and so unbearable was the sadness I felt on entering the oratory, that I had to muster up all my courage" *Life* ch. 8, 7). In this regard, Kavanaugh notes that the problem probably came more from lack of technique than from laxity or indifference.[9]

Early in 1554, at the age of thirty-nine, Teresa came in touch with a Spanish translation of *The Confessions of St. Augustine*. The reading of this book together with a kind of emotional shock she experienced on seeing an image of the wounded Christ with Mary Magdalene at his feet began what we have come to call her "second conversion." Never again was she to doubt her love of God nor to turn aside from the resolution to serve him with all her strength. These two incidents initiated her into the realms of a more passive prayer and the experience of mystical graces. In this way, she began the interior journey which led outwardly to the reform of Carmel and to the writing of works on prayer that have yet to be surpassed.

Teresa's teaching on prayer is contained most basically in three major works: *The Book of Her Life* (ch. 11–22), *The Way of Perfection*, and *The Interior Castle*.

A summary of her teaching is succinctly expressed in a well-known definition found in the *Life*. "Mental prayer in my opinion is nothing but an intimate sharing between friends; it means taking time frequently to be alone with Him who we know loves us" (*Life* 8, 5). In *The Way of Perfection* she offers a justification for her conviction.

> Remember how Saint Augustine tells us about his seeking God in many places and eventually finding Him within himself. Do you think it matters little for a soul with a wandering mind to understand this truth and see that there is no need to go to heaven in order to speak with one's eternal Father or find delight in Him? Nor is there any need to shout. However softly we speak, He is near enough to hear us. Neither is there any need for wings to go to find Him. All one need do is go into solitude and look at Him within oneself (*The Way of Perfection* 28, 2).

Since God dwells within the soul it must be a place of beauty. *The Interior Castle* pictures it as a splendid dwelling "made entirely out of a diamond or of very clear crystal, in which there are many rooms. For in reflecting upon it carefully, we realize that the soul of the just person is nothing else but a paradise where the Lord says He finds His delight" (*The Interior Castle* 1, 1).

Teresa is convinced that every person has the capacity to realize this presence of God. Her life, the meaning of her reform, and her major works actualize this experience.

Teresa began to write the story of her life when she was approaching fifty. She had been practicing the prayer of recollection, and receiving mystical graces for almost ten years. The *Life* was written in obedience to confessors who were fearful, mistrustful, and perhaps ignorant of the depth and scope of the religious experience of this woman who had no access to theological education, and whose reading of spiritual books in Spanish had ceased after the Inquisition had forbidden the publication of any books on prayer in the vernacular. This last measure not only robbed her of spiritual nourishment but initiated a kind of crisis in which she complained to God, but which in reality led her to trust her own spiritual experience:

> When they forbade the reading of many books in the vernacular, I felt that prohibition very much because reading some of them was an enjoyment for me, and I could no longer do so since only the Latin editions were allowed. The Lord said to me: 'Don't be sad, for I shall give you a living book'. I was unable to understand why this was said to me, since I had not yet experienced any visions. Afterwards, within only a few days, I understood very clearly, because I received so much to think about and such recollection in the presence of what I saw, and the Lord showed so much love for me by teaching me in many ways, that I had very little or almost no need for books. His Majesty had become the true book in which I saw the truths (*Life* 26, 5).

Without the help of any literary or theological education Teresa developed her doctrine of prayer from her own personal story. In what would have been considered a very unorthodox statement in a time when a veritable panic surrounded mysticism and the experience of God was seen as anything but normative, she expresses her own clear conviction.

> I know a person who hadn't learned that God was in all things by presence, power and essence, and through a favor of this kind that God granted her she came to believe it. After asking a half-learned man—he knew as little as she had known before God enlightened her—she was told that God was present only by grace. Such was her own conviction that even after this she didn't believe him and asked others who told her the Truth, with which she was greatly consoled.[10]

The whole meaning of Teresa's reform, and the dynamic behind the indefatigable zeal with which she founded new Carmelite convents in Castile and beyond, was motivated by her desire to enable others to find the deep center of God's presence that she had found within herself. To attain that union with God for which we were all created was for her the meaning of the church, the focus of its teaching, the wellspring for apostolic service, and the sure antidote to arid arguments and abstract conceptualizations of theologians so often devoid of devotion. Her own spiritual journey did not follow a steady ascent to heights of perfection nor did it describe a system of clearly defined steps and stages. But rather, not unlike the roads she traveled, it passed through deep, lush valleys, across arid plains and swirling rivers in order to reach the destined and desired goal. What she required of those who would set out on this royal but rugged road was the courage to begin, the determination to continue, the generosity to persevere, and perhaps above all the trust in God's merciful love that never abandons us along the way.

In August of 1566, seven years after the Index had been published by the Inquisition, Teresa wrote *The Way of Perfection* in response to the nuns of St. Joseph's (the first reformed Carmel) who asked that she share with them her experience of prayer. To compensate and console them for having been deprived of spiritual books written in the vernacular, she encourages them, with a clear reference to the Index, and not without a note of irony, to "hold fast . . . for they cannot take from you the Our Father and Hail Mary." The censor who read the book was quick to note in the margin of the first edition, "It seems she is reprimanding the inquisitors for prohibiting books on prayer."[11] Believing that all the secrets of the contemplative life are contained within the prayer taught us by Jesus, she wrote this kind of primer on prayer in the form of commentary on the Our Father. Its tone is conversational, addressed as it was to the nuns of St. Joseph's.[12]

In 1577, Teresa aged sixty-two, was firmly grounded in the truth of her own experience. Although the opposition to the reform had reached its height, it did not ruffle more than the surface of her soul. Fifteen years of intense activity had gone by since she founded the monastery at St. Joseph's which initiated the reform. On June 2, Trinity Sunday, Teresa began to write *The Interior Castle* which was to be her most mature work on prayer. In comparing it to the *Life*, she declares that "it is composed of finer enamel and more precious metals; the goldsmith was not so skillful when he made the first." But before the work was completed, Teresa was to lay it aside to undergo yet more trials.

Later in the summer she was to learn of the papal nuncio's dismissal of her with the remark that she was a "restless and wandering female . . . a gad-about who under the cloak of piety has invented false doctrines, left the enclosure of her convent against the orders of the Council of Trent and her own Superiors and gone about teaching as though she were a professor (como maestra) contrary to the injunctions of Saint Paul who said that women were not to teach."[13] Moreover, about the same time a kind of popular pamphlet denouncing her work and containing veiled references to various "crimes" was circulated, raising more suspicions about her character and reputation. Teresa's response to false witness is characteristic of her deeply rooted peace. "I am so accustomed to it (the false witness) that it is not surprising that I do not feel these things. . . . It's as though I had a block of wood inside me on which the blows rain down without touching my heart" (*Letters* ccv). In October the nuns at the convent of the Incarnation were excommunicated by the Provincial of the Calced Carmelites for electing Teresa as prioress. Back in Toledo, not yet knowing the outcome of the excommunication, she resumed her writing and on November 29 laid down her pen. Although five months had passed, the actual time she was engaged in writing was only two.

The Interior Castle is Teresa's final synthesis on prayer. Thoroughly convinced and having experienced that human beings are created in the image and likeness of God, Teresa pictures an interior castle with many mansions in the depths of the soul. In its deepest center dwells "His Majesty." Prayer is the door that allows entry, and the journeys through the various mansions deepen and expand the growing friendship with God. In the end, God becomes the very dwelling in which the soul rests. The pathway to the final dwelling is made possible by a generous response to the invitations of Christ's grace. A growing self-knowledge and humility lead the soul to know both its own beauty as well as its own fidelity . Good books, friendships, trials and meditation on the humanity of Jesus become the means for an ever-deeper movement toward the center. Like the silkworm that spins its own cocoon in which it dies in order to emerge transformed as a small white butterfly, Teresa sees the soul entering into Christ where it dies to itself and becomes one spirit with him. Far from seeing the final dwelling as a place of blissful rest, the new life is experienced in having "put on the mind of Christ Jesus," enabling it with new strength to serve and enable the kingdom of God.

Rather than seeing the call to union with God as something extraordinary and offered only to privileged souls, Teresa is certain that all are called to discover and experience the center where God dwells, keeping watch and waiting for the hour to give. We may put off the time by our own attachments and lack of determination. "Since we do not succeed in giving up everything at once, this treasure as a result is not given to us all at once. May it please the Lord that drop by drop He may give it to us, even though it cost us all the trials in the world. . . . For God does not deny Himself to anyone who perseveres" (*Life* 11, 3, 4).

Teresa's teaching on prayer was not developed or brought to maturity outside of the context of her times. The founding of Carmelite convents in which nuns could grow in friendship with Christ, which she felt to be at the heart of the Christian message, was an urban phenomenon. Teresa wanted the reform to be in the midst of city life, and it was chiefly for this reason that she avoided the rural areas. Moreover, in Catholic Spain of the sixteenth century she needed the support of patrons and the approbation of both civil and church authorities.

Teresa in Conflict with Societal Mores

Teresa's reformist approach to prayer as growth in intimate friendship with God who has first loved us, and her belief that all persons were called to experience such friendship, was to bring her into conflict with the societal mores of her day. Two situations, in particular, militated against her central thesis: the social inequality between "Old Christians" (those of "untainted blood") and Judeoconversos (Christianized Jews), and the condition of women.

1. *The Social Inequality*

Teresa's earliest biographers, who were her contemporaries, point out that she was born of noble lineage. In the process for her canonization, it was taken for granted that she was of an "Old Christian" family—a "pure-blooded" Spaniard. To suppose that any sanctity and heroism could possibly be found in one with Jewish or Moorish blood would have been inconceivable.[14] However, recent research has now proven without doubt that Teresa had Jewish blood. Her grandfather and father, silk merchants in Toledo, were Judeoconversos who, after having been obliged to do public penance in 1485, moved to Avila after having purchased false certificates which acknowledged them as "Old Christians" and true hidalgos—men of honor and "pure blood." Here they changed their name from Sanchez to Cepeda, and Teresa's father married into an hidalgo family, hoping perhaps to better erase his past. Whether or not Teresa knew of this is not clear, but the indisputable fact casts a new light on her preoccupation with "honor," the pursuit of which she considers to be a major obstacle to a life of prayer. Her denunciations of "honor," expressed with irony and sometimes bordering on harshness, are not unlike those uttered by the secular social critics and non-conformists of her day (Egido, p. 14).

In the early chapters of the *Life*, Teresa recounts her own preoccupation with honor and the importance of a good reputation. An early flirtation with a cousin caused her father to send her to a convent boarding school lest her honor be tainted. She readily acknowledges that her concern was only in terms of outward appearances—of what others would think of her and how they would judge her. Entrance into the Incarnation did not initially free her from such preoccupation. The convent itself included levels of social standing, titles of noble lineage, and varying economic backgrounds. It was only after Teresa's "second conversion" at age thirty-nine that she took up an irrevocable stance in her evaluation of social approval—"the chain no file can sever."

In attacking "honor," Teresa knew that she was calling into question that strongest social principle of the established order of her day. Egido points out that her statement "I have always esteemed virtue more than lineage" contains a revolutionary axiom which would have been considered subversive and dangerous.[15]

The convents of the reform actualized what Teresa had come to know of true honor—that of serving God in imitation of Christ who lost a thousand honors (*The Way of Perfection*, 3, 7). Here there would be no titles or marks of distinction, no references to noble lineage. No hint of discrimination would be found in the constitutions, and the contempt for the world which she insists upon in those who would enter was aimed specifically at this social aberration that marginalized a whole class of persons with "mixed" or "impure" blood. In this way, she went against the mentality of most religious orders of her time which prohibited entrance to anyone descended from Moorish or Jewish blood.[16] Here then was a counter-cultural way of living religious life in direct opposition to the fetishes of honor which had become the power principle in both the civil and church society.

In the tapestry of Teresa's writings as a whole, the contempt in which she held prestige and its privileges is threaded over and over in a continuous pattern. A distillation of all her convictions is summed up in a statement to her sisters at St. Joseph's: "The soul's profit and what the world calls honor can never go together" (*The Way of Perfection*, 36, 3).

2. The Condition of Women

Teresa's critique of the situation of women in sixteenth century Spain is much more understated than that which is leveled against honor. Perhaps she herself was of the generally held opinion that women were by nature inferior to men. Her struggle may also have come in part from the fact that she herself was a woman and resented the restrictions and domestic enclosure enjoined upon them. She speaks of "womanish tears," of her inability to express herself "because she is a woman," and that "just being a woman is enough to have my wings fall off." She wonders that good men should oppose "a little woman, wretched, weak, and fearful like myself." She notes that it is especially bad for women to try to raise up the spirit, because they are more susceptible to illusion. Her views on the status of married women is especially dim. She remarks that because they must live in accord with their calling (that is, totally subject to the pleasure and whim of their husbands) they should not attempt to reach freedom of spirit and be content to advance "at the speed of a hen"—though she does not hold this for religious. Here we sense her resentment at the social conditioning of women which in part led her to choose religious life where at least she would enjoy some measure of independence.

When Teresa later reflects on marriage and the way in which it kept women psychologically immature and incapable of developing their own gifts and talents, she notes that religious life was a way of promoting greater liberty of spirit and a freedom from subjection. She speaks to the nuns of "the great grace God has given them in choosing them for Himself: He has spared them being in subjection to a man who is often the cause of their losing their life and God be thanked if he did not make them lose their souls too."

She frequently sought out "competent men of learning" with whom to consult. Without a doubt both a desire for verification on one hand, and a fear of the Inquisition with its mistrust of spiritual experience on the other, was behind much of this concern. But what also seems to be true is the deep resentment she felt at being deprived of such learning because she was a woman, though for the most part it is disarmingly hidden in a vocabulary of submission. Very likely it is for this reason that the *Life* escaped condemnation, though it was submitted three times to the Inquisition. Moreover, her thinly veiled criticism of male ecclesiastics to whose judgment she was constantly subjected, though often expressed with humor and a touch of irony, is a telling commentary on her views about unearned prestige and empty honor.

> It (the soul) sometimes laughs to itself when it sees seriously religious and prayerful persons making a big issue out of some rules of etiquette which it has already trampled underfoot. They claim that this is a matter of discretion and of the prestige accompanying their office so that they might bring about more good. The soul knows very well that they would bring about more good in one day than they would in ten years if for the love of God they thought a lot less of the prestige or office (*Life* 21, 9).

Teresa knew that she could not change the system or structures—but that does not mean that she approved of them. She was not above using political shrewdness nor of feigning submission if in so doing she could carry out the reform. In recounting the story of how the monastery of St. Joseph was founded, she recalls how she accepted a severe reprimand with "apparent" humility.

> I saw clearly that in some matters they condemned me without any fault on my part, for they said I did it so as to be esteemed or to become famous and other similar things. . . . None of what they said caused me any disturbance or grief although I let on that it did so as not to give the impression I didn't take to heart what they said to me (*Life* 36, 13).

Many years later in July of 1581, just a year before her death, Teresa in a letter to Gratian indicates that she felt such tactics were still called for. "If the General sees we are obedient and if, from time to time, we show him some little civility in token of our submissiveness, no harm will come to us."

The general opinion of churchmen in the sixteenth century regarding the spiritual capacities of women was clearly a matter of doctrinal certitude. Any attempts to declare otherwise was met with belittling and scornful replies that bordered on contempt. Even the spiritual writer Francisco de Osuno, whose book *The Third Spiritual Alphabet* had initiated Teresa into the meaning of the prayer of recollection, was not above such opinions.

> Since you see your wife going about visiting many churches, practicing many devotions, and pretending to be a saint, lock the door; and if that isn't sufficient, break her leg if she is young, for she can go to heaven lame from her own house without going around in search of these suspect forms of holiness. It is enough for a women to hear a sermon and then put it into practice. If she desires more, let a book be read to her while she spins, seated at her husband's side.[17]

Teresa reacted strongly against this mistrust of women, of the low opinion in which they were held, and of their apparent incapacity for pursuing a life of prayer.

> You will hear some persons frequently making objections: there are dangers; so-and-so went astray by such means; this other one was deceived; another who prayed a great deal fell away; it's

harmful to virtue; it's not for women, for they will be susceptible to illusions; it's better they stick to their sewing; they don't need these delicacies; the Our Father and the Hail Mary are sufficient (*The Way of Perfection,* 21, 2).

Rooting her own convictions in the scriptures she does not consider it a boldness for women to desire to contribute to the building up of the church as she proposed to do in establishing the reform. In a prayer to God she petitions with undeniable logic.

> It seems bold that I think I could play some role in obtaining an answer to these petitions. I trust, my Lord, in these Your servants who live here, and I know they desire and strive for nothing else than to please You. For You they renounced the little they had—and would have wanted to have more so as to serve You with it. Since you, my Creator, are not ungrateful, I think You will not fail to do what they beg of You. Nor did You, Lord, when You walked in the world, despise women; rather, You always, with great compassion, helped them. And you found as much love and more faith in them than you did in men. . . . Is it not enough, my Lord, that the world has intimidated us . . . so that we may not do anything worthwhile for You in public or dare speak some truths that we lament over in secret, without Your also failing to hear so just a petition? I do not believe, Lord that this could be true of Your goodness and justice, for You are a just judge and not like those of the world. Since the world's judges are sons of Adam and all of them men, there is no virtue in women that they do not hold suspect. I do not speak for myself . . . but because I see that these are times in which it should be wrong to undervalue virtuous and strong souls, even though they are women (*Way of Perfection* 3, 7).

In an even more daring passage in response to the criticism of the papal nuncio that in teaching and writing on prayer she is going against the injunction of St. Paul who admonished women to learn in silence, not teach nor use authority over the man (1 Tim 2:11–12), she confides her doubt to Christ who answers: "Tell them they shouldn't follow just one part of scripture but that they should look at other parts, and ask them if they can by chance tie my hands" (*Spiritual Testimony* 15, July 1571). Here Teresa appeals to an important hermeneutical principle but has the audacity to use Christ himself as her theological source.[18]

While Teresa struggled with many churchmen to find a way in which her experience of God might enable a revisionist approach to prayer that would bring the reality of God's presence into the lives of all persons as a decisive fact, she was not without the support of many men with whom she worked in mutuality and collaboration. Surely the best known of these is John of the Cross who, more than Teresa perhaps, suffered at the hands of those who opposed her teaching, and encouraged her most to trust the experience she had difficulty in naming theologically. It was truly in learned men such as John of the Cross that she found kindred spirits who did not find or believe God's action and favor to be weighted in terms of men when they encountered women whose gifts equaled and perhaps surpassed those of their own.

The Contribution and Challenge of Teresa Today

Contemporary women and men can find a model of courage and commitment in Teresa of Avila as they seek to find full acceptance and acknowledgment of their gifts and pastoral insights in the service of the church. To allow this recognition to happen will be to declare frankly that our experience of God today is one that not only challenges societal and church structures but calls for the reformulation of church teaching so as to allow for such an experience.

Based on the teaching authority of the scriptures, Vatican II defined the church as the people of God and reaffirmed the universal call to holiness, the vocation of all the baptized to further the mission of the church, and the servant role of leadership. It enunciated these principles of equality by citing, among others, the baptismal formula quoted by St. Paul in the letter to the Galatians, "In Christ Jesus there is neither Jew nor Greek, slave nor free, male nor female" (Gal 3:28).

All of these movements of the Spirit call for spiritualities of liberation and the consequent exposure of idols and ideologies that, in the name of the Christian God, have thwarted the egalitarian teaching of the gospel. It has called the church to lay aside its triumphalism, to examine its hierarchical structures and distinctions, and to develop new criteria with which to model the mutuality and collaboration of all God's people in the transformation of society.

Segundo Galilea reminds us that "St. Teresa undertook the reform of Carmel precisely in order to make the religious life a sign of liberation from all the idols of her time."[19]

The basis of that reform, as has been pointed out, was her teaching on prayer which in turn provoked a critique of societal mores which posed as formidable obstacles in the church as well.

Women religious today, as in the world of Teresa, are not desirous or willing to break away from the long history of consecrated life which has borne so much fruit. But, like her, they are desirous and intent to enrich that life still more by bringing their own experience of God to bear upon its continued growth. This calls, of course, for the willingness to discern not only the calls of grace but the call to an on-going conversion as well if that experience of God is to bear witness in holiness of life and apostolic zeal.

In the sixteenth century when women were viewed as inferior to men by nature and incapable therefore of spiritual equality, Teresa was not beyond feigning submission in order to further the experienced and contrary convictions that were at the heart of her reform. Feminists today are critical of this kind of cultural manipulation that plays into an ideology that needs to be exposed for what it is. Yet the temptation remains, especially when the structural system of patriarchy continues in the church with the blessing of doctrinal authority and under the guise of God's ordaining will.[20]

Is such political shrewdness the price exacted of religious women today in order to carry out the ministries to which they feel called and within which they discover the face of God? Or rather, does the very mission of the church, which is to form a divine/human community of justice and peace, demand that they commit themselves to courageous confrontation in pursuit of that mutuality which acknowledges and actualizes the equality of men and women in all aspects of its life?

Conclusion

Teresa of Avila was both a daughter of the church and a child of her times. This was to be both the cause of her joy and the arena of her struggle. Her belief and conviction that all persons are called to experience the demanding reality of an intimate friendship with God was the passion of her life and the hallmark of her zeal. Without such a friendship there can be no true witness to the incarnate faith of the gospel that is liberating even as it liberates.

Haunted by a Jewish heritage that would disclaim her lineage, she had to hide her real identity and attack the "bore-worm" of racial purity by appealing to the only true honor that matters—that of Jesus whose only worldly honor was gained in losing it. As a woman deprived of any theological education and not able to read even the Bible in the vernacular, she turned to the "living book" within her—the presence of the living God.

The pursuit of God as experienced in life and in the reality of history has been a struggle in the Christian church from its very beginnings. The prophetic words of Jesus uttered in complaint to the Pharisees who asked for a sign in testifying to the truth of his message are sounded anew in every age: "You know how to interpret the appearance of the sky, but you cannot interpret the signs of the times" (Mt 16:3). To be able to discern the word and action of God's Spirit in our own time requires that we be rooted in the best traditions of our past, but it also demands that our own lives be so in touch with God that we can trust the deepest desires of our own hearts in charting a future not yet clear to us. In pursuing these longings so that they become "habits of the heart," we would do well to ponder the words of Teresa in speaking of her own Order's call to a continual renewal.

> Let it never be said of them, as it is said of some other Orders, that they do nothing but praise their beginnings. It is we who are the beginners now; but let them continually strive to be beginners too, in the sense of growing better and better all the time (*Foundations*, 29).

NOTES

1. See Robert N. Bellah, et al., eds., *Habits of the Heart: Individualism and Commitment in American Life* (San Francisco: Harper & Row, 1986), p. vii.
2. See Richard Crashaw, "The Flaming Heart."
3. See Teofanes Egido, O.C.D., "The Historical Setting of St. Teresa's Life," *Carmelite Studies*, Vol. 3: Centenary of St. Teresa (Washington, D.C.: ICS Publications, 1980), p. 129.
4. For a detailed study of this history, see Fernand van Steenberghen, *Aristotle in the West: The Origins of Latin Aristotelianism*, tr. Leonard Johnston (Louvain: Nauwelaerts, 1955).
5. See Aristotle, *Politics*, Book 1, Chapter 5.
6. See Rosemary Ruether, *Sexism and God-Talk* (Boston: Beacon Press, 1983), pp. 80–81.
7. Segundo Galilea, *The Future of Our Past* (Notre Dame, Indiana: Ave Maria Press, 1945), p. 85.
8. See Kieran Kavanaugh, O.C.D., "*The Book of Her Life*: Introduction," in *The Collected Works of St. Teresa of Avila*, Vol. 1, tr. Kieran Kavanaugh, O.C.D., and Otilio Rodriguez, O.C.D. (Washington, D.C.: ICS Publications, 1976), p. 4.
9. See Kavanaugh, Vol. 1, p. 4.
10. *The Interior Castle*, 5, 1, 10. See Ciriaco Moron-Arroyo, "I Will Give You a Living Book: Spiritual Currents at Work at the Time of St. Teresa of Jesus," *Carmelite Studies*, Vol. 3: Centenary of St. Teresa (Washington, D.C.: ICS Publications, 1980), pp. 95–112.

11. The original autograph of *The Way of Perfection* which contains this note is preserved in the royal library of the Escorial.
12. See Morron-Arroyo, pp. 110–111.
13. Critical edition of the works of St. Teresa by P. Silverio de Santa Teresa, vol. 5, p. 246, n. 2.
14. See Egido, p. 137.
15. See Egido, p. 165.
16. A proviso issued in 1566 for all the Calced Carmelites, just four years after the first foundation of the reform, indicated specifically that only those would be received who were daughters of praiseworthy parentage, not illegitimate, nor of Jewish or Moorish blood.
17. Francisco de Osuno, *The Third Spiritual Alphabet*, quoted in *The Collected Works of St. Teresa of Avila*, Vol. 2, tr. Kavanaugh and Rodriguez, p. 23.
18. See Moron-Arroyo, p. 109.
19. Galilea, p. 86.
20. See Sonya A. Quitsland, "Elements of a Feminist Spirituality in St. Teresa," *Carmelite Studies*, Vol. 2: Centenary of St. Teresa, pp. 19–50.

Keith J. Egan

The Symbolism of the Heart
in John of the Cross

Catholic France once prided itself on its devotion to the Sacred Heart of Jesus, but this devotion underwent a decline in the aftermath of the Second World War especially among the young. When young Catholic actionists in France were surveyed, their objections to this devotion signaled the eventual loss of the heart as an effective religious symbol.[1] In so doing, French youth anticipated attitudes that surfaced after Vatican II in North America. Commercialism and a slogan-ridden society have trivialized the heart and robbed the heart of its power to symbolize much of anything let alone religious realities. If the heart is to become an effective religious symbol once more, it is necessary to identify resources that can facilitate its retrieval. It is my conviction that the writings of John of the Cross have a contribution to make in achieving this recovery.[2] As a mystic and as a poet, Juan de la Cruz, 1542–1591, had access to a rich world of symbols. Moreover, this saint and doctor of the church has used the heart extensively and adeptly to communicate symbolic meaning.

In this essay I prefer to speak of the heart as a symbol rather than as an image or a like designation. I do so under the influence of the psychology of Carl Jung[3] who has opened up the psychic dimensions of the symbol and under the guidance of Mircea Eliade's rediscovery of the symbol in his exploration of the primitive mentality.[4] This growing appreciation of the dynamics of the symbol has been continued in theology by David Tracy[5] and philosophically by Paul Ricoeur.[6] This essay tries to show that heart for John of the Cross is a symbol akin to the notion of symbol espoused by these contemporary thinkers, and, in fact, is an archetypal symbol in the language of Philip Wheelwright who describes archetypal symbols as

". . . those which carry the same or very similar meanings for a large portion, if not all, of mankind."[7]

While John of the Cross constantly uses symbolism in his poems and in his commentaries, he is best known for the symbol night, dark night, which he so effectively used in the poem "Noche Oscura." However, John is not a poet and writer of a single symbol. Following the lead of the Song of Songs tradition, he constantly makes use of bridal symbolism. He also appropriates the symbol of the mountain as in his commentary *The Ascent of Mount Carmel* and the symbol of fire as in *The Living Flame of Love*. John of the Cross is a writer of many symbols but, in these pages, concern is for his use of the heart as a symbol.

Though John of the Cross does not, in every instance, use heart in the most complete sense of a symbol as articulated above, he generally uses *corazón, seno, pecho, entrañas, vientre* in a way that communicates undertones of symbolic consciousness. There are, in addition, uses of heart by John that reflect what Lucien-Marie de St-Joseph has called John's use of a symbol as a "re-creation of experience," with an "affective charge" that translates an intuition of the spirit and which communicates reality.[8] Thus John of the Cross demonstrates extensively Karl Rahner's theory of symbolic reality. As Annice Callahan has shown, Rahner perceived reality as symbolic and has found words like heart to be primordial words that are symbols.[9]

At first, a study of John of the Cross' use of the heart as symbol appeared to be anything but promising. Nowhere does heart appear in the subject index or in the index of the principal figures of speech in the widely dispersed three volume English translation by E. Allison Peers of the writings of John of the Cross.[10] Of not much more help is the second edition of John's works translated by Kieran Kavanaugh and Otilio Rodriguez where there are only seven references to heart in the index.[11] The project becomes brighter when one consults a Spanish concordance of John's writings which has one hundred and eighty-seven citations to the usual Spanish word for heart, *corazón*.[12] Brother Dermot Conlon, OCD, who has been working on a concordance to the Kavanaugh-Rodriguez translation, adds nearly a hundred more references to heart than appear in the above concordance.[13] Father Regis Jordan's computer search of the Kavanaugh-Rodriguez text, that does not include the poetry at the back of the book, has about two hundred and eighty-seven references to the English word heart[14] while the Spanish text breaks down to *corazón* (248), Latin *cor* (11), *seno* (13), *pecho* (4), Latin *venter* (1), *vientre* (2), and *entrañas* (2).[15] One must be cautious of attempts to establish a precise enumeration of the heart in John of the Cross' writings because of the differences in what can be rendered as heart in English and what various textual aids pick up as heart from the texts.[16] What can be said is that this lyrical poet used the symbolism of the heart regularly, even frequently, to sing of God's love in his poems and to describe in his commentaries the journey to union with God in love. The rootedness of this usage in the scriptures and John's extensive use of the symbolism of the heart are the concern of the rest of this essay.

The Word of God

Father Barnabas Ahern wrote of John of the Cross that "the Bible colors every page he wrote, simply because the Bible was woven into the fabric of his life. Among all the moderns, he stands as the Saint of the Bible."[17] John of the Cross' symbolic consciousness, his theological teachings, his language and his symbolism are thoroughly shaped by the Hebrew-Christian scriptures[18] with about two-thirds of his citations coming from the Old Testament.[19] It should be noted that this biblical influence applies both to his poetry and to his commentaries.

It is not surprising that John of the Cross reflects in his writings the Bible's frequent use of the symbolism of the heart. Joseph Grassi states that "in the Bible, the word/image for heart is found close to a thousand times."[20] While it is not known what specific copy of the Bible John used, this much is certain: he used and mastered the Latin Vulgate.[21] Consultation of a modern concordance to the Vulgate shows that it contains more than fourteen long columns of citations to *cor*, the usual Latin word for heart.[22] The word of God, it is clear, was the major resource for John of the Cross' spirituality and thoroughly shaped his use of the symbol heart.

Mystic and Poet of the Heart

This Spanish mystic and poet was most fully symbolic in his use of the heart when he tried to translate into language his mystical experience. For this mystical teaching John of the Cross has often been called *doctor mysticus*,[23] but John was more than a teacher of mysticism. John of the Cross was himself a mystic, in fact, a mystic's mystic. His experiences of intimate union with God, celebrated in his poetry and interpreted in his commentaries, reveal John's mystical encounters with the divine. Yet, one must keep in mind that his gifts of mystical experience and his gifts as a poet converge in him, rather than rival each other as has been the case at times for some Christian poets, e.g, in the struggles of Raïssa Maritain and Thomas Merton.[24] John of the Cross never apologized nor, as far as we know, agonized over the appropriateness of communicating his mystical experience in poetry, even in the poetry of a bridal mysticism that had roots in the prophetic imagery of love and in the Song of Songs.

In his prologue to *The Spiritual Canticle*, John stated that the stanzas of his poem ". . . were composed in a love flowing from abundant mystical understanding" (CW, 409). His prologue to *The Living Flame of Love* speaks of stanzas that ". . . treat of a love within this very state of transformation that has a deeper quality and is more perfect" (CW, 578). John of the Cross was a mystic whose experience took him into the depths of his being. As a poet he was able to describe that inner terrain with apt symbolism. A modern disciple of John, Edith Stein, affirmed his practice when she said that ". . . it is through poetry that the soul is most adequately described. . . ."[25]

It took the poets of Spain to rediscover John of the Cross in this century. Decisive in this recovery has been the work of Dámaso Alonso.[26] Moreover, the high regard that modern Spanish poets have for John's poetry was expressed by Jorge Guillén in his Charles Eliot Norton lectures at Harvard University in 1957–58: "San Juan de la Cruz is the briefest great poet in the Spanish language, perhaps in world literature."[27]

In John of the Cross' writings God's activity is manifest in a way that transcends expected manifestations of Christian grace. With his poetic genius he was able to report and recreate his experience of God in poetic symbolism that evokes for others a taste of this experience. At times he used the heart as symbol to express this experience in poetic form. In his poem, "Noche Oscura," one hears that he had "no other light or guide/ Than the one that burned in my heart" (*en el corazón ardía*) (CW, 711). In the "Cántico Espiritual," John asked: "Why, since you wounded/This heart, don't you heal it?" (*corazón*) (CW, 713). In the justly celebrated eleventh/twelfth stanza of the same poem,[28] John of the Cross sang of his mystical encounter with Christ:

> O spring like crystal!
> If only, on your silvered-over face,
> You would suddenly form
> The eyes I have desired,
> Which I bear sketched deep within my heart (*mis entrañas*) (CW,
>   713).

A crown to the mystical experience of John of the Cross is that represented in his poem "The Living Flame of Love." Although untrained in Spanish poetry, I suggest that this poem not only records John's most profound mystical experience but may be a candidate for consideration as his finest poem. Such a consideration may further exemplify the convergence in John of the Cross of mysticism and poetry. John made the claim himself for this encounter with God when he wrote that it had a deeper quality and was more perfect than his previous experiences of spiritual marriage (CW, 578). Final judgment for the quality of this poem must be left to those with the expertise to make such judgments.[29] In any case, the symbolism of the heart appears in the fourth and final stanza of the "The Living Flame of Love":

How gently and lovingly
You wake in my heart (*mi seno*),
Where in secret You dwell alone;
And in your sweet breathing,
Filled with good and glory,
How tenderly You swell my heart with love! (CW, 579, 718).

In this poem and in the event it records there is a newness to John's use of heart symbolism. One might have expected John to have used *corazón* or *pecho* or *entrañas* in this stanza. Instead, John used the word *seno*, used nowhere else in his poetry, to express the experience that took place in the "deepest center" of his soul. It is as if John reached for a symbol that transcended his use of other symbols for deep inner experiences. John may well have been suggesting a feminine/maternal dimension to the union with God expressed in the above stanza. *Seno* can be translated not only as the breast or heart of the human person but also as the womb.[30] The history of the word certainly contains maternal meanings,[31] although I have been unable to find evidence for maternal symbolism precisely at the time of John of the Cross. The issue deserves further investigation by a philologist trained in sixteenth century Castilian.[32] An argument that so precise a poet as John of the Cross would use *seno* in the second line of the above stanza merely to rhyme with *lleno* seems unlikely to me. Rather the message of this stanza calls for feminine symbolism: a receptivity to God's love and a swelling of the breast/womb with this love. If the direction of my argument is correct, John of the Cross was a most discriminating practitioner in the western heart tradition, a poet who reached for precisely the right symbol to report and recreate a very special event in his life. Here and elsewhere John of the Cross was a person with a profound feminine disposition in the Jungian sense of these words.[33] As a mystic and as a poet, John of the Cross used the symbolism of the heart with a rare sensitivity for the world of archetypal symbols.

A Representative of the Tradition

Like the Bible and the subsequent western heart tradition, John of the Cross used the heart to symbolize a full range of inner human realities and activities. Through the heart John explored what the soul is, what its capacities are, and what the soul does. In his commentaries John admittedly turned to the terminology of sixteenth century scholasticism when he tried to offer his readers theoretical precision. He even offered his readers an apology for doing so. In the prologue to *The Spiritual Canticle*, he says:

I hope that, although some scholastic theology is used here in reference to the soul's interior converse with God, it will not prove vain to speak in such a manner to the pure of spirit (CW, 409).

However, in his poetry and in his commentaries, John of the Cross made generous use of symbols in order to connect his readers to his experience and to his imaginative exploration of the journey to union with God in love. The symbol of the heart served John of the Cross well as a poet and also as a corporate spiritual director in his other writings.

As in the Bible and in the tradition, John of the Cross used the heart with both its negative and positive connotations. Thus the heart is a place where melancholia and heaviness can be present (CW, 141, 167). At times the heart is possessive (CW, 247) and can be attached to what keeps it from growth (CW, 246, 247). The heart endures sorrow (CW, 416), and the heart is a place where evil might grow (CW, 252) and which can be preoccupied with pleasure (CW, 262). In other words the heart endures human folly and weakness.

The heart is also a way of describing the geography of the inner person. The heart symbolizes not only the soul itself but also its faculties of intellect and will (CW, 113, 445–456). The heart knows, comprehends (CW, 113, 442) and also loves as we shall see below. However, I have not found John of the Cross describing the third faculty, memory, as heart. For him the heart is a place for devotion, meditation, prayer, and faith (CW, 275, 302, 326, 277, 288). At their annual meeting in the summer of 1987 David Tracy urged the members of the College Theology Society to turn to Greek philosophers as a way of recovering a language for the soul. I add to this advice an invitation to turn to John of the Cross as a key resource for the recovery of symbols like the heart to explore "The Anatomy of the Soul" as Dicken entitled a chapter of his study of Teresa of Avila and John of the Cross.[34]

Not a few readers have been intimidated by John of the Cross' challenge that they struggle for a radical freedom of the heart. Yet, John's call is to a freedom for the sake of love. In a letter to a long-time spiritual directee, Mary of Jesus, the prioress at Cordoba, John of the Cross, having reminded her that she was a follower of the "naked Christ," set out his doctrine of freedom on behalf of love in the following words.

> For he who is poor in spirit is happier and more constant in the midst of want, because he has placed his all in nothingness, and in all things, he thus finds freedom of heart. O happy nothingness, and happy hiding place of the heart! For the heart has such power that it subjects all things to itself; this it does by desiring to be subject to nothing and losing all care so as to burn the more in love (CW, 697).

This lyricism prepares one to encounter John's call to forsake "a slave's heart" for the sake of a "liberated heart" (CW, 80). It also enables one to hear his call to abandon possessiveness which ". . . like a bond, fastens the spirit to earth and does not allow it freedom of heart" (CW, 247). John preaches detachment for the sake of "great liberty" (CW, 247) because detachment brings ". . . freedom of the heart for God" (CW, 248), whereas attachment impedes one's heart from turning to God (CW, 280). Those who search for God, as John would have them search, need freedom of heart. Of this John vividly reminds his readers in these words.

> Since seeking God demands a heart naked, strong, and free from all evils and goods which are not purely God, the soul speaks in this and the following verses of the freedom and fortitude one should possess in looking for Him (CW, 429).

With freedom like this, one can direct one's heart to God (CW, 249), center one's heart on God (CW, 245) and keep one's ". . . heart fixed on Him" (CW, 664). Although there is a tradition that sees Teresa of Avila as a guide for those advanced in the spiritual life while John of the Cross is for beginners,[35] John's doctrine of freedom of the heart is surely for those who have a heart courageous enough to ". . . be a friend of the passion of Christ" (CW, 675).

John of the Cross is a doctor of desire. He challenges the human person to let desire be purified of all that keeps one from centering one's heart entirely on God. This purification or liberation of desire is accomplished by God as one hears in *The Ascent of Mount Carmel*.

That heart symbolized the human heart that is attached to worldly things. To undertake the journey to God the heart must be burned and purified of all creatures with the fire of divine love (CW, 75).

For John of the Cross the journey to God is a journey to a transformation of the human person in love, with the soul "inwardly transformed in the fire of love" (CW, 578). John's story, his own and that to which he beckons his readers, is of a transformation of human seeking into the deepest of God-given desires. His message is pithily stated in one of his sayings: "Deny your desires and you will find what your heart longs for" (CW, 667).

Everything is for the sake of love since "at the evening of life, you will be examined in love. Learn to love as God desires to be loved . . ." (CW, 672). The human heart is made for love, to be an "enamored heart" (CW, 422), a heart inflamed like fire (CW, 422, 491), and the heart must know how to be a lover's heart (CW, 425).

Since "purity of heart is nothing less than the love and grace of God" (CW, 355), this purity is worth all the suffering that the heart must endure to grow in love. Until the soul possesses its loved one, it

is like an empty vessel waiting to be filled, or like a hungry man craving for food, or like a sick person moaning for health, or like one suspended in the air with nothing to lean on. Such is the truly loving heart (CW, 444).

This suffering is like being stolen by God and, in the imagery of the Song of Songs, it is a wounding of the heart. It is a suffering that prepares one to seek God's beauty as we hear from *The Spiritual Canticle*.

The soul, desiring to be possessed by this immense God, for love of whom she feels her heart is robbed and wounded, unable to endure her sickness any longer, deliberately asks Him in this stanza to show her His beauty. . . . She makes this request by displaying before Him the sickness and yearning of her heart . . . (CW, 448).

John of the Cross knew what it was like to be loved intensely by God. With his poetic gift he was able to speak of this experience in a telling and daring way. Thus we hear that the "touches of love" caused by "the Beloved in your heart are enough to take away your life" and that "these touches so impregnate the soul and heart with the knowledge and love of

God that she can truthfully say she conceives . . ." (CW, 442). God's impregnation of the human person has deep roots in the Christian tradition, a tradition going back to Mary of Nazareth and to early eastern mysticism.

"In Its Deepest Center!"

The journey to union with God in love took John of the Cross into his "deepest center" where he experienced God's penetrating love in the way that he described that event in his poem, "The Living Flame of Love" (CW, 578–579, 717–718). Yet, this "awakening" in the "substance of the soul which is its heart" is "entirely beyond words" (CW, 646). John's use of the Spanish symbol *seno* to communicate a feminine dimension of this his most profound experience of God has been discussed above. However, one may note here that, in his commentary, this event of consummation brings the soul to the place where ". . . its sole occupation now is to receive from God" (CW, 582). One should also keep in mind that for John the soul is feminine not only as a Spanish word (*alma*) but because of the female character in the Song of Songs, a tradition which profoundly shaped John's language and symbols.

As the soul nears the awakening of "The Living Flame of Love," it (she) may receive the gift of transverberation,[36] an experience perceived as a piercing of the heart by an arrow or dart that is "all afire with love." This piercing is as if there ". . . were a sharp point in the substance of the spirit, in the heart of the pierced soul." This is a ". . . wound which seems to be in the middle of the heart of the spirit. . . ." John of the Cross described this soul as ". . . converted into the immense fire of love which emanates from that enkindled point at the heart of the spirit" (CW, 599).

Conclusion

These pages are indicative rather than exhaustive of Juan de la Cruz' use of the symbolism of the heart in his poetry and in his writings of spiritual direction. In fact, all of John's writings are spiritual direction since even his poetry was offered to friends and directees for edification in the deeper meaning of this word. The profound mystery recognized in John's poetry led to requests by his directees for explanations of his poetry, explanations that took the form of commentaries (CW, 408, 577). This essay has not been able to communicate fully John's use of the heart. Rather, its aim has been to share some glimpses of this master of symbol turning to the heart. Watching him use the symbolism of the heart, readers of John of the Cross may understand better the creativity of his poetry and other texts. It is further hoped that this essay adds evidence to the other essays in this book of the vibrancy of the heart tradition, the retrieval of which can make a contribution to the remythologizing of religious language at the end of the twentieth century.

John of the Cross knew thoroughly the Bible's use of the symbolism of the heart and is a worthy successor of those who wrote of the *leb somea*, the listening heart (1 Kgs 3) and the "heart from which shall flow streams of living water" (Jn 7:38). John of the Cross belongs to a tradition enriched by Augustine who explored the restless heart and Benedict who bade the readers of his rule to listen with the "ear of the heart."[38] John was a gifted listener whose mystical experience and poetic genius gave him an original and creative way of using the symbolism of the heart. He was a bold interpreter of the heart tradition, daring enough to picture God's own heart sharing an equality with the human heart.[39]

> The soul no longer fears, since from henceforth the King of heaven acts in a friendly way toward it, as toward His brother and His equal. In revealing to it, in gentleness and not in furor, the might of His power and the love of His goodness, He communicates to it from His heart strength and love . . . (CW, 647–648).

John of the Cross, saint and doctor of the church, thus stands as an effective resource in the retrieval of the heart as a religious symbol.

NOTES

1. André Dérumaux, "Crise ou évolution dans la dévotion des jeunes pour le Sacré-Coeur?" *Le Coeur, Études Carmélitaines* (Paris: Desclée de Brouwer, 1950), pp. 296–326.
2. Research for this essay was made possible through the Dehon Fellowship at Sacred Heart School of Theology, Hales Corners, WI, for which award I thank the priests and brothers of the Sacred Heart.
3. Carl G. Jung, et al., *Man and His Symbols* (New York: Dell, 1968), passim.
4. Mircea Eliade, *Images and Symbols: Studies in Religious Symbolism*, trans. Philip Mairet (New York: Sheed and Ward, 1969), pp. 9–12.
5. David Tracy, *The Analogical Imagination: Christian Theology and the*

Culture of Pluralism (New York: Crossroad, 1981), pp. 205–206, 281–287.

6. Paul Ricoeur, *The Symbolism of Evil*, trans. Emerson Buchanan (Boston: Beacon Press, 1969), pp. 3–18, 347–357.

7. Philip Wheelwright, *Metaphor and Reality* (Bloomington: Indiana University Press, 1962), p. 111.

8. Lucien-Marie de St-Joseph, "Expérience Mystique et Expression Symbolique chez Saint Jean de la Croix," *Polarité du Symbole, Études Carmélitaines* (Bruges: Desclée de Brouwer, 1960), pp. 38, 42, 37.

9. Annice Callahan, R.S.C.J., *Karl Rahner's Spirituality of the Pierced Heart: A Reinterpretation of Devotion to the Sacred Heart* (New York: University Press of America, 1985), pp. 37–53.

10. *The Complete Works of Saint John of the Cross*, trans. E. Allison Peers, 3 vols., 2nd ed. (London: Burns, Oates and Washbourne, 1953), vol. 3.

11. *The Collected Works of St. John of the Cross* (=CW). Trans. Kieran Kavanaugh and Otilio Rodriguez, 2nd ed. (Washington, DC: Institute of Carmelite Studies, 1979).

12. Luis de San José, comp., *Concordancias de las Obras y Escritos del Doctor de la Iglesia, San Juan de la Cruz*, 2nd ed. (Burgos: El Monte Carmelo, 1980).

13. Dermot Conlon, OCD, Institute of Carmelite Studies, 2131 Lincoln Rd., NE, Washington, DC, 20002.

14. Regis Jordan, OCD, Monastery of Christ-on-the-Mountain, Hinton, WV, 25951.

15. In the Kavanaugh-Rodriguez text some renderings as heart are approximations of the Spanish text, e.g., *unica* as wholehearted. *The Spiritual Canticle* (B), 31, 9. CW, p. 534. The Spanish text used for this study is Juan de la Cruz, *Obras Completas*. Ed. Simeon de la Sagrada Familia, 2nd ed. (Burgos: El Monte Carmelo, 1972).

16. The enumeration of citations in various editions of the writings of John of the Cross is further complicated by what may or may not be included in the editions, e.g., whether or not both versions of the *Cántico Espiritual* are included in the count.

17. Barnabas Ahern, "The Use of Scripture in the Spiritual Theology of St. John of the Cross," *The Catholic Biblical Quarterly* 14 (1952), 6–7.

18. See my study of "The Word of God in *The Living Flame of Love*" to be published in a forthcoming collection of studies in honor of John of the Cross by the Institutum Carmelitanum, Rome.

19. Jean Vilnet, *Bible et Mystique chez Saint Jean de la Croix, Études Carmélitaines* (Bruges: Desclée de Brouwer, 1949), p. 35.

20. Joseph A. Grassi, *Healing the Heart: The Transformational Power of Biblical Heart Imagery* (New York: Paulist Press, 1987), p. 1.

21. Kieran Kavanaugh, ed., *John of the Cross, Selected Writings*, "The Classics of Western Spirituality" (New York: Paulist Press, 1987), pp. 28–32.

22. *Novae concordantiae bibliorum sacrorum iuxta Vulgatam versionem critice editam*, ed. Bonifatio Fischer, 5 vols. (Stuttgart-Bad Cannstatt: Frommann-Holzborg, 1977), vol. 1. *Cor* appears some 863 times in the Latin Old Testament and 211 times in the New Testament for an approximate total of 1,074 times that *cor* occurs in the Vulgate Bible.

23. John of the Cross was declared a doctor of the church on August 24, 1926 by Pius XI. *Acta Apostolicae Sedis* 18 (1926), 378–381. The designation *doctor mysticus* does not appear in this document but occurs often in subsequent literature, e.g., Andrew Louth, *The Origins of the Christian Mystical Tradition* (Oxford: Clarendon Press, 1981), p. 180.

24. Raïssa Maritain, "On Poetry as Spiritual Experience," *Raïssa's Journal* (Albany, NY: Magi Books, 1974), pp. 373–377; Thomas Merton, "Poetry and the Contemplative Life," *The Commonweal* 46 (1947), 280–286; Thomas Merton, "Poetry and Contemplation: A Reappraisal," *The Commonweal* 69 (1958), 87–92.

25. Edith Stein, "Spirituality of the Christian Woman," *Essays on Woman*, vol. 2: *The Collected Works of Edith Stein* (Washington, DC: Institute of Carmelite Studies, 1987), 88.

26. Dámaso Alonso, *La poesía de San Juan de la Cruz*, 3rd ed. (Madrid: Aguilar, 1958).

27. Jorge Guillén, "The Ineffable Language of Mysticism: San Juan de la Cruz," *Language and Poetry: Some Poets of Spain* (Cambridge: Harvard University Press, 1961), p. 79.

28. Eleventh stanza in "Cántico Espiritual," A (CW, 713) and twelfth stanza in version B (CW, 411).

29. See Gerald Brenan, *St. John of the Cross: His Life and Poetry* (Cambridge: Cambridge University Press, 1973), p. 103, where "Noche Oscura" is called John's most perfect poem. The latest Spanish edition of Brenan's book has not been available to me.

30. E. A. Peers, et al., ed., *Cassell's Spanish-English, English-Spanish Dictionary*, 3rd ed. (London: Cassell, 1964). See *seno*. *Seno* appears outside of the poem and commentary *The Living Flame of Love* only in the commentary *The Spiritual Canticle*, B, 1, 10 (CW, 419).

31. *Diccionario de la lengua Castellana . . . por La Real Academia Española*, 6 vols. (Madrid, 1726–1739), 6, 79–80. See also María Moliner,

ed., *Diccionario de uso del Español*, 2 vols. (Madrid: Editorial Gredos, 1966–67), 2, 1134. *Seno* is derived from the Latin *sinus* which can have a maternal meaning. P.G.W. Glare, ed., *Oxford Latin Dictionary* (Oxford: Clarendon Press, 1982), pp. 1771–1772.

32. While a 1611 A.D. dictionary has no maternal meaning for *seno*, it points to *seno's* derivation from the Latin *sinus*. Sebástian de Covarrubias, *Tesoro de la lengua Castellana* (the 1611 first edition in a 1943 facsimile.) I thank Dr. Gerald Gingras of Saint Mary's College for his help in exploring the meanings of *seno* and also Ms. Gisela Terrell of the Irwin Library, Butler University, for a copy of the entry on *seno* from the Covarrubias facsimile.

33. M.-L. von Franz, "The Anima: The Woman Within," *Man and His Symbols*, op. cit., pp. 186–198.

34. E. W. Trueman Dicken, *The Crucible of Love: A Study of the Mysticism of St. Teresa of Jesus and St. John of the Cross* (New York: Sheed and Ward, 1963), pp. 327–351.

35. John Chapman, *Spiritual Letters*, 2nd ed. (New York: Sheed and Ward, 1935), pp. 265–266.

36. For Teresa of Jesus' experience of the transverberation, see *The Collected Works of St. Teresa of Avila*, 3 vols. (Washington, DC: Institute of Carmelite Studies, 1976, 1980, 1985), 1: 193–194; 2: 368, 492.

37. *Sancti Augustini Confessionum, Libri XIII*, ed. L. Verheijen, "Corpus Christianorum, Series Latina, XXVII" (Turnhout: Brepols, 1981), 1, 1, 1.

38. *RB 1980, The Rule of St. Benedict*, ed. Timothy Fry (Collegeville, MN: The Liturgical Press, 1981), Prologue.

39. For other statements of John's doctrine of equality with God through love, see CW, 520, 528, 536, 559 (all in *The Spiritual Canticle*, B).

Wendy M. Wright

"That Is What It Is Made For": The Image of the Heart in the Spirituality of Francis de Sales and Jane de Chantal

Within the Salesian tradition of spirituality parented by Jane de Chantal (1572–1641) and Francis de Sales (1567–1622) the heart is a central image.[1] It is the image most used in that tradition to attempt to portray, in a visual and affective manner, who God is, who the human person is, and how they are intimately related to one another.

But the heart is not a cleanly etched Salesian image. Nowhere in the writings of de Sales or de Chantal is there an attempt either to define the term heart or to develop a systematic theology or anthropology based on their understanding of what the heart image conveys. Rather, it is an image of multivalent richness, a term at once evocative and suggestive, ripe with associative meanings. They use it assuming that others will grasp its significance almost intuitively and that others will flesh out the image with their own associations. When Francis de Sales asserts quite simply that "heart speaks to heart,"[2] he rests confident in his own and his readers' felt knowledge that there *is* an affective language, a language of hearts, that is learned experientially. He assumes a way of knowing that derives from a sensitivity to the way in which one's own and others' "hearts" move, what the person yearns for and wraps himself or herself around, which is, in fact, a sensitivity to a divine knowledge that transcends the individual. Heart is a wholistic and diffuse image that in Salesian use conveys a sense of the central and ultimate dynamic of both the human person and of God.

It is virtually impossible to turn to a page of Francis' or Jane's writing which does not contain some reference to the human heart or the heart of God or of Jesus or which does not use affective language associated with the image of the heart. Considerable scholarly effort has gone into documenting the references to the heart in the writings of Francis de Sales and much has been done to explore in these writings the richness of the heart as metaphor and the way in which contemporary doctrinal, devotional and cultural conceptions of the heart shaped de Sales' thought.[3] What I would like to do in this brief chapter is to draw, as it were, a word-picture of the Salesian spiritual world which is, in fact, a world of hearts.[4] As suggested, it will be a picture that captures the Salesian heritage not only through the features of Francis de Sales but through the visage of Jane de Chantal as well.

The Human Heart

Jane and Francis were part of the early seventeenth century flowering of Christian humanism on French soil. They breathed the bracing air of Catholic reformation devotion, were fed by theological food that affirmed an intrinsic correspondence between human and divine, and were watered by cultural springs that celebrated the full range of human ingenuity and artistry.[5] He was a bishop and charismatic preacher, she was a young widow who came to him for spiritual direction. Together they discovered a mutual love of God and founded a religious congregation for women—the Visitation of Holy Mary—of which Jane became first superior.

In an era of humanism one begins one's venture into the spiritual by beginning with human experience. For Francis and for Jane the human person was made by and for God. Discovered as the central impulse within the person was a capacity to return to God. This impulse, which they identified as a desire or an insistence of the good, was the foundation of all Salesian thought. For them, the created image and likeness to God may have been wounded in the fall of the first man and woman but it was not effaced. They believed that the unleashing of innate human desire and God-directedness was the primary task of each person's life.

It was particularly in the heart (conceived as the dynamic core of the person) that this God-directedness was located. "May God live in my heart for that is what it is made for," Francis prayed.[6] The heart was the "seat of love"[7] and love was both the way and the goal of the whole venture of human life.

The Salesian heart is a thoroughly baroque image, full of movement and vitality, restless in its action, reaching beyond its present spatial and temporal confines like the ceiling of a baroque church which draws the eye and mind upward in a celebration of infinite expanse.[8] Yet it is also a thoroughly human heart. While the baroque aesthetic may soar to the heights of heavenward aspiration it is always grounded in what is of earth. The baroque celebrates human capacity and ingenuity, is sensual in its enjoyment of color, line and mass, and revels in the drama of human emotion. So too the Salesian heart. It is a principle of life: as a womb of the soul[9] it begets love, as the "stomach of understanding" and a source of milk it is an organ associated with nourishment.[10] The Salesian heart is, among other vital things, a fountain that pours its waters of reason out over the whole person,[11] a garden in which virtuous seeds are sown,[12] a tree,[13] a place that burns with the light and heat of spiritual fire.[14]

Most importantly, the Salesian heart breathes. With the restless motion of baroque sensibility the heart expands and contracts according to the actions of love. In de Sales' longest and most theoretical work, *Treatise on the Love of God*, he presents his teaching on the two motions of the heart in love. He calls them the "love of complacence" and the "love of benevolence." While his thoughts on love and its movements are complex and deserve a more careful analysis, suffice it to say here that these two loves are, on the one hand, a love that is receptive and draws God's life into itself and, on the other, a love that is active and pours out praise and love of God.[15] In the exercise of these two interrelated motions of love the heart breathes in and breathes out: it inspires and aspires.

> Complacence draws God's delights into the heart . . . but the love of benevolence causes the heart to go out of itself and to breathe forth the scent of lovely perfume, that is, all sorts of sacred praise.[16]

This life-giving and life-enhancing heart of humanity is sacred space. It is the element of the human person in which the divine image is most clearly reflected. It is to the entirety of the person what the tabernacle or inner sanctuary is to the architecture of a whole church.

> As soon as a person gives a little attention to divinity a sweet feeling within the heart is experienced which shows that God is God of the heart. . . . If some misfortune strikes fear into our heart, it immediately turns to divinity. . . . This pleasure, this confidence that the human heart naturally has in God certainly comes from nowhere else than the congruity between God's good-

ness and our soul. . . . We are created in the image and likeness
of God.[17]

The Heart of God

The diastolic and systolic rhythm of the human heart pulses in concert with the heart of God. In Salesian thought God *is* love and the divine
heart is the source and womb of that love. Divine love, as depicted in
Francis' *Treatise on the Love of God,* is so gracious, so intent upon calling
back into itself all that it has created out of its fullness, that it too desires
and yearns with heartfelt emotion for union with humankind.

> 'You shall love the Lord your God with all your heart, all your
> soul and all your mind. This is the first and greatest command-
> ment.' Good God! How amorous the divine heart is of our love!
> Wouldn't it have been enough to give us permission to love Him
> as Laban permitted Jacob to love his fair Rachael and to gain her
> by services? But no! He makes a stronger declaration of His
> passionate love for us and commands us to love Him with all our
> power. . . .[18]

Similarly, even the intimate motions within the trinitarian life of God
are depicted in language which echoes the restless and vital Salesian language of the human heart.

> The eternal Father sees the infinite beauty and goodness of his
> own essence . . . vividly, essentially and substantially expressed
> in his Son. The Son reciprocally sees that his own essence, good-
> ness and beauty are originally in his Father as in their Source and
> fountain. Could it be possible for this divine Father and his Son
> not to love one another with an infinite love? . . . Since the
> Father and the Son are not only equal and united but even one
> and the same God, goodness and unity, how great must be their
> love for one another! . . . This divine love of the eternal Father
> for His Son is practiced in one sole aspiration sent forth recipro-
> cally by the Father and the Son. . . . The Father breathes forth
> this love and so also the Son breathes it forth . . . this spiration is
> but one spiration or only one spirit sent forth by the two who
> breathe.[19]

The Heart of Jesus

God's eternal heart and the created heart of humankind find their life and breath in a corresponding movement of desire. Yet the history of each man or woman's love-relationship with God is unique and the paths taken to effect a true meeting of hearts are often circuitous. Guidance is needed along the way. While Salesian thought is basically optimistic about human capacity to love in a radical God-directed way, it is neither naive nor does it stretch the theological confines of Catholic orthodoxy. It asserts that there is a mediating reality between human and divine which allows human potential to achieve its fullness. It teaches that much discipline and serious formation are necessary for the human person to become what it was created to be. Francis and Jane call upon a wide range of techniques and approaches from the repertoire of ascetic praxis and prayer in order to facilitate the transformation of the human heart into a heart that breathes in union with God. At their root all these practices seek to open the heart so that the whole person, in thought, intent and deed, will become utterly responsive to the most subtle fluctuations of the divine breath.

The passion underlying this opening of the heart is captured beautifully in a spontaneous passage penned by Jane while she was still newly under Francis' direction:

> Lord, consume me, ingest me, annihilate me in yourself. I want nothing but God; to rest in him, completely, being strengthened more and more to serve him by my total dependence on his divine Providence, always more firmly anchored in the faith of his true word and completely abandoned to his mercy and care. Oh eternal and fatherly goodness! My heart opens itself to you![20]

The model for this transformation and the mediator between the worlds of divine and human hearts is the heart of Jesus Christ. Jesus for Francis and Jane is a living presence, a reality to be experienced and lived into more and more fully as one's life unfolds. The heart of this living Jesus belongs to God and comes to live in humankind so that all hearts might be united with their creator. What is the quality of this Christ-heart as Jane and Francis perceived it? The Salesian Jesus is perhaps best seen in a passage in Matthew's gospel which presents the Lord as inviting all to come and learn from him for he is gentle and humble of heart.[21] From a Salesian perspective this is not a sentimental depiction but one full of vigor and challenge. For the words of this Jesus are part of a discourse in which the mysterious identity of the child of God is revealed as being one of gentleness and humility, an identity that ushers in the reign of God while

overturning the values of the world. It is an identity that Salesian spirituality asserts is crucial to the enfleshing of divine life in creation. Later in her
life as the mother superior of the Order of the Visitation, Jane de Chantal
wrote to her sisters in religion of the power of possessing the qualities of
humility and gentleness.

> My sisters, how great a value humility is! It is the virtue loved
> best by our Jesus Christ and our divine mistress, his glorious
> mother . . . humility attracts the eyes and heart of the Lord to
> us. But it must be a more interior than an exterior humility. He
> does not tell us to learn the latter from him but the former:
> 'Learn from me,' he tells us, 'for I am gentle and humble of
> heart.' Oh God! My sisters, what is rarer than a truly humble
> heart for one always discovers that such a heart is more lowly
> than can be imaged. Believe me, my dear daughters, to possess a
> grain of true humility is to possess a treasure and money that can
> buy heaven and the heart of God.[22]

> As for gentleness of heart, my dear daughters, this is a heart
> which does not resist anything and is not angry at anything done
> to it, that bears all, endures all, that is compassionate and full of
> affection for its neighbor and that does not have any bitterness in
> it. No, I am not talking at all about a heart of flesh but a heart
> [united with God's will and] of the superior part of the soul.
> Therefore, contradictions, persecutions, obstacles and difficul-
> ties which come to a truly gentle heart are immediately weakened
> as soon as they approach it.[23]

It is through transformation by and into Jesus that a man or woman
attains a heart that is utterly responsive to the heart that created it, a heart
open and vulnerable enough to beat in rhythm with the heart of God. For
Francis and Jane this deep transforming reality begins first and foremost
interiorly. Francis describes it in his *Introduction to the Devout Life:*

> 'Be converted to me with your whole heart,' God said. 'My son,
> give me your heart.' Since the heart is the source of our actions,
> as the heart is so are they. When the divine Spouse invites the
> soul, he says, 'Put me as a seal on your heart, as a seal on your
> arm.' Yes, for whoever has Jesus Christ in his heart will soon
> have him in all his outward ways.
>   For this reason . . . I have wished above all else to engrave
> and inscribe on your heart this holy and sacred motto, 'Live

Jesus!' . . . With St. Paul, you can say these holy words, 'It is no longer I that live but Christ lives in me.' In short, whoever wins a person's heart has won the whole person.[24]

This unfolding sacred presence is cultivated in many ways, chiefly through mortification and prayer. Prayer, gentle and humble, is the place of most intimate contact with the divine. It is the place where the person lays his or her head against the heart of God and listens to the rhythm of the life pulsing there. Salesian practice in prayer, no matter what "methods" it employs, is directed toward enabling this listening to occur. Through it, heart speaks to heart. Two examples of advice on prayer will suffice to show the inventive manner in which Jane and Francis teach this sensitizing of the human heart.

In her *Réponses,* a collection of recorded conversations that Jane held with her spiritual daughters, she writes of the traditional practice of meditation on the mysteries of Christ's life, death and resurrection which involves preparation, imaginative re-creation of a mystery, and a brief spoken response or colloquy.

After placing ourselves in the presence of God, as our blessed Father taught in his 'Philothea' [the *Introduction to the Devout Life*], by a simple act of faith in His complete presence in all places and hiding ourselves in His divine goodness like a little chick under its mother's wing, gathering ourselves completely into ourselves in this way in order to see Him in our hearts (for we are taught that He dwells there in a most unique way) . . . we must begin very gently and simply to consider our first point, moving as soon as we are able to the colloquy with affectionate words on the proposed subject.

And when our affections are moved, we do not need to increase our words but stop a bit, savor them and impress them gently on our hearts by simply gazing at whatever our Lord does in the mystery. At other times we might speak a few words to Him on the subject or, better yet, speak words of love, abandonment, compunction and other such things as we are moved. But they must be spoken gently and beautifully, letting them slip into His divine heart as though they were meant to be heard by Him alone.[25]

This impressing on the heart of various images of Jesus as seen in the mysteries of faith is formative. The power of image cumulatively to draw the worshiper into participation in the qualities and way of life formulated by the image is an ancient wisdom known to the Christian tradition of prayer. Salesian prayer drew on this wisdom. In an early letter of spiritual direction written by Francis de Sales to Jane de Chantal when she was reflecting on what she experienced as a call to religious life, he describes the practice of entering imaginatively into the wounds of Christ. It is implied that this entry gives the devotee access to the heart of Christ.

> . . . go farther and farther, my dear daughter, in establishing your holy purposes and resolutions. Plunge your thinking deeper and deeper into the wound of Our Lord where you will find an abyss of reasons which will confirm you in your generous enterprise and will make you realize once again that the heart that dwells anywhere else, that builds its nest in any other tree than the cross, is empty and worthless. Oh God! How happy we will be if we live and die in this holy tabernacle.[26]

Human Hearts and the Love of God

While the heart is the seat of sacred love and is made for the aspiring and inspiring work of going to God, human loves are not at all disdained in Salesian thought. In fact, in keeping with the tenor of Christian humanism, they are celebrated. All love is believed to have its origin and end in God. And all love, if rightly ordered, is seen as capable of leading a man or woman deeper into the mystery of the divine.

In the Salesian spiritual world human hearts are capable of recognizing in each other's rhythmic motion the heartbeat of God. The hearts of friends especially aspire and inspire in concert with their mutual desire for God.[27] Much is made of friendship by Jane and Francis both theoretically and in practice. They themselves shared in one of the most ardent of relationships which gave substance and companionship to each of their unique religious histories.[28] We have as evidence of that friendship many of the letters they exchanged.[29] One example from Francis will serve to show the affectionate and heartfelt nature of their union and the intent to which they understood their relationship as given by and directed toward love of God.

> . . . from the first time that you consulted me about your interior life, God granted me a great love for your spirit. When you confessed to me in greater detail, a remarkable bond was forged in my soul that caused me to cherish your soul more and more. This made me write to you that God had given me to you, not thinking it would ever be possible for the affection that I felt in

my spirit to be increased—especially by praying to God for you. But now, my dear daughter, a certain new quality has emerged which it seems I cannot describe, only its effect is a great interior sweetness that I have to wish for you a perfect love of God and other spiritual blessings. No, I am not exaggerating the truth in the least, I speak before 'my hearts' God and yours. Each affection is different from others. The one I have for you has a certain quality which consoles me infinitely and, if all were known, is extremely profitable to me.[30]

They also claimed many others as cherished friends. In fact, they considered all their spiritual directees as well as their special companions as friends in God. One letter written by Jane to Noel Brulart, Commandeur du Sillery, reveals quite clearly the manner in which the Salesian world perceived the spiritual life. The letter was written in 1634, more than a decade after Francis' death. Noel Brulart was a wealthy patron of the Order of the Visitation co-founded in 1610 by Francis and Jane. The affection Jane feels for her correspondent is representative of the genuine love of friendship that pervades all Salesian writing. The letter reveals the way in which she experienced love for others and love for God as intimately intermingled.

My very honored and most dearly beloved brother,
. . . You wouldn't believe how much comfort it gives me to know that you are praying for me. To my knowledge, I don't think I ever fail to remember you, especially at holy communion, and I never want to fail in this. I am sure that the merit of holy communion is a worthy response to the genuine, incomparable love God has given you for our blessed Father [the late Francis de Sales] and his dear Visitation, and for myself in particular, it seems, even though I don't deserve it. Really, as imperfect as I am, God has willed to unite my heart intimately with yours; for this I shall ever bless His divine goodness.
. . . God be praised for all His graces, especially for having given you a heart which, in my opinion, is fashioned after His own most sacred one. In truth, my very dear brother, your heart is capable of touching ours by its incomparable love. Apparently, you have drawn this love from the inexhaustible love of our divine Savior, for neither human considerations nor the power of nature could bring about anything like it. It is the most precious gift imaginable. I believe it was obtained for you from the fa-

therly heart of God through the tender love that our blessed
Father has for his dear Visitation.

. . . I know that all you wish from us is fidelity to our
vocation and, by this means, a deep union of our hearts with
yours. . . .[31]

A union of hearts. This is the ideal Salesian relationship, a union
forged out of a mutual desire for the fullness of love found in God. For love
and its motions are, in Francis' and Jane's perception, both means and
end. In the cultivation of affective, God-centered unions the living presence of Jesus comes to be enfleshed in the world.

So vivid was Francis' and Jane's vision of a world of transformed
hearts living the Christ life in a web of sustaining and caring friendships
that they founded a religious community based on this ideal. The Visitation of Holy Mary was created to be a small "kingdom of charity" where
women, each called to a radical intimacy with God in prayer, lived out
their shared vocation. It was an unusual foundation for its time.[32] It had no
specific work as its charism except the living out of this vision of the
transformed heart through prayer. The Visitation invited an unusual collection of women—the infirm, the elderly, the widowed, women whose call
was not to a harsh monastic regime, but whose hearts were filled with
longing for God. Their vocation was not at all ascetic in the physical sense.
Rather, theirs was to be a life of the surrender of the heart, a slow and
unobtrusive metamorphosis into the loving capacity of the creator. In a
letter of greeting written from Paris in 1619 to the Visitandine community
in Annecy, Jane joyously communicates the Salesian spirit:

> Since our Lord, in His goodness, has gathered our hearts into
> one, allow me, my dearest Sisters, to greet you all, as a commu-
> nity and individually, for this same Lord will not allow me to
> greet you in any other way. But what a greeting it is! The very
> one that our great and worthy Father taught us: LIVE JESUS!
> Yes, my beloved Sisters and daughters, I say the words with
> intense delight: LIVE JESUS in our memory, in our will and in
> our actions! . . . [Have] a spirit of gentle cordiality toward one
> another, a spirit of recollection of your whole being toward our
> Divine Master . . . strive for that loving union of hearts which
> brings about a holy peace and the kind of blessing we should
> desire to have in the house of God and His holy Mother.[33]

The entire process of formation within the Visitation was conceived as
"winning the hearts" of the sisters by showing forth the qualities of the

gentle, humble Jesus in the arts of governing and spiritual direction. Many of Jane's letters to superiors within the order are concerned with instilling these maternal arts.

> I beg you, my dear sister, govern your community with great expansiveness of heart: give the sisters a holy liberty of spirit and banish from your mind and theirs a servile spirit of constraint. If a sister seems to lack confidence in you, don't for that reason show her the least coldness, but gain her trust through love and kindness. Don't entertain thoughts against any one of the sisters but treat them all equally. Lead them, not with a bustling, anxious kind of concern, but with a care that is genuine, loving and gentle. I know there is no better way to succeed in leading souls. The more solicitous, open and supportive you are with them, the more you will win their hearts. This is the best way of helping them advance toward the perfection of their vocation.[34]

The Crucified Heart

A union of men's and women's hearts mutually inspired by and aspiring toward the heart of God: this is the Salesian vision of the reign of God realized, however imperfectly, in human society. It is a vision of the continually emerging presence of Jesus, the coming to birth of the heart of Christ in the hearts of humankind. But the love that flows from the heart of the Salesian Christ is not simply a love that experiences beauty and delight but a love that suffers and dies in the pursuit of love's consummation. The Salesian heart, of Jesus and of humankind, is a crucified heart, willing to be broken and pierced for its beloved, a heart opened so wide that nothing can fail to enter whether it be delight or sorrow.

This heart of immense proportion gathers the fullness of human experience into it so that all such experience might ripen and be transformed. In the process, the heart itself breaks and dies. Francis and Jane draw upon differing metaphors to describe the centrality of the crucified heart in Salesian spirituality. At the end of the *Treatise on the Love of God*, his lengthy work that aches with the passion of divine love, de Sales has a brief but concise chapter entitled "Mount Calvary Is the Academy of Love." In it he states:

> Mount Calvary is the Mount of lovers. All love that does not begin with Our Savior's passion is frivolous and dangerous. . . . Love and death are so mingled in [His] passion that we cannot have one in our heart without the other. Upon Calvary one can-

not have life without love nor love without the death of our redeemer.[35]

Similarly, a passage always much esteemed in Visitation literature as being central to the spirit of their community quotes Jane as saying:

'For myself, I believe that there is a martyrdom of love in which God preserves the lives of his servants so that they might work for His glory. This makes them martyrs and confessors at the same time. I know,' she added, 'that this is the martyrdom to which the daughters of the Visitation are called and which God will allow them to suffer if they are fortunate enough to wish for it.'

     A sister asked how this martyrdom would be realized. 'Give your absolute consent to God and you will experience it. What happens,' she continued 'is that divine love thrusts its sword into the most intimate and secret parts of the soul and separates us from our very souls. . . . But this is intended for generous hearts who, without holding themselves back, are faithful to love. Hearts that are weak and capable of only a little love and constancy are not martyred by our Lord.'[36]

This martyrdom of love which takes place primarily in the heart is, of course, a martyrdom which, in the spirit of the earliest Christians, seeks identification with Jesus through participation in his agony on the cross, which is at one and the same time a death and a birth.

This somewhat impressionistically drawn word-portrait of Salesian spirituality reveals its world as a world of hearts. Interconnected by their common natures, the divine heart and human hearts bridged by the human-divine heart of Jesus are the generative and vitalizing organs of a life which is at once spiritual and earthly. Together they breathe, they desire and they die. Together they form a reality, at once vivid and creaturely, yet which opens wide onto the uncreated and limitless expanse of the divine.

NOTES

1. I have argued elsewhere that the Salesian tradition, generally understood in scholarly circles to be derived primarily from the experiential synthesis achieved by Francis de Sales, has not one parent but two.

Jane de Chantal's imprint upon the whole of that tradition is distinctive and formative. See the introductory chapter in *Francis de Sales and Jane de Chantal: Letters of Spiritual Direction*, Classics of Western Spirituality Series, ed. Joseph Power and Wendy M. Wright (Mahwah, New Jersey: Paulist Press, 1988).

2. *Oeuvres de Saint François de Sales, Edition Complète* (Annecy: Monastère de la Visitation, 1892–1964), XII, Lettres 2, 321.

3. John A. Abruzzese in his study, *The Theology of Hearts in the Writings of St. Francis de Sales* (Rome: Institute of Spirituality, Pontifical University of St. Thomas Aquinas, 1983), has very thoroughly discussed the saint's doctrinal presentation on love using the heart as a synthesis. Henri Lemaire's *Étude des images littéraires de S. François de Sales* (Paris: Éditions A. G. Nizet, 1969), is a useful compendium of Salesian imagery.

4. It should be noted and kept in mind that the imagery of the heart, as basic as it is to the Salesian vision, is not the only imagery employed to describe the spiritual life or nature of God. There is an almost sensuous luxuriance of imagery in that tradition, especially in de Sales' work, which on first impression can obscure the underlying dominance of the heart image. Jane de Chantal's writing is not so self-consciously rhetorical in its employment of metaphor and simile as is her companion's. Her style is much less ornamental. This is in part due to their difference in education. On his education see Elisabeth Stopp, "St. Francis de Sales at Clermont College" in *Salesian Studies*, 6 (Winter 1969), 46–63 and James Langelaan, *Man in Love With God: Introduction to the Theology and Spirituality of St. Francis de Sales*, unpublished paper, Hyattsville, MD, 1976. On the education of women in this period and its possible influence on the spiritual teaching of Jane, see Wendy M. Wright, "St. Jane de Chantal's Guidance of Women" in *Salesian Living Heritage*, Vol I, No. 1 (Spring 1986), 16–28 and Vol II, No. 1 (Spring 1987), 10–22.

5. On the Christian humanism of this era see the works of Henri Brémond, *L'Humanisme dévot* (1580–1660), Vol. I of *Histoire de la fin des guerres de religion jusqu'à nos jours* (Paris: Bloud et Gay, 1921), Eng. trans. *A Literary History of Religious Thought in France* (London: Society for Promoting Christian Knowledge, 1930); *Autour de l'humanisme d'Erasme à Pascal* (Paris: Editions Bernard Grasset, 1937); Julien Eymard d'Angers, *L'humanisme chrétien au XVII esiècle: St. François de Sales et Yves de Paris* (La Haye: Martinus Nijhoff, 1970); Cecelian Streebing, *Devout Humanism as a Style: St. François de Sales' Introduction à La Vie Dévote* (Washington, D.C.: Catholic University of America Press, 1954). It should be noted that I have not followed Brémond

in distinguishing de Sales' brand of humanism as "devout humanism" and in seeing it as practical and popular rather than speculative and aristocratic as Brémond sees other types of Christian humanism. With Julien Eymard d'Angers I agree that the distinction is spurious, that there is one Christian humanism presented sometimes theologically, sometimes as praxis.

This period in the history of Christian spirituality is interesting especially because it represents the merging of a rigorous Christian ascetic tradition which in some ways is very world-denying and an intellectual tradition (both theological and philosophical) which is world-affirming.

6. Ste. Jeanne Françoise Frémyot de Chantal, *Sa Vie et ses oeuvres* (Edition authentique publiée par les soins des Religieuses du Premier Monastère de la Visitation Sainte Marie d' Annecy), III, *De Beatification et canonization de Saint François de Sales*, 124.

7. *Oeuvres*, VI, *Les Vrays Entretiens spirituels*, 56.

8. I am thinking particularly of the ceiling frescoes (both in Rome) of Il Gesu, which depicts the triumph of the name of Jesus, and of S. Ignazio which portrays the entrance of St. Ignatius into paradise. Both are stunning examples of illusionist technique that enable the worshiper-viewer to enter into the unconfined expanse of baroque space. I use the term "baroque" here in the general sense of the aesthetic style that seems to characterize European visual arts during the seventeenth century and which is notable in its visual realism, its preoccupation with the passions of the soul and its sense of the infinite (expressed in an exploration of light, space and time).

9. Cf. *Oeuvres*, V, *Traité de l'Amour de Dieu*, 310–11. I am indebted to Abruzzese for the labor of sifting through the corpus of Francis' work and identifying these varied qualities of the heart.

10. *Oeuvres*, XXV, 25 and IV, *Traité*, 261–62.

11. *Ibid.*, V, *Traité*, 262–63.

12. *Ibid.*, 265.

13. *Ibid.*, III, *Introduction à la vie dévote*, 323.

14. *Ibid.*, IV, *Traité*, 79 and 113.

15. For a more detailed discussion of the loves of benevolence and complacence which are focused upon in Book V of *Treatise on the Love of God* refer to Abruzzese, pp. 89ff and Joseph F. Power, OSFS, "Love of Benevolence and Liturgy" in *Salesian Studies*, III, No. 1 (Winter 1966), 27–40 and III, No. 3 (Summer 1966), 5–14.

16. *Oeuvres*, V, *Traité*, 9.

17. *Ibid.*, 136.

18. *Ibid.*, IV, 112.

19. *Ibid.*, 203–208.
20. *Sa Vie et ses oeuvres*, II, *Petit Livret*, 12–13.
21. Matthew 10:25ff.
22. *Ibid.*, II, *Entretiens*, 285.
23. *Ibid.*, 318. The superior part of the soul Jane refers to is understood to be the arena of human and divine interaction.
24. *Oeuvres*, III, *Introduction*, 216–17.
25. *Réponses de notre sainte Mère Jeanne-Françoise Frémiot, Baronne de Chantal fondatrice et première supérieure de l'ordre de la Visitation Sainte Marie, Sur les règles, constitutions et coutumier de l'Institut* (Annecy: Imprimerie de Aimé Burdet, 1849), 511–14.
26. *Oeuvres*, XIII, Lettres 3, 186. The power of image in spiritual formation is discussed in Margaret R. Miles' book *Image As Insight: Visual Understanding in Western Christianity and Secular Culture* (Boston: Beacon Press, 1985). See especially Chapter 2 in which she attempts to construct a hermeneutics of visual imagery that can enhance our understanding of historical (and contemporary) spirituality.
27. Friendship is, in the Salesian tradition, a type of love. Drawing on classical definitions of love, de Sales describes friendship as a love sustained by equals which is characterized by its mutuality and freedom of communication. The saint likewise characterizes marriage as a relationship in which the love of friendship is uppermost. He is psychologically and philosophically sophisticated in his analysis of the wide variety of friendships that can exist between people. See *Oeuvres*, III, *Introduction à la vie dévote*.
28. On their nineteen year friendship see Wendy M. Wright, *Bond of Perfection: Jeanne de Chantal and François de Sales* (New Jersey: Paulist Press, 1985). Chapter 3 of this work contains a theoretical examination of friendship in the Christian heritage.
29. Francis' extant letters to Jane are numerous and can be found throughout volumes XI–XXI of the Annecy edition of his collected works. Only a few stray missives from Jane's side of their correspondence can be found in the Plon edition of her collected writings or in the new critical edition of her letters, Jeanne-Françoise Frémyot de Chantal, *Correspondance*, édition critique et annotée par Soeur Marie-Patricia Burns, (Paris: Centre d'Etudes Franco-Italien, Les Editions du Cerf, 1986–). Volume I covering the years 1605–1621 is now available.
30. *Oeuvres*, XII, Lettres 2, 354.
31. *Sa Vie et ses oeuvres*, VII, Lettres 4, 306–313.
32. It was one of the few religious communities established specifically for women and not placed under the authority of a men's order. I have suggested elsewhere that this significantly colored the spirituality of

the Visitation. See Wendy M. Wright, "St. Jane de Chantal's Guidance of Women" in *Salesian Living Heritage* as well as the introduction to *Frances de Sales and Jane de Chantal: Letters of Spiritual Direction*.

33. *Sa Vie et ses oeuvres*, IV, *Lettres 1*, 290–91.
34. *Sa Vie et ses oeuvres*, VIII, *Lettres 5*, 556–57.
35. *Oeuvres*, V, *Traité*, 346.
36. *Sa Vie et ses oeuvres*, I, 356–57. The source of this quote is Mother Madelaine de Chaugy's *Life* of Jane.

Mary Quinlan, R.S.C.J.

Madeleine Sophie Barat's Doctrine of Interior Life

Madeleine Sophie (1779–1865), foundress of the Society of the Sacred Heart, taught a doctrine centered on devotion to the heart of Jesus but with some particular emphases which were especially her own. Most characteristic of her spiritual teaching was her insistence on the importance and the possibility of leading a truly recollected life, no matter how many and distracting one's occupations might be. Her own life, spent entirely in very demanding administrative duties, yet allowed her to experience mystical prayer, and she herself was the best example of the spirituality she inculcated in others. We know her spiritual teaching from the many volumes of her letters and conferences as well as from the Constitutions of her congregation and from the recollections of those who knew her during the more than six decades of her leadership of the order, so that, although she never wrote any theoretical work on spirituality, we have ample material on which to base an assessment of her doctrine.

Early Spiritual Formation

Her understanding of devotion to the Sacred Heart evolved over many years. As a ten year old child in the little Burgundian town of Joigny, she first saw images of the Sacred Heart of Jesus and of the Immaculate Heart of Mary. Her brother Louis, eleven years her senior, had gone to Paris to participate in the clandestine ministry during the revolution of 1789. He was eventually imprisoned during the Reign of Terror but before that he had sent the pictures to his parents to give them courage and hope. The daily family prayers recited before these images in which Sophie and

159

her parents entrusted Louis to God's care made a deep impression on the child and came to be the focus of her devotion.

When the Reign of Terror had ended and Louis, now a priest, returned to Joigny in 1795, he found Sophie a mature, charming, and intelligent fifteen year old. He was now convinced that she was destined for some outstanding service in the church, and he persuaded their parents to allow him to take her to Paris with him, there to continue her education, which he had overseen since her early childhood, and to give her a thorough spiritual formation.

For Sophie, the following five years in Paris, where she lived with her brother and at times various young women in a sort of novitiate under Louis' direction, constituted an orientation period of extreme severity, only somewhat mitigated by the interest she took in her religious studies. Already well trained in the classics and liberal arts and a gifted linguist, she now devoted hours every day to mastering the writings of the fathers of the church, the classics of western spirituality, and, above all, the scriptures. Throughout her life she drew on these sources for the development of her spiritual teachings and attained a breadth of view which enabled her to direct women of all types of personality with a sureness of touch and a freedom which allowed each person to grow in the way that was natural to her. In the almost sixty years that Madeleine Sophie spent as superior general of her congregation, she exercised enormous influence not only on her own religious but also on the thousands of people who came to her for advice and direction. If she had not had such a solid knowledge of spirituality, she probably would not have been able to elaborate a doctrine of such profundity and simplicity. Out of all her experience came an original synthesis of insights drawn from many spiritual traditions. In one sense her spiritual formation ended quite early as she took up the responsibilities of leadership of the congregation when she was still in her twenties, but in another sense she never ceased to be a pupil of those who, in her view, were the surest guides to whom she listened with great humility. Thus her spiritual formation was lifelong.

Religious Vocation

During the years in Paris, Sophie felt herself attracted to the contemplative life and planned to become a Carmelite when circumstances would allow it. But Joseph Varin, a priest who became acquainted with her in Paris and felt impelled to assist in the founding of an order of women to be dedicated to educational work, thought as Louis Barat did that Sophie's unusual gifts of mind and heart seemed to indicate that she was called to a more active service in the apostolate. At the end of the revolutionary period, all convent schools in France had been destroyed and the Catholic education of women was virtually unprovided for. Therefore, the priests whom Sophie knew and whose judgment she trusted urged her to collaborate in establishing an order which would have as its special work the education of girls. They did not propose that Sophie should found a new order but that she should give leadership in the forming of a French branch of a congregation, the *Dilette di Gesù*, just then being established in Rome. Thus it was that Sophie, without actually intending it, laid the foundation of what was to become a separate congregation, the Society of the Sacred Heart.[1]

But it was not merely the arguments of others that convinced Sophie that this was her vocation. Before she had met Joseph Varin and while she still felt herself called to be a Carmelite, she was at prayer one day and seemed to see a large monstrance raised high above the earth, and before it was a throng of people in adoration. She understood obscurely that she would have a mission, along with others, to raise up such a host of worshipers from all parts of the world (HC 176–77). Probably the memory of this experience helped to persuade her that she ought to concern herself with the apostolate of education. In the event, the schools which developed under her leadership had as their principal task the inculcation of faith and, when solid foundations had been laid, the development in the pupils of true devotion to the Sacred Heart which would be a source of grace to all.[2] Thus the vision of adorers from the ends of the earth was to be fulfilled.

Devotion to the Sacred Heart

In the course of many years, Saint Madeleine Sophie sought to penetrate ever more deeply into the meaning of devotion to the Sacred Heart. As Margaret Williams, R.S.C.J., who has made a careful study of the writings of the saint on this subject, has pointed out, the foundress, besides using scriptural sources, turned to the medieval mystics, to the prayer-books of the sixteenth century, to the writings of the Jesuits of the following century such as Nouet and Lallemant, and to the works of Francis de Sales, Eudes, and Bérulle. From the latter and from the French school in general, she learned to meditate on the interior dispositions of Jesus in order to unite herself to them. Apart from these sources, she attached great importance to the tradition of Paray-le-Monial and "knew by instinct what role the revelations made to Margaret Mary Alacoque would play in future developments of the devotion."[3]

In the mind of Madeleine Sophie, the devotion to the Sacred Heart was closely linked to devotion to the Blessed Sacrament. From the tradition of Saint Margaret Mary there came an emphasis on reparation, the practice of the Holy Hour in preparation for the First Friday of the month which was to be celebrated as a day of special devotion, and the use of various prayers and other acts of devotion intended to draw people to the love and worship of Jesus in the Blessed Sacrament. When the Society of the Sacred Heart was developing its way of life in the first quarter of the nineteenth century, these aspects of devotion to the Sacred Heart were exerting a powerful influence in the church—and not less so on the first generation of Religious of the Sacred Heart. Most of them had had personal experience, or had heard of it from their parents, of desecrations of the eucharist, not to mention the guillotining of people who insisted on professing their faith during the revolution of 1789. For the early members of the Society of the Sacred Heart, then, it was natural to respond to the appeal of Jesus for love and reparation and to associate it with his presence in the Blessed Sacrament. Mother Barat herself was so convinced of the value of adoration of the Blessed Sacrament that she would have preferred to give to it the time assigned to the recitation of Office if that had been possible at the time of the approval of the Constitutions in 1826. Through her influence the custom of making a half-hour of mental prayer daily before the Blessed Sacrament grew up; it was part of the hour and a half of mental prayer provided for in the order of day.

Interior Life

As greatly as Mother Barat esteemed formal prayer, she once said that interior life is more than prayer, by which she meant that the constant recollection of God's presence at least through an obscure awareness throughout the activities of the day was of major importance in the development of prayer. Such an awareness was of the essence of devotion to the Sacred Heart as she conceived of it. She spoke of interior life as the constantly renewed recollection of the presence of God for whom we act, a recollection which she thought of as equivalent to the entire sacrifice of oneself.[4] Yet she never ceased to point out how easy and delightful is the life of a person who is truly given over to the action of God. One time in writing to one of the religious she said:

Few give themselves over to the Holy Spirit, and what a mistake we make in not being among the privileged few! Believe me, it costs much more to stay in a miserable mediocrity in which one belongs neither to God nor to oneself. It is like swimming between two currents; it is difficult and dangerous. Hurry up and plunge into mid-stream. The Holy Spirit will then carry you and you will get to port much more quickly.[5]

And she said in one of her conferences:

A soul who is thus given no longer walks, she flies; the greatest sacrifices cost her nothing, and the heaviest crosses no longer weigh her down. What am I saying? The cross is her happiness; she loves it, desires it, because God permits that a soul who is thus given over, handed over, to him instead of feeling the sufferings which accompany the cross, no longer tastes anything but its consolations (CON I 118).

Apropos of this passage, Mary Wolff-Salin, R.S.C.J., draws attention to the importance of this joyous interpretation of spiritual experience when one is reading Mother Barat's letters and conferences; otherwise, the emphasis she places on suffering might suggest a dolorism which is entirely at variance with her optimistic and joyful outlook on the spiritual life. She was a realist and she knew by experience how joy, sorrow, anxiety and trust can coexist at the same time in a person. She expressed the whole range of emotions in referring to her own experience. The warning about dolorism is well made.[6]

In another part of the conference quoted above, Mother Barat exclaimed:

If only it were given to me, if I were not unworthy, to speak to you of the happiness of a soul who surrenders to the Holy Spirit fully and with no reserve! If I could tell you what happens within her, if I could picture for you her joy! It is not she who acts, it is God; she only moves, only walks, by his inspiration. Everything becomes easy for her. She experiences no more difficulties, meets with no more obstacles. The Holy Spirit enchains such a soul. She is his; he binds her to himself (CON I 118).

The dominant note in Mother Barat's spiritual direction of others was joyful freedom in dependence on God. The following passage may illustrate the point:

Be in peace about the state of your soul and your manner of prayer; only love and do what you please. The essential thing and the proof of true love is forgetfulness of self and of one's own interests to think only of those of the loved one. . . . So what difference does it make how you pray provided that your heart is seeking the one you love (LR III 227)?

When Mother Barat was seventy-eight years old, writing to a religious who had been her close friend and confidante for many years and who had evidently asked for some advice, Mother Barat sketched out joint spiritual direction for her friend and herself:

> Let us both ask Jesus to enlighten and guide us. Oh, my daughter, how weak, ignorant and subject to error we are if his divine Spirit does not take hold of us and lead us. At my age, which ought to have given me knowledge of a good many things, I am always aware of my own insufficiency, my nothingness, my mistakes if I act without dependence on the Spirit of Jesus; how many times I have to regret it! So here is the spiritual direction for the two of us: let us repress our natural activity, let us act under the eyes of Jesus and according to his impulsion; let us forget and annihilate the self and we will have fulfilled the precepts, even the counsels, and all the rest will be given to us.[7]

The Holy Spirit

As is already evident, Mother Barat's devotion to the Sacred Heart can hardly be separated from her desire to live always under the guidance of the Holy Spirit. Perhaps this emphasis on the Spirit is the most characteristic aspect of her own piety. One tries in vain to divide these two strands of her thought. As Margaret Williams, R.S.C.J. has put it:

> Through experience [Mother Barat] found the role of the Holy Spirit in the devotion to the Sacred Heart; she expressed it in such an all-pervasive way that it is, perhaps, the most distinctive note in her spiritual doctrine. There is hardly a letter or conference that does not refer to the Holy Spirit, usually in the phrase "Spirit of Jesus" or "Spirit of his Heart." At first reading this phrase seems often to be generic or impersonal, but in its use it points to the Sanctifier, the third Person of the Trinity, and in many sentences it is linked to the Sacred Heart: "The Spirit of Jesus who dwells always in an interior soul united to the divine Heart will know at the right moment what to do, to decide, to counsel" (SMS 512).

Just as there was a close connection in the mind of the foundress between devotion to the Sacred Heart and an inner life lived under the guidance of the Spirit, so too the Spirit drew her to an inner penetration of the gospels. She was absorbed in the mysteries of Christ as they came before her in the course of the liturgical year, although she always returned to the contemplation of the passion and also had special insight into the incarnation of the word of God which filled her with awe and humility. Thus her inner life revolved about the mysteries of Jesus always in view of the revelation of his love.

Interior Life and the Work of Education

As we know from her first vision of the Society as it might be one day, Mother Barat viewed the work of education in the light of faith—the faith of those who carried it on and those who received it. It was obvious to her that the real success of the work could come only if the religious practiced a true interior life. She certainly valued their natural gifts and urged them to prepare themselves seriously for their apostolate, but she did not consider talent enough. In a letter to Mother d'Avenas who was later to become a famous teacher and director of studies she wrote:

> If only you knew how much the Society needs holy and learned women you would hurry up and become one. Here in the Roman novitiate we have a number of saints but not a single scholar— not one! It is all very well to lay the foundations of solid virtue, but only the union of virtue with learning will give our work its perfection. Unite these two things closely, my daughter, and you will understand the full extent of your vocation (LR II 361).

The type of educational work for which the Society was best known in the lifetime of Mother Barat and long thereafter was that of boarding schools for girls of affluent families. The foundress recognized the pressing need of good Christian education for young women who were likely to become leaders in their social milieu. She wanted them to exercise a beneficent influence, and she therefore held up to them ideals of service, self-sacrifice and strong faith. But she was equally concerned about the education of poor children and wished never to found a boarding school unless there were an accompanying school for children of modest means. In her view, the financial gains from the boarding schools were required to support the schools and other works for the poor. Without this concern for the poor, she would have thought that the Society failed to care for those dearest to the Heart of Jesus. Similarly, she wanted the work of retreats to be given much attention, since this was a means of inculcating a spirit of faith and prayerfulness in women of whatever social class who came to the convent seeking spiritual help; this was one of the most significant ways in which the Society could spread the knowledge and love of Christ (CRL 97).

Over and above these formal ministries, the members of the Society were to consider as a means of making known God's love all contacts with lay people whom they might meet in the course of their duties (CSSH #238). For many of the religious this became a heavy if beloved apostolate and for no one more so than for Mother Barat whose decades of residence at the rue de Varenne had brought her into contact with people of every kind who came to her with a variety of needs. She once remarked that she felt more like a minister of state than a cloistered religious. No doubt her charm and wisdom as well as her patent holiness drew people to her. She herself set the example of this ministry—what might be called the ministry of friendship. The incidents which illustrate her attitude to it are so numerous that it is difficult to choose one to stand as an example of all of them, but the following anecdote seems to sum up the spirit in which Mother Barat carried on this apostolate.

It happened that one day when a large crowd of visitors were attending a ceremony at the convent on the rue de Varenne (now the Rodin Museum), a poor elderly woman joined them and by chance fell into conversation with Mother Barat. They agreed that they would see each other soon again, but when the old woman came for her next visit the portress thought it would be enough to give her an alms and send her away. This happened several times until Mother Barat by chance learned of it. She was distressed about it and gave orders that whenever her friend came she was to be called immediately. After that, the two of them often sat together talking animatedly. On one occasion the portress, who must have been somewhat lacking in human feeling, was shocked to see Mother Barat rise and remove her warm petticoat from under her skirt and give it to the poor woman. For Mother Barat the spirituality of the heart knew no bounds of class or financial status. She comforted duchesses in their trials and also provided for the spiritual welfare of their coachmen. No one who could benefit from what she called "a little word about God" or a small gift was left outside the range of her care and concern.

But with all her love for people and her burning enthusiasm for the work of education, Mother Barat never ceased to teach her daughters that zeal should not lead them to think that prayer was of less importance than activity. A thought often expressed by her occurs in one of her letters: "It is certain that our vocation is or should be as contemplative as it is active. I could even say that the former [aspect] must dominate and sustain the latter" (LS II 28).

Contemplation in the Midst of Action

The tension between the contemplative and active aspects of the life was plainly felt by the foundress and was perhaps more acute in her case because she carried a burden of responsibility as superior general for almost six decades, until her death at the age of eighty-five, and for most of her life was strongly drawn to mystical prayer. She often experienced ecstasy and lost contact with whatever was going on about her. She always tried to hide or ignore these incidents, but if she had to speak of them she sometimes laughingly said that Jesus had played a trick on her and sometimes she excused herself by saying that she was tired or unwell. The religious understood both her raptures and her unwillingness to speak about them, so they learned to act as if these episodes were not taking place. The marvel was that with all these occasions of being swept away from the realities around her, Mother Barat had a precise knowledge of everything that pertained to her duties and was a close observer of persons for whom she was responsible.

Her experience of prayer enabled her to lead others who were gifted with unusual modes of contact with God. The ultimate experience of prayer for her seems to have occurred when she felt herself in direct contact with the persons of the Holy Trinity. She seldom spoke of those moments but certain remarks in her direction of others suggest that she knew from experience what such contact meant. Once in writing to Mother Goetz who was to be her successor as superior general and who was afraid of the increasing responsibilities which fell to her, Mother Barat encouraged her to put her trust in the Heart of Jesus and then she added a few words describing how the Trinity animates nothingness by the divine Spirit. And on another day, writing to a religious who was passing through a time of pain and darkness, she told her that if she had known, even for a moment, true union with the Trinity, she would then taste so much joy in heavenly things that she would no longer hesitate and nothing would be capable of distracting her from the love of Jesus (SMS 512).

But Mother Barat did not lead others to points beyond which they were called by grace. She was careful in her direction, lest someone should fall into illusion. She preferred to have them pray simply and humbly without either fearing or desiring the great trials experienced by some of the mystics. She always encouraged fidelity to the action of the Holy Spirit, knowing that in the practice of interior life lay safety and the right balance between action and contemplation, according to their vocation. If she encountered in a humble and obedient religious some exterior manifestations of extraordinary grace, she tried to keep these phenomena hidden as much as possible. Like all true mystics and especially like Teresa of Avila from whose writings she had learned so much, Mother Barat valued God's action in itself but approached its external manifestations with critical acumen. Once, on hearing about someone reputed to have mystical experiences, she wrote to Eugénie de Gramont, long headmistress of the school on the rue de Varenne and a woman of great sense and executive ability: "I will believe in visions, Eugénie, when you have them. Let me know right away" (SMS 509)!

On the other hand, in the presence of real mysticism she was full of reverence and joy. She hoped that all the religious, seeing the effects of grace in women who were particularly holy, would imitate their virtues. She especially thought that in old age the religious should give their major attention and energies to prayer, as she would have wished to do herself. But that joy was withheld from her. She accepted as God's will the Society's refusal to release her from her duties as superior general even when, at the age of eighty-four, she begged the councillors to do so, in order, as she put it, to give her a little leisure to prepare for death. They could not think of it. She therefore continued to the end to give that example of contemplation in the midst of action which is the particular way in which the Society has always glorified the Heart of Jesus.

NOTES

1. Jeanne de Charry, R.S.C.J., *Histoire des Constitutions de la Société du Sacré-Coeur,* vol. I: *La Formation de l'Institut* (=HC) seconde édition révisée (Rome: privately printed, 1981), p. 219. Translations of passages from this and other works in French are mine.
2. *Constitutions and Rules of the Society of the Sacred Heart* (1815) (=CSSH) #349 in the 1987 edition.
3. Margaret Williams, RSCJ, *Saint Madeleine Sophie: Her Life and Letters* (=SMS) (New York: Herder and Herder, 1965) p. 441.
4. *Conférences de la Vénérable Mère Madeleine Sophie Barat* (=CON) 2 vols. (Roehampton, England: privately printed, 1900) I, 367.
5. *Lettres choisies de Notre Sainte Mère, addressés aux Religieuses* (=LR), 5 vols. (Rome: Maison Mère, 1928–57), II, 339.
6. M. R. Wolff-Salin, R.S.C.J., *A Conception of the Religious Life: A Study in the Original and Present Spirit of the Society of the Sacred Heart of Jesus* (=CRL): A Thesis presented to the Faculty of Theology of

the Catholic University of Louvain as partial requirement for the doctorate in theology, 3 vols. Part One: *The Thought of Saint Madeleine Sophie* (Louvain: privately printed, 1973), p. 33.

7. *Lettres Choises de notre Bienheureuse Mère pour les seules Supérieures* (=LS). 5 vols. (Rome: Maison Mère, 1922–65), II, 116.

Robert Faricy, S.J.

The Heart of Christ in the Writings of Teilhard de Chardin

A strong personal devotion to the heart of Jesus Christ risen and glorified lies at the foundation of the whole edifice of Pierre Teilhard de Chardin's philosophy and theology.

Teilhard's rethinking of the formulation of Christian doctrine crystallized around his practical religious commitment to the heart of Christ. During the four decades that he worked out his ideas, his explicit love for the heart of Jesus animated his philosophical and religious thinking and writing. As a result, not only Teilhard's spiritual teaching but all his philosophical and religious writings have, as their almost invisible foundation, the real symbol of the heart of the risen Christ.

Pierre Teilhard de Chardin was born in 1881 in the dark gray town of Clermont in central France. He was baptized and sacramentally nurtured there in the dark gray twelfth century church of Notre Dame du Port. He began his career as a Jesuit and scientist early, collecting the rocks from the somber gray stone that lies around Clermont and of which the town is built, and imbibing the strong nineteenth century devotion to the Sacred Heart of Jesus.

Seventy-five years after his birth, and soon after his death on Easter Sunday, 1955, in New York, his ideas burst like flares in the dark Catholic sky before Vatican II. Those ideas provided the theological framework and main concepts for *Gaudium et spes, The Pastoral Constitution on the Church in the Modern World*, held today as the Second Vatican Council's most important and most influential document. Teilhard's writings provided most of the principal ideas for post-Vatican II theology of original sin, of human progress, and of Christian involvement in the world. They have greatly influenced all the important Catholic theological currents in the second half of this century: in particular the theology of liberation, environmental theology, and the theology of prayer.

In these pages I would like to show how the new and brilliantly shining ideas we have received from Teilhard were founded in the dark gray stone of his lifelong and intense personal devotion to the heart of Jesus.

As early as 1919, Teilhard sees that the key to synthesis in Christian spirituality is the humanity of Jesus, his human flesh. And he writes in his private journal:

That the Spirit of Christ be the Soul of our souls, it is first necessary that it be the Flesh of our flesh. He does not achieve our unity in his Spirit spreading over us except by holding us together in the fabric of his flesh underpinning our corporeal existence.[1]

Some months later, Teilhard grasps that his principle of synthesis that has been operating in his reflection is the heart of Jesus. He admits this to himself in his journal:

Although I never really analyzed it before, it is in the Sacred Heart that the conjunction of the divine and the cosmic has taken place. . . . There lies the power that from the beginning has attracted me and conquered me. . . . All the later development of my interior life has been nothing other than the *evolution of that seed*.[2]

Years later, looking back, Teilhard understands clearly the importance in all his spirituality, written reflections, essays and books of the devotion to the Sacred Heart, the seed planted early in his own heart. And he sees that the heart of Jesus is both the heart of matter, of the whole material world, and also of the spiritual-theological question of Christian synthesis. The heart of Jesus is the heart of matter and, therefore, the "heart of the matter." Teilhard writes in a letter of 1952:

I have read *The Heart of the Matter* by Graham Greene. A study in despair. Why never a study on hope? . . . The title would be wonderful for me (although with a quite different meaning) for an essay I am dreaming to write since some time. . . . The appearances of God from and in the "Heart of Matter." I shall explain this to you.[3]

In fact, not long after that letter, Teilhard writes an essay entitled, "The Heart of Matter." In it, he discusses the role of the Sacred Heart devotion in his personal spirituality and in his spiritual doctrine.

> Everybody knows the historical background of the cult of the Sacred Heart (or the Love of Christ): how it was always latent in the Church, and then in the France of Louis XIV assumed an astonishingly vigorous form which was at the same time oddly limited both in the object to which it was directed ("Reparation") and in its symbol (the heart of our Savior, depicted with cautiously anatomical realism!).
>
> The remains of this narrow view can still, unfortunately, be seen today. . . . I was not yet "in theology" when, through and under the symbol of the "Sacred Heart," the Divine had already taken on for me the form, the consistence, and the properties of an ENERGY, of a FIRE. . . .[4]

Teilhard's Early Devotion to the Sacred Heart

In the same essay, "The Heart of Matter," an essay devoted to a description of the history of his inner psychological experience through the years, Teilhard gives predominant attention to the place of the heart of Jesus Christ in his life. The God that Teilhard's mother taught him to revere in his childhood was an incarnate God, the Word incarnate. As his mother introduced him prayerfully to the humanity of Jesus Christ, Teilhard found a center for his world (*HM*, 42–43). In his devotion to the Sacred Heart, Teilhard's love for the world and his yearning for the Absolute came together. The Sacred Heart synthesized his "pagan" side and his "Christian" side by personalizing the world, centering the world in the heart of Christ. At the same time, God was "universalized," because God's love could be understood as radiating everywhere from the human heart of Jesus (*HM*, 45–49).

Long before Teilhard began to study theology in the Jesuit order, he writes, his love for the Sacred Heart had begun to bring into synthesis his "upward" impulse toward God and his "forward" impulse toward progress, toward the world-to-be-built, toward the world in evolution into the future.

The apparent divergence between the two fundamental components of human life, the upward component of worship of God and the forward component of involvement in the world, constitutes the basic problem of all Teilhard's philosophical and religious thought as well as the mainspring of his own personal spirituality and his spiritual teaching. He was both a

Christian and a lover of the world, both a priest and a scientist, a man of God and a man of his time. How could he avoid being torn between the vertical vector of his inner self, the drive upward toward God, and the horizontal vector, the drive forward toward accomplishment in this world? How could he synthesize faith in God and faith in the world?

Teilhard writes to a friend in 1916 that the reconciliation between Christianity and the contemporary spirit "has always been the problem of my interior life—a little like the question of Rome for Newman . . .; I mean the reconciliation of progress and detachment, of the passionate and legitimate love of this great earth and the single-minded pursuit of the kingdom of heaven."[5] In another letter of the same day, Teilhard says, "And once again I was conscious within myself of the inspiration that calls me to the great work of reconciling the supreme and absolute love of God with the lower (but still legitimate and necessary) love of life embraced under its natural forms."[6]

The coming together of these two currents, love for God and love for the world, was responsible for the progress and also for the struggles of Teilhard's interior life. Only in a unified concept of Christ and the world could he find peace and room to grow. And Teilhard was quite conscious that his own life, at a personal level, furnished at least the elements of a solution to "the great spiritual problem that right now is troubling the front ranks of mankind," the bringing together of "the upward" and "the forward,"[7] the "Christian point of view" and the "human point of view."[8]

In the last ten years of his life, from the end of World War II until his death, Teilhard formulates the problem as one of two faiths: faith in God and faith in the world.[9] And he finds their synthesis in Jesus Christ risen— even more exactly, in the heart of the risen Jesus.

Teilhard's passion for God existed as far back as he could remember, a certain "love for the Invisible One" (*HM*, 41). This love for God merged with his love for the world; in a sense, it "materialized" his love for God. The "materialization" of Teilhard's passion for God found its religious expression in his attachment to the humanity of Jesus, especially under the real symbol of Jesus' human heart (*HM*, 41–43).

The negative aspects of the Sacred Heart devotion, as practiced in nineteenth century France and down into this century, never hemmed Teilhard in. He was aware of the tendencies to be obsessed with sin and to isolate the Heart of Christ in a closed-in sentimentality. But his own attachment to the Sacred Heart took shape as a concentration of all the physical and spiritual reality of Jesus Christ risen in one definable object, his heart. This freed Teilhard because it showed him, gave him, the absolute and steady Center of a changing world. He had a firm place to stand and a Center of synthesis (*HM*, 43–44).

For Teilhard, the Divine, through the symbol of the Sacred Heart, took on the form of a Fire that has the capacity to transform everything, not a destructive fire but the creative Fire that burns in the human heart of God become human (*HM*, 47). "Christ, his Heart, a Fire, capable of penetrating everything—and which, little by little, spreads everywhere" (*HM*, 47).

We can find Teilhard's love for the heart of Christ in the letters he wrote to his mother in 1915 and 1916 when he was a young priest. During these few early years, Teilhard's original ideas began to take shape in his earliest essays.[10] We can find his attachment to the heart of Christ not only implicitly in those essays, but explicitly in the letters he wrote home. The "cosmic Christ" of Teilhard's early essays is the Sacred Heart of his letters to his mother. Since Teilhard's spiritual life, at the time of the essays, is rooted in his attachment to the Sacred Heart, the cosmic Christ of his theological formulations loses nothing of his human particularity. It is not so much Christ who is cosmic as the cosmos that is Christic, grounded in a Person who is human as well as divine, centered on the heart of Christ.

"This is the time," Teilhard writes his mother in 1915, "for each one of us and for all of us together to allow ourselves to be ruled by the Heart of Our Lord. He must find us . . . ready for whatever he might will. And we should want nothing so much as to remain *united* to him, accepting what he sends and doing whatever he wishes."[11] And a month later: ". . . love of *his Will*, wanted for its own sake as *coming from his Heart* and as our surest binding to him—I wish you that, little mother."[12]

In these letters, as in all of Teilhard's writings, especially from this point on in his life, the emphasis lies not on truth, intellectual understanding, thinking—but rather on love, the will, and acting. It is easy to find here the influence of Teilhard's devotion to the heart of Christ. It led Teilhard in his theological reflection to part from the intellectualist neo-Thomism in which he had been trained and that dominated Catholic theology until the Second Vatican Council in favor of a voluntarist perspective that emphasizes love and doing rather than truth and understanding. The primacy of love in Teilhard's spirituality has its origin in his prayerful union with the heart of Christ.

A letter of December 1915 remarkably foreshadows the doctrine of Teilhard's spiritual classic, *The Divine Milieu*.[13] And it indicates that *The Divine Milieu*'s teaching is anchored in Teilhard's love for the heart of Jesus. He speaks of "complete abandonment of the will to Our Lord. Nothing is more intimate to us than our will, tastes, likings. To love and look for these things in Our Lord is to *find what is deepest in him*, his Heart, and it is to encounter him in the surest and most profitable way." He then anticipates *The Divine Milieu*'s doctrine on communion with God in and through all things: "Surest because nothing should at any moment be able to shake us from that true communion that God gives us in his action on us through everything, everyone, every event. And also most profitable, because everything in our lives becomes material for supernatural growth, and because a thousand unpleasant realities *are* transfigured *at the touch of God's greatly loving hand.*"[14]

Teilhard's whole intellectual effort was to unify. He wanted to show how reality is one because all things come together under one Head, in one Heart. We can see that search for unity, and where Teilhard always found it personally, in another letter to his mother, in 1916. "The Sacred Heart has been good to me in giving me the one desire to be united with him in the totality of my life."[15]

Teilhard writes to his mother that "love of the Sacred Heart" is the best way "to give brightness to our lives, to transform them."[16] And he writes of the need for "communion with the desires of the Sacred Heart."[17]

Later Life: The Retreat Journals of 1939 to 1950

Like all Jesuits, Teilhard de Chardin made a retreat of eight or ten days every year. And like most Jesuit priests even today, after he had finished his formation years, he made his annual retreat in private and in complete silence. He always kept a retreat journal. Sometimes the entries are only brief notations, perhaps coming to just a few pages for eight or ten days—but they are always comprehensible and revealing. Teilhard wrote them for his own eyes only; they tell us a great deal about his life with the Lord.

Many of Teilhard's retreat journals have been lost. We do not have, for example, the journals from his retreats during the long years he spent in China in geological and paleontological research. But we do have the retreat notes from 1939 through Teilhard's last retreat, in 1954, plus three earlier retreats from the 1920's.[18]

One of Teilhard's most interesting sets of retreat notes comes from his 1948 retreat at Les Moulins, France, from August 30 to September 7. Teilhard is sixty-eight years old. His health is poor. His heart condition results in a physically-felt anxiety that can put him to bed for days at a time. His approaching death is on his mind.

His retreat notes for the first day begin: "First Day. Without HIM, nothing. My inconsistency. No retreat last year: there was my close call through sickness and my coming to a tangential point with death. Through death, I contacted God. And this year it's in an atmosphere of physical anxiety that I try to put myself back into the Divine Milieu." Certainly there is at least a hint of depression in these lines.

Teilhard's concern, however, is not with his health, but to center himself on Jesus, "Jesus only," he writes, "only Jesus." He continues, "His Holy Presence ought to gradually absorb me. Here's the point: I feel myself really in conflict, as if that Presence, precisely, were less present to me. That these days, gently, put me back in Him, to Him!"

He asks himself that if he's not immersed in Jesus, then what does he have to offer others who come to him and who judge by his words that he has truly come through into the light? "Oh that I might drown in You, Universal Jesus, by trust now in this present instant. . . . Oh Jesus, that I be not just a clanging cymbal. Oh Jesus, help me to end well." And Teilhard prays that the end of his life be a witness that seals his claim and his faith that there exists an end-point of love that has universal import. "Communion through death (Death-Communion)." On this first day of retreat, Teilhard has brought together his concern with his coming death, and his need to live more in the presence of Jesus.

The retreat continues: "Second Day. Again: to live in the Existence." Teilhard then reminds himself that this is the only thing necessary. "If we really lived in the Existence of Christ-Omega, the rest would follow immediately."

The expression "Christ-Omega" is common in Teilhard's writings, in his private journals as well as in his writings written to be read by others. He takes the word "Omega," the last letter of the Greek alphabet, from Christ's description of himself in the New Testament Book of Revelation as the Alpha and the Omega. Teilhard uses it to indicate that the risen Christ is the end, the end-point, of the world. Christ-Omega, in Teilhard's christology, is the risen Jesus in his role as the future focal point of the convergent evolution—now principally social—of the world.[19] Teilhard understands the world not as having been started off by a Creator in the past, but rather as being created by being drawn into the future by the Creator God acting in and through the risen humanity of Jesus. And Jesus stands ahead of us, in the future, Omega. He *is* the Future, the future of everyone and of the world, a future with a face.

Teilhard can hope precisely because his future is some One, a Person, Jesus. And this same Jesus is present here and now, in Teilhard's life, in his retreat, in each present moment, as the ground of his hope. So when he writes in his notes "Christ-Omega," he means that, facing his death, and in the face of his own inconstancy, he hopes—wants to hope more—in Jesus, living in the Lord's presence.

There follows a short phrase: "Life in centration . . . all the way to excentration." The words "centration" and "excentration" are found in Teilhard's published writings, especially in *The Divine Milieu*.[20] They name the first and second steps of his three part dialectic of Christian life, death, and life-to-come. The three parts, or steps, or phases of the dialectical process are named by Teilhard: centration, excentration, supercentration.[21]

First, centration. Our first duty is to develop ourselves, to grow as persons. Secondly, excentration. We cannot reach our limits of personal growth without going out of ourselves and uniting in love with others. We grow not by working for our own fulfillment but by dying to self, by taking up the cross, by losing ourselves for the sake of the kingdom. Excentration can result from our own discipline and motivation, or it can come from outside us in the form of crosses we cannot avoid: sickness, failure, misunderstanding, death.

Finally, supercentration. The fragmentation we undergo in the excentration phase breaks us into pieces, so to speak, so that the Lord can put us together this time less centered on ourselves and more centered on him, super-centered on Jesus Christ. These are, of course, the three phases of the paschal mystery: the public life of Jesus, his death on the cross, his resurrection. They are the three eschatological phases of the world: history, the end of the world, the world to come. They are the three phases of our human existence: life here, death-as-passage, life-after-death.

Teilhard is aware, on this second day of his retreat, that he is elderly and not well, diminishing: that his life is in the excentration phase, headed toward the most radical excentration, his coming death. And he moves into the third day.

Like all Jesuits, Teilhard is following the spiritual exercises of Saint Ignatius Loyola for his retreat. The Spiritual Exercises have four "weeks" or sections. The "first week" (and Teilhard is in the "first week" here in the first three days of his retreat) has the retreatant look at his own sins and sinfulness, repent, and ask for God's healing forgiveness. A consideration of the fact of death often comes into the "first week" as a sobering factor to help the retreatant repent and reform.

Still in the "first week," Teilhard gives the title "Contact of Purification" to the short entries, about twelve handwritten lines, for the third day of the retreat. The first two lines read, "Heart of Jesus = Center of Jesus = Universal Center of the convergent universe." Teilhard here continues his second day's consideration of Christ-Omega. And he adds a new element: Jesus is Omega, the center of the whole world's convergent movement into the future toward its end-point where Christ as Omega waits for it; and, further, the center of that Center is Jesus' own heart, the human heart of the risen Christ.

The notes for the third retreat day conclude: "—the disturbing factor in my own spiritual situation: that the Pan-Presence of Christ makes me so *frightened*, undoubtedly because of my conviction that even the worst will happen. However, in fact: (1) my trust should count on a favorable directioning of chance events; and, (2) at worst, I should accept and love every Communion with Death."

By the "Pan-Presence of Christ," Teilhard means the universal presence of the risen Christ through the universal influence of his creative love. This creative love radiates out from Jesus risen, from his heart, as he—as Christ Omega—draws all things to himself precisely through the force of that creative love. That is how Teilhard interprets and rethinks theologically the Pauline doctrine of creation in Christ.

Moreover, the same risen Jesus radiates the creative force of his love out from his presence in the eucharist.[22] The physical heart of Jesus, at the world's end-time focal point and in the eucharist, affects all reality, and every part of reality, through love. And it results in the "Pan-Presence of Christ," a presence through influence.

Jesus, then, is everywhere, omnipresent—through love. This leaves Teilhard frightened; he is afraid of what the Lord will ask, might ask. But he understands that the random factor, the fact of chance (including adverse chance), in no way eliminates divine providence. By his universal influence, Jesus can give his own providential direction even to adverse chance happenings. And so Teilhard can trust in Jesus Christ for his life and for what will happen to him.

The worst that can, will, come is his death. He sees this as a passage to fuller life, as the excentration necessary for the final super-centering on Jesus in the life to come. He wants, then, to embrace death, to fully accept his coming "Communion with Death." Not because death is evil, the worst evil of all and the last enemy to be conquered, but because death stands as the only passage out of this life to new life with Jesus in the world to come.

In an "N.B." at the beginning of his notes for the fourth day, Teilhard writes, "Retreat conceived as a deepening of contact with God-Christ Omega." He specifies that this contact with Christ-Omega takes the forms of "(1) contact of existence; (2) contact of dependence (consistency); (3) . . . the human (the *forward*); (4) . . . the Christian (the *upward*); (5) of interiorization: Inward; (6) of excentration—Pan-Communion."

Teilhard understands the purpose of his retreat as a deepening of his personal relationship with Jesus Christ who holds him in existence, and on whom he does in fact depend and wants to (psychologically) depend more so that he can be more consistent in his behavior. Teilhard wants a deeper relationship with Jesus in and through all things: the human (the "forward," this world, everyday events), and the Christian (prayer, Mass, specifically religious activities). He hopes the retreat will interiorize his contact with Jesus, make it more important in his inner life. And he knows this means the cross, suffering, excentration; he wants contact with Jesus also in excentration, in *all* things ("Pan-Communion").

Teilhard writes the words "forward," "upward," "inward," and "Pan-Communion" in English rather than in French. They have become almost technical terms for him, and there are no one-word French equivalents.

He adds to his fourth day notes: "—the supreme virtue: *total Trust.*" Trust, of course, is the main virtue traditionally associated with devotion to the Sacred Heart. Teilhard gives it, however, his own nuances, calling trust "the specific operative holding-on to a personalized Cosmogenesis." In the genesis (evolution, ongoing history, movement forward) of his life, of the world around him, of the cosmos, Teilhard sees and hangs on to the universal love of Jesus Christ risen; that hanging-on is his act of total trust.

The retreat's fifth day turns out to be a "first Friday." In keeping with the traditional practice of observing the first Friday of each month in honor of the Sacred Heart, a practice particularly important in the Jesuit order, Teilhard surely said the Mass of the Sacred Heart. His entries are sparse and repetitive of previous days. "One must distinguish a double unitive action: to Humanize (forward); to Christify (upward) (Omega)." And this equals: "Christocentric omnipresence, all day."

I do not know what Teilhard has in mind when he writes "all day." I suspect he means that he is (we are) called to live all day, each day, in the presence of Jesus risen because our union with him is at both "levels" of life, the upward and the forward, and together they include everything. What seems significant to me is that Teilhard gives the fifth day the title "1st Friday. Sacred Heart." He prays about his union with Jesus in terms of his own devotion to the Sacred Heart.

The sixth day is headed, "Presence of Mary (Sacred Heart); the Day, place of Our Lady (the feminine)." There follow only a few lines. "To continue to plunge, through a series of concentric circles, into the Fundamental Omnipresence,—towards the Center of the World." And a cryptic sentence that readers can decode in any way they wish: "I've built an airplane (according to the plans), but how can I fly 'this airplane'? That is what everyone is waiting for from me." Finally: "to recognize Christ-Omega, to enter into communion, even in what spoils life or casts a shadow over it."

But what does Teilhard pray about on this sixth day of his retreat? Judging from the day's heading, he prays about the presence of the Blessed Virgin Mary in his life, and this in reference to the Sacred Heart. The day seems to be centered on a prayerful consideration of the place of Mary, and of "the feminine," in Teilhard's life, all somehow in the framework of Teilhard's personal devotion to the heart of Jesus.

What connection in Teilhard's mind does the Sacred Heart have with Mary? From these retreat notes, we can say only that there is an important connection. We can say more, however, if we refer to other writings of his.

In the first place, "the feminine" for Teilhard is not an abstract principle, but a universal principle concretized in individual women, in the church as bride and mother, and in a particular and almost primordial way in the Blessed Virgin Mary. The feminine, as concretized—especially in Mary—symbolizes for Teilhard certain qualities of the forward movement of the world toward Christ-Omega: materiality, darkness, mystery; and also: the progressive transcendence of the material through unification in love.[23] The connection between the feminine and the Sacred Heart, then, lies in the area where they intersect conceptually: the area of evolution (the feminine) toward Christ-Omega (the Sacred Heart).

The seventh day is entitled, " 'Excentration'; 'Christifieri'." The second half of the heading, "Christifieri," is a Latin neologism I can find nowhere else in all Teilhard's writings. It would seem to be more or less synonymous with "Christogenesis," world evolution seen as moving toward Christ-Omega as its center and future focal pole of attraction.[24] "Christifieri," however, seems to apply to the individual, to Teilhard, rather than to the world; it seems to mean Christogenesis on a personal basis.

The entry for the seventh day has only four words. "Re-meditate the Golden Glow" (the words "the Golden Glow" are in English). "The Golden Glow" appears in only one other place in Teilhard's notes and writing, on a "holy card" of the Sacred Heart, written on both sides, that was found after his death among the things on his desk. On the front of the picture is written, "Jesus, the Heart of the World, the Essence and Motor of evolution." On the back is a kind of litany, a series of titles or appreciations for the Sacred Heart, such as, "Sacred Heart, Motor of evolution, heart of evolution," and "the altar of God, the Center of Jesus," and "the heart of the heart of the world." Also: "Heart of Jesus, Heart of Evolution, unite me to yourself." And finally, "The Golden Glow."[25]

We can only guess at what the Golden Glow is. Most probably, the phrase evoked for Teilhard the universal influence of the love that radiates from the human heart of the risen and glorified Christ.

The eighth day has no heading. The entries consist of four brief paragraphs that discuss the meaning of Christian faith, for today and for the future, regarding death. Faith in Jesus Christ (in Christ-Omega) should give us more energy than others have, "both to live and to die! Or is that it?" Someone who thinks only about death and about self-crucifixion will little by little lose taste for living. "We have been put into the world not to die, but to live,–to exit from this World, to emerge from it." "After all," Teilhard concludes, our faith today "perhaps can make us more *sensitive* (that does not mean more *vulnerable*)" than the faith of our forerunners "to suffering, to doubt, and to Death."

The ninth day, like the eighth, has no heading. The notes sum up much of what has gone before. Teilhard desires to "go to the deepest of the circles of the Presence: to be in the state of pure dependence on Christ-Omega,—in the fullest communion (although) in the greatest weakness" (in Teilhard's French: *"archi-communiant dans l'archi-faiblesse"*). He repeats the words "centration" and "excentration," making "excentration" equal to *"Christifieri."* He wants to live "in an atmosphere of supreme abandonment and trust," with that "trust which is the most generalized form of the love of Evolution, of the Golden Glow."

Other annual retreats from the 1939–1950 retreat journals mention the Sacred Heart, although to a much lesser extent than Teilhard's 1948 retreat. In his 1939 retreat, the seventh day falls on a first Friday. He writes, *"The Sacred Heart:* Instinctively and mysteriously since my infancy: the *synthesis* of Love and Matter, of Person and Energy. From this, there has gradually evolved in me the perception of Omega—of the universal holding together in unity." Teilhard states clearly here that his conception of Omega—and this includes Omega as philosophical concept (the polar focus of convergent evolution) as well as the theological concept of the risen Christ as personal Omega—has derived directly from his attachment to the Sacred Heart.

In fact, he makes no real distinction at all between Jesus as Sacred Heart and Jesus as Christ-Omega, not even from the point of view of personal piety. This seems clear from the next entry in his journal notes for the 1939 retreat. "I would like to spread, effectively, the attraction (I do not want to say the word, 'devotion,' much too sentimental and too weak) to the universal Christ, to the *true* heart of Jesus."

The 1940 annual retreat notes have the phrase, "Sacred Heart—Personal Heart of the Cosmos," and Teilhard's journal for the retreat of 1943 states: "The Sacred Heart is the Center of Christ, who centers all on himself."[26]

Teilhard finds his own Center, his strength and stability, in the heart of Jesus. The notes for the sixth day of his 1945 retreat begin, "Yes, the vertigo of fragility and of instability. There remains the all-surrounding hand and heart of the Universal Christ. Come to me *one more time* on the changing and shifting waters. Why do you fear, you of little faith?"

The 1950 retreat notes contain a lament: Teilhard finds the Ignatian Spiritual Exercises too confining, too narrow especially in the last part of the Exercises which treats of Jesus Christ risen. He understands Jesus not only as risen, but as centering the whole universe on himself, drawing it to himself as its personal Omega point. It is Jesus' heart as the center of the Center of every person and of all things, and of all history that the devotion to the Sacred Heart should emphasize.

The Development of Teilhard's Spirituality
of the Heart of Jesus

Teilhard de Chardin's spirituality of the heart of Jesus evolves from the traditional piety of the Sacred Heart devotion as he learned it from his mother and as the devotion to the Sacred Heart was practiced in the late nineteenth and early twentieth centuries. But as early as 1916, Teilhard has a firm understanding of the heart of Christ that sees Jesus' heart as filling the world with the power of Christ's love. In that year, Teilhard writes the poetic essay, "Christ in the World of Matter."[27] In it, he describes in three stories three mystical experiences of a friend. In the first story, the friend gazes at a picture of the Sacred Heart. This seems to be the traditional picture of the Sacred Heart that has Jesus offering his heart, the same picture that was on the "holy card" found after Teilhard's death with his personal "litany" written on it. As the friend looks at the picture, the outlines of the figure dissolve and the power of the love of the Sacred Heart fills the world. "The entire universe" is "vibrant."[28]

Jeanne Mortier, Teilhard's secretary, friend, and confidante, assured me before she died that the "friend" of the story was Teilhard himself, and the story accurately describes a mystical experience that he himself had. That experience, surely, underlies the development of Teilhard's understanding of the Sacred Heart.

Around 1920 Teilhard already understands the Sacred Heart as a living symbol that brings into synthesis the two basic directions between which twentieth century culture appears to be torn: the upward and the forward.

In the real symbol of the heart of Christ, detachment and progress, prayer and action, love for God and love for the world are reconciled. The Sacred Heart no longer stands only for the love of Jesus for us, but also for the unifying meaning and force of that love as it unites and gives greater meaning to all our best hopes, aspirations, and efforts.

By the time of his 1939 retreat, Teilhard sees the heart of Jesus Christ risen as the heart of him who stands as the Omega point of Teilhard's Christology, the heart of him who draws all things to himself as the future focus of all evolution's convergence. In an essay of 1940, Teilhard explains how his concept of the Universal Christ is "born from an expansion of the heart of Jesus."[29] And in the 1940's and 1950's Teilhard describes Jesus' heart as the heart of the Heart of the world, and the center of the Center of the universe.

In 1951, in one of the journals in which he wrote his theological insights, ideas for essays, and notes from his reading, Teilhard sums up his view of the heart of Jesus Christ risen as the heart of the world. The problem "is to find a heart for the world, and to identify it with the heart of Christ."[30] Two weeks later, on the feast of Christ the King, Teilhard notes in his journal, "The great secret, the great mystery, is this: there is a heart of the world (a fact we can arrive at through reflection), and this heart is the heart of Christ (a fact of revelation)."[31] This secret, this mystery, Teilhard writes, has two levels that correspond to the level of human reflection and to the level of divine revelation: "–a center of convergence (the universe converges toward a center),–a Christian center (this center is the heart of Christ)." And he adds, "Perhaps I am the only person who can say these words, but I feel they express what everyone and what every Christian feels already."[32]

NOTES

1. *Journal 26 août 1915–4 janvier 1919* (Paris, 1975), p. 369.
2. Cahier, F., October 17, 1919, quoted in P. Schellenbaum, *Le Christ dans l'energétique Teilhardienne* (Paris, 1971), p. 192.
3. Letter from Rome, October 10, 1948, in *Letters to Two Friends (1926–1952)* (London, 1972), pp. 188–190. Teilhard wrote the letter in his own English. But what must have struck him is that "the heart of matter" and "the heart of the matter" are the same in French, "le coeur de la matière."
4. "The Heart of Matter," in *The Heart of Matter,* tr. R. Hague (London, 1978), pp. 42–44, hereafter referred to in the text as *HM*.
5. Letter of March 15, 1916, quoted in H. de Lubac, *La pensée religieuse du Père Teilhard de Chardin* (Paris, 1962), p. 349. On Teilhard's interior life, see H. de Lubac, *Teilhard de Chardin, the Man and His Meaning,* tr. R. Hague (New York, 1965), pp. 13–88.
6. *The Making of a Mind,* tr. R. Hague (London, 1965), p. 114.
7. "The Heart of the Problem," *The Future of Man,* tr. N. Denny (London, 1964), p. 261.
8. "L'intégration de l'homme dans l'univers," fourth lecture, 1930, unpublished notes.
9. See R. Faricy, *Teilhard de Chardin's Theology of the Christian in the World* (New York, 1967), pp. 25–28, for an outline analysis of Teilhard's formulation of the two faith problems from 1945 to 1955.

10. These essays are collected in *Writings in Time of War* (London, 1968).
11. Unpublished letter of June 4, 1915, quoted in Schellenbaum, *op. cit.*, p. 187.
12. Unpublished letter of July 2, 1915, *ibid.*
13. Tr. N. Denny (New York, 1960), paperback.
14. Unpublished letter of December 9, 1915, quoted in Schellenbaum, *op. cit.*, p. 188.
15. Unpublished letter of February 9, 1916, *ibid.*, pp. 188–189.
16. Unpublished letter of July 8, 1916, *ibid.*, p. 189.
17. Unpublished letter of June 28, 1916, *ibid.*
18. These unpublished retreat journals can be found at the Jesuit spiritual center at Chantilly, France, just north of Paris. A typed copy of the retreat journals from 1944 through 1954 is at the office of the *Fondation Teilhard de Chardin* in Paris.
19. Regarding Christ-Omega, see C. Mooney, *Teilhard de Chardin and the Mystery of Christ* (New York, 1966), especially pp. 22–86; R. Faricy, *The Spirituality of Teilhard de Chardin* (Minneapolis, 1981), pp. 32–46; *ibid.*, *Teilhard de Chardin's Theology of the Christian in the World*, *op. cit.*, pp. 67–122.
20. *Op. cit.;* see especially pp. 71–88.
21. These three dialectical phases of Christian personalization are concisely described in Teilhard's essay, "Reflection on Happiness," in *Toward the Future*, *op. cit.*, pp. 117–120.
22. This is the theme of much of the material in Teilhard's essays in *Hymn of the Universe* (London, 1965), paperback.
23. See "The Eternal Feminine," in *Writings in Time of War*, *op. cit.*, pp. 171–202; H. de Lubac, *The Eternal Feminine*, tr. R. Hague (London, 1971), pp. 7–129; C. O'Connor, *Woman and Cosmos: The Feminine in the Thought of Pierre Teilhard de Chardin* (Englewood Cliffs, 1971); R. Faricy, "Jung and Teilhard on the Incompleteness of God," *The Teilhard Review*, 21 (1986) 69–84, especially pp. 79–81.
24. The term "Christogenesis" first appears in Teilhard's writings for publication in 1938 in *The Phenomenon of Man*, tr. N. Denny (London, 1959), paperback in 1965. It shows up after that in several essays. See Mooney, *op. cit.*, pp. 160–168.
25. This litany can be found published at the end of the collection of his essays, *Christianity and Evolution*, tr. R. Hague (London, 1969), pp. 244–245.
26. In the entries for the retreat's first day.
27. Published in *Hymn of the Universe*, tr. S. Bartholomew (London, 1965), pp. 41–55.
28. *Ibid.*, p. 43.

29. "The Awaited Word," in *Toward the Future* (London, 1975), p. 98.
30. Unpublished journal number 6, p. 106, quoted in P. Wenisch, "Teilhard de Chardin et la dévotion au Sacré-Coeur," *Paray-le-Monial*, 11, number 11 (1976), p. 25.
31. *Ibid.*, p. 112, quoted in *ibid.*, p. 25.
32. *Ibid.*

Michael Downey

Region of Wound and Wisdom: The Heart in the Spirituality of Jean Vanier and l'Arche

Christian living is motivated by a way of viewing things.[1] The Spirit illumines the mind and guides the heart, enabling Christians to live by vision and hope. Christian spirituality is concerned with the ways in which the Spirit works in human life, calling forth various forms of Christian living born of different ways of viewing things and diverse approaches to making sense out of the practicalities of Christian living.

With this in mind, we may speak of the life of Jean Vanier and the communities of l'Arche in terms of a spirituality of the heart. Vanier's mode of perceiving and being is shaped in great measure by a conviction about the priority of the heart in human and Christian living. The precise nature of the heart, the centrality of which gives rise to a particular way of perceiving and being at l'Arche (its spirituality) is the subject of this essay. In what follows Vanier's understanding of the heart will be explained, using the following strategy.

A brief biography of Vanier will be provided as well as a short introduction to the communities of l'Arche.

Since Vanier's understanding of the heart is influenced by several significant persons and events, it will be necessary to examine these. Of particular importance is Vanier's encounter with handicapped persons who have influenced his understanding of heart in a crucial way.

To appreciate Vanier's understanding of the heart his own view must be seen in light of more traditional formulations. Though influenced by traditional philosophical and theological insights, Vanier's view of the heart is spelled out in much simpler terms.

Vanier's way of seeing the heart lends to a unique view of the importance of friendship, justice and contemplation in Christian life. It also provides for understanding the basis within which both action and contemplation are rooted. These elements will be highlighted.

By way of conclusion, a synopsis of Vanier's contribution to a spirituality of heart will be offered.

Vanier and l'Arche: In Brief

A Canadian, born in Geneva, Switzerland, on September 10, 1928, Jean Vanier is one of five children of the late nineteenth Governor-General of Canada, Georges Philias Vanier, and his wife, Pauline Archer Vanier. Many things could be said about Jean Vanier, even in a very brief biographical sketch such as this. Let it suffice to nod in several directions.

After serving in the Royal Navy, as well as in the Royal Canadian Navy, Vanier resigned his commission in 1950.

Sometime after his resignation from the navy, Vanier joined l'Eau Vive, a small community of students, predominantly lay, situated in a poor neighborhood near Paris, close to the Dominican community of Le Saulchoir. Shortly after his arrival at l'Eau Vive, Vanier was asked to direct the community when ill-health forced the resignation of his friend and teacher, Dominican Thomas Philippe. Vanier directed the community under adverse circumstances for approximately six years, at which point he himself resigned from the directorship.

In 1962, Vanier successfully completed his doctoral dissertation in philosophy at l'Institut Catholique de Paris. Upon completion of his dissertation, *Le Bonheur: Principe et Fin de la Morale Aristotélicienne*,[2] Vanier began teaching philosophy at Saint Michael's College in Toronto.

Shortly after beginning his career as a professor of moral philosophy, Vanier moved to Trosly-Breuil, France, at the suggestion of his friend and former teacher Thomas Philippe. There he bought a small, dilapidated house which he called l'Arche, the Ark—Noah's Ark. After visiting a number of institutions, asylums and psychiatric hospitals, Vanier welcomed two mentally handicapped men, Raphael and Philippe, into his home on August 4, 1964.

From the seed sown in Trosly-Breuil in August 1964, l'Arche has grown to include over eighty communities worldwide, representing over two hundred family-like homes. Small in number, loose in structure, the communities of l'Arche are founded upon the belief in the uniqueness and sacredness of each person, whether handicapped or not. Motivated by the affirmation of the primacy of the beatitudes in Christian and human living, the gifts of each person are to be nurtured and called forth with predilection for the poorest, weakest, and most wounded in community and society. The handicapped and their "assistants" (the non-handicapped) live together in the spirit of the beatitudes.

Influences upon Jean Vanier

To gain a comprehensive understanding of how Vanier views the heart it is necessary to look to several persons and events which have influenced his understanding of the human person, because, for Vanier, the person *is* the heart.

1. *Thomas Philippe.* Jean Vanier claims that no individual has been more influential in his own view of the human person in relation to God than the French Dominican, Thomas Philippe.[3] It was Thomas Philippe who directed l'Eau Vive when Vanier first joined the community. It was he to whom Vanier went time and time again for counsel and direction during his early adulthood. It was during a visit with him and at his suggestion that Vanier decided to welcome two mentally handicapped men to live with him. And it is Thomas Philippe who, until this day, remains chaplain of the l'Arche community at Trosly-Breuil and Vanier's own "spiritual father."[4] At the level of Vanier's own understanding, the influence of Thomas Philippe appears mainly in five areas. First of all, Philippe's own Thomistic foundation is very influential in Vanier's development, especially regarding the role of the gift of wisdom as the apex of the spiritual life, and the role of the gifts of the Holy Spirit in completing and perfecting the theological virtues: faith, hope and charity. Second, the place of the heart at the center of the person, together with the importance of the affective and the knowledge which comes through this medium, in contradistinction to rational knowledge. Third, the place given to the weak and the little in God's plan of salvation, and the notion of the evolution of the human person through stages of life. Fourth, in the understanding of the human person and all creation as mystery. Finally, Thomas Philippe's influence on Vanier is perceived in his concentration on the mystery of the divine childhood, and the agony and passion of Jesus, as well as the relationship between Jesus and Mary.

2. *The Study of Aristotle.* While living at l'Eau Vive, but after the resignation of Thomas Philippe due to ill health, Vanier studied philosophy at l'Institut Catholique de Paris. The focus of his studies was Aristotle, the Greek philosopher whose influence on Vanier's own thinking he recognizes even today. Vanier's dissertation gives evidence that he judges

Aristotle's views to be incomplete in themselves. They need to be completed by Christian insights (*LB* 420–421). It must not be overlooked, however, that Vanier honors the merits of a purely Aristotelian ethic, even if he clearly favors a specifically Christian view. Vanier's study of Aristotle is of significance in the development of his thought because it is indicative of ideas and questions appreciated and retained. This is particularly evident in that the notions of justice, friendship, and contemplation, the three highest virtues according to Aristotle, are part of the vision which continues to animate the communities of l'Arche. Such notions are nuanced considerably, however, due to the primacy which Vanier attributes to love as the highest activity of God and, consequently, of the person. This affirmation also gives rise to Vanier's opinion that the philosophy of Aristotle needs to be surpassed. Happiness, for Vanier, is not to be defined as the mind's clear gaze toward unchanging, eternal reality, but rather as love's act through which one participates in the very life of God.

3. *The Influence of Georges Philias Vanier.* Georges P. Vanier, nineteenth Governor-General of Canada, died on March 5, 1967. Jean Vanier was thirty-eight years old at the time of his father's death. Two years later, Vanier published a short book on his father's life entitled *In Weakness, Strength.*[5] Not a detailed biographical study, this short work attempts to illustrate the spiritual sources in the life of Georges Vanier. Vanier spells out the contours of his father's spiritual life by the articulation of various spiritual themes. In this domain lies the most formidable influence of Georges Vanier upon his son. These include (a) God's strength in human weakness, (b) perseverance, (c) littleness, (d) providence, (e) the role of Mary, (f) the primacy of love, and (g) unity (for a fuller treatment of these see *IWS*).

It is of interest to note that Vanier's book about his father is indicative of many of the attitudes and tensions which become important features later on in the work which he himself does, the attitudes he adopts, and the problems he confronts. For example, the contrast between the fear which characterized Georges Vanier's religious life before his conversion to deep Christian faith in 1938 and the primacy of love in his life after that point illustrates a tension about which Jean Vanier grows increasingly aware, as evidenced in his work entitled *Be Not Afraid*, which is, in large part, a treatment of the dynamics of love and fear.[6] Vanier's references to his father's distaste, on the one hand, for obtuse theological discussions and, on the other hand, his desire to grow in childlikeness and simplicity are indicative of the problems which Jean Vanier himself confronts in the attempt to build communities wherein are joined persons richly endowed with intellectual ability and persons sometimes deeply wounded in terms of mental capacity. Jean Vanier's treatment of his father as one who gave himself to the primacy of love, attentive at the same time to the claims of justice, is illustrative of the values appreciated and retained throughout his own life and work. His exposure of his father's deep attachment to and affection for his own religious tradition, while at the same time remaining open to the truth within other religious traditions, gives evidence of Jean Vanier's own commitment to the idea of the primacy of the human person beyond religious and cultural differences. The interplay he points out between the active and contemplative dimensions of his father's life is indicative of the struggle which Jean Vanier and l'Arche face anew each day in the communal praxis of l'Arche. Finally, the treatment Vanier gives to the theme of power and weakness as one of the foundations of his father's spiritual life, as well as to his father's increased awareness in old age of God's special predilection for the poor, is suggestive of Jean Vanier's own attitude toward what is primary and fundamental in the spiritual life.

4. *The Influence of Handicapped Persons.* The decisive revelation of Vanier's vocation occurred in his encounter with the handicapped people in 1964. It was as a result of this meeting that Jean Vanier's understanding of the human person was clarified. Vanier writes that his life with handicapped people has taught him far more about living and about human relations than any theory or writing.[7] The decisive event, the pivot around which his life and writings turn, is the meeting of Jean Vanier, Raphael and Philippe in 1964. It is to this event that one must look in an effort to appreciate Jean Vanier's view of the human person and of the heart.

Of the handicapped people of l'Arche, Vanier writes: "They have taught me much about human nature and the real meaning of human existence, the true value of love, of wonder, and even of contemplation" (*EH* 39). What Vanier could not find satisfying in the sophisticated theory of Aristotle, he stumbled upon, as if by surprise, in the struggles and half-audible sounds of these two handicapped men. Vanier had learned the systems of thought which emphasize the rational and intellectual capacities of the person. Post-World War II Europe had impressed upon him the importance of efficiency and technology in national and international development. What he had not yet learned prior to the encounter of 1964 is that while the person is comprised of the abilities of the intellect (head), and a great capacity for efficiency and productivity (hands), he or she is, more importantly, a being with a heart (*EH* 42, 47). In their woundedness and affliction, while not exhibiting capacities of the head or hands, handicapped persons demonstrate tremendous qualities of heart: celebration, forgiveness, tenderness, and compassion. For Vanier, the person is comprised of head, hands, and heart.[8] The handicapped people of l'Arche enabled Vanier to uncover insight into the third, and most important, of these dimensions.

Books, papers, lectures, retreats or conferences of Jean Vanier begin or end with a note of gratitude to the handicapped people of l'Arche, for, in his perception, they have taught him about being human and being Christian. In the preface to *Be Not Afraid*, Vanier writes: "I have learned more about the Gospels from handicapped people, those on the margins of our society, those who have been crushed and hurt, than I have from the wise and the prudent" (*BNA* viii). It is to them that he looks primarily for insight into the nature of the person and the heart.

How does Vanier explain the insight into the nature of the heart which he has derived from the handicapped? According to Vanier, the handicapped person has been wounded (*EH* Preface 1). In the mind or the body the handicapped person bears the mark of suffering in a very visible way. The mentally handicapped person, for example, bears a wound in the brain or nervous system which causes slow, retarded or bizarre activity or behavior. Because of this wound and the behavior and activity which result, the handicapped person is afflicted with another wound, far more painful than the first. This deeper wound is an enormous affective frustration which results from the rejection, ostracization, and alienation precisely because of the mental or physical wound.[9] Parents, family, neighbors, and society at large very often reject the handicapped person, and this brings about deep anxiety and suffering.

The wounds of the handicapped person place him or her in a position of weakness (*EH* 39–42). Handicapped people, and especially mentally handicapped people, are not self-reliant. They need help and assistance in the most ordinary affairs of daily living. In contemporary western culture, with its emphasis upon technology, productivity and competition, handicapped persons are generally viewed as a burden. From this point of view, which finds its early proponents in the Greek philosophers Plato and Aristotle, they are the weak ones who must be carried along through the provision of suitable living conditions, special schools and institutions (*EH* 39–42). Their quite obvious weakness and suffering is perceived as a personal as well as a corporate liability.

The handicapped person is aware of his or her wound and consequent weakness. According to Vanier, "The great suffering of the handicapped person is consciousness of his handicap, his consciousness that he is different than others and because he is different he is not loved."[10] The anguish which results from this awareness of being different from others is frequently far more severe than the anguish of the physical or mental wound itself.

Because the handicapped person is wounded in mind and/or body, he or she is often unable to do or accomplish much with the head or hands. As a result, the handicapped person relies much more on the third constitutive element of human nature: the heart (*EH* 42, 47). Handicapped persons, deprived of the possibility of accomplishing great things with the head or the hands, are richly endowed with qualities of the heart: joy, celebration, forgiveness, tenderness and compassion. It is precisely within this domain that the handicapped person is capable of making great progress.

When Vanier first began l'Arche he understood his mission as one of providing shelter and comfort for people who were not capable of doing much or of making any significant progress.[11] But he quickly found that these handicapped persons, given a warm and loving environment of acceptance and friendship, could make great progress and could advance quickly in the domain of the heart (*JVA* 11). Further, as Vanier quickly learned, in its domain they are often the teachers of the clever and the robust.

5. *The Encounter with the Third World.* Vanier visited India in 1970 with the hope of beginning a l'Arche community there. While in India he came into contact with the legacy of Mohandas Gandhi. The writings and teachings of Gandhi had a significant impact on Vanier. The awareness of the divisions in the world, and the real obstacles to universal justice and friendship, take on increasing significance in the thought and writings of Jean Vanier, and have emerged as a prominant theme in his writings after his contact with India and the legacy of Gandhi. His contact with India enabled him to find in another person of a different religious tradition his same aspirations toward a community of justice and friendship which secures the rights and dignity of the human person, no matter how lowly or despised the person may be. The means to building this community of justice and friendship, for Vanier as for Gandhi, lie in love, gift of self, gentleness and non-violence: the spirit of the beatitudes, or *ahimsā* in Gandhi's terms. Vanier remains nonetheless Christian throughout, and his encounter with the legacy of Gandhi intensified and deepened his experience of, and commitment to, Jesus Christ and the gospel as he himself testifies (*EH* Preface 1–2).

6. *The Influence of the Gospel.* Jean Vanier's reading of the gospel, and its influence upon him, predate the foundation of l'Arche. It is difficult to determine at what point in life the gospel became an influential factor in Vanier's development. Likewise, it is difficult to pinpoint specific scriptural texts which have influenced him. The influence of the gospel is, rather, all-pervasive; it was Vanier's original inspiration and has remained his consistent inspiration, even as his views have evolved.

Vanier has written that he began l'Arche in the context of a Christian faith response:

I began l'Arche in 1964, in the desire to live the Gospel and to follow Jesus Christ more closely. Each day brings me new lessons on how much Christian life must grow in commitment to life in community, and on how much that life needs faith, the love of Jesus and the presence of the Holy Spirit if it is to deepen. Everything I say about life in community . . . is inspired by my faith in Jesus.[12]

In the life of each Christian there are particular gospel themes which have an influential and formative role. The gospel themes which are found attractive and nourishing will vary, at least in part, according to the personality of each individual. Though in the case of Jean Vanier the gospel's influence is all-pervasive, we can nonetheless discern three gospel themes which are prominent in his life and writings: (a) the agony and passion of Jesus, (b) the hidden life of Jesus, Mary and Joseph at Nazareth, and (c) the centrality of the beatitudes in Christian discipleship. The specifically Christian spirituality of l'Arche lies in the interplay of these three gospel themes with the Aristotelian triad of friendship, justice and contemplation—nuanced by the primacy of love.

The Person Constituted by Heart

Vanier does not treat the notion of heart at any length in the doctoral dissertation on Aristotle. However, he does give evidence of his perception, even at the time of its writing, that Aristotle's rather singular focus on reason and intellect stands in need of a corrective (*LB* 418–421). Such a focus leaves out of its scope the great majority of people who could never attain human fulfillment and perfection because of lack of intellectual ability, education or leisure (*LB* 419). Further, the priority given to the powers of intellect, especially in contemplation, leaves little room for the affective dimension.

His objections to Aristotle's vision give indication that Vanier understood the human person in a different light. His vision was even at the time of his study of Aristotle developing around the notion of the heart as that which is the foundation or base of the human person, though this did not emerge clearly until his experience of encounter with the handicapped people of l'Arche.[13]

Vanier's experience with the handicapped enabled him to fill out what he saw as lacking in Aristotle. In Raphael and Philippe, Vanier perceived two men who, by Aristotelian standards, could never arrive at a point of fulfillment. From this perspective these men would be incapable of performing a fully human act, to say nothing of their incapacity for virtue, or the highest virtue of contemplation. Yet, Vanier sensed in them something very deep, good, and worthy. Not exhibiting the ability for greatness in Aristotelian terms, they were nonetheless capable of living very simple and joyful lives with deep compassion, joy and an ability to forgive, reconcile and celebrate (*EH* 45–46). With very little intellectual ability, or ability to produce things by the work of their hands, these men, and later the women of l'Arche, taught Vanier that there is something deeper, richer, more profound and fundamental to the human person than the intellect (*EH* 47). By their very lives, these men and women were living examples that it is indeed possible to live a human and happy life without the riches of the intellect. They taught Vanier that there are other values than those of the mind, and those of efficiency and productivity (*EH* 45).

Vanier then perceived in the little child, and in the very old, many of the same qualities and characteristics that he had encountered in the mentally handicapped (*CG* 79). He also noticed many of the same qualities in people in crisis and distress of all kinds. All of these persons found themselves in positions of vulnerability, and therein manifested extraordinary human qualities. Situations of vulnerability, which cause one to live at the most basic level of one's existence, which Vanier calls the heart, can strengthen and evoke the qualities of the heart and provide the occasion for a deepening of communion (*EH* 42, 48). Often it is only when one is stripped of all the strengths and arguments of the intelligence, and deprived of the ability to create and produce through the work of one's hands, that one is able to see the essentials of human existence, that which lies deepest. Beneath the levels of intellect, and all of the spheres of language, communication and symbol, there lies the heart, which all have in common. Vanier expresses this by saying that "a person is the heart," the qualities of which must be developed by all (*BNA* 12). Because all persons have the capacities of the heart, this provides the common basis and groundwork for true advancement and progress among peoples. The notions of compassion, joy, reconciliation, forgiveness and celebration, which stem from what is deepest and most central in the person, are finally the dimensions which internally unite and vivify the human person. Furthermore, it is the development of the capacities of the heart which makes possible the unity of people desired by all (*BNA* 12 ff). What is needed, according to Vanier, by way of a solution to the massive difficulties throughout the world is a revolution of the heart, of love and compassion (*EH* 102).

The Aristotelian foundation of Vanier's view is not to be underestimated, even if this did not satisfy Jean Vanier. It is from the handicapped person that he learns that there is a basis or core within the human person which he calls heart, which needs to be nurtured in the child, at the beginning of everyone's life, and with which mature adults and adolescents need to be in touch. When he turns to people in situations of crisis or distress, and those living in poverty, he brings about a type of synthesis between the Aristotelian foundation and what he has learned from the handicapped. It is precisely when their vulnerability is revealed that non-handicapped persons are most in touch with the heart and thus that they are able to realize the virtues that Aristotle exalts, such as love for truth, communion in friendship, freedom, and desire for justice. They take on a new tone in light of the gospel, but they are fundamentally the Aristotelian virtues, given a new basis in what Vanier calls heart.

Learning from History

For Vanier, the heart is mystery and as a result constitutes the person as mystery. He writes: "The secret of the heart is so impenetrable, so extraordinary—the place where God resides in each one of us" (*SNH* 1). A thorough appreciation of Vanier's understanding of heart necessitates see-ing his view in light of more traditional formulations because of the influ-ence which these have had upon him. The similarities between Vanier's thought on the heart and these more traditional formulations have been treated elsewhere.[14] A brief survey must suffice here.

The first element from history which is helpful in understanding Vanier's view is the image of the heart in Christian spirituality. The heart connotes the root of diverse personal functions. It describes the origin and source of all thoughts, desires, intentions, but is more fundamental than any one or combination of them. Though in the seventeenth-century French school of spirituality the term "heart" comes to be associated with the will, and more particularly with the emotions, throughout the bulk of the history of Christian spirituality the heart is viewed as the basis and unifying foundation within the human person. It is also understood to be affective inasmuch as it is open to the pull of God's love through the indwelling of the Holy Spirit.

A second element is found in the scholastic tradition. Scholasticism distinguished between *voluntas ut natura* and *voluntas ut ratio*.[15] The former describes the natural tendency within human nature toward the good, while the latter refers to the deliberative pursuit of specific objectives and ends. Aquinas does not use it frequently, but the term is used in scholasti-cism more broadly in description of the radical, fundamental, primitive, drive toward the good within each person. This impulse is prior to thoughts and voluntary actions. *Voluntas ut natura* is an affective tension. It is to be distinguished from the quest for the good and the true which entails deliberation, judgment and choice. This radical impulse toward the good and the true at the deepest level of the person remains operative throughout one's life. *Voluntas ut natura* indicates a unity prior to any distinction or separation of human operations. It is, thus, a synthetic concept. It is important in understanding human cognition and activity as well as the spiritual life. The term expresses the understanding that there is in the human person a fundamental tendency to fulfillment and with which all thought, choice and action must remain in touch.

A third factor from history which aids in appreciating Vanier's view on the heart is the Thomistic understanding of the role of the gifts of the Holy Spirit in the person, particularly the gift of wisdom. In the thought of Thomas Aquinas, God's presence resides in the soul through creation. In addition to this, there is a presence which is supernatural through the bestowal of the Holy Spirit. This bestowal is accompanied by an infusion of sanctifying grace. The theological virtues of faith, hope and charity enable one to strive for the supernatural end as an agent endowed with the ability to perceive and to pursue the divine good. By means of the moral virtues of prudence, justice, temperance, and fortitude one is able to include in this pursuit the human enterprise elevated by grace. Both the theological and the moral virtues are supernatural. However, their principle lies within the person and, as such, the activities of these virtues are human activities.

The gifts of the Holy Spirit may be understood as permanent dispositions within the soul. By means of these dispositions the person may be moved by another, by God, from outside himself or herself. Because the grasp on the supernatural life is tenuous, the gifts are needed to complement the theological and moral virtues. In Aquinas' view of the spiritual organism, the theological virtues have priority. They unite the person to the end pursued, God. This end is sought through the exercise of theological virtues, primarily charity. However, because the hold on the supernatural life is so insecure, the promptings of the Holy Spirit are necessary so that the person might move toward the supernatural end. This movement of the Holy Spirit also gives shape to the exercise of the moral virtues which allow one to act in the supernatural life according to the human mode. The moral virtues under the influence of the gifts of the Spirit are expressed in the activity of the beatitudes.

A final point regarding the Thomistic view of the gifts is crucial for understanding Vanier's view of the person as heart. The Holy Spirit acting through the gifts, the preeminent of which is wisdom, does not prompt one to do what reason in and of itself would require. Thus, the mentally handicapped person, whose ability to reason may be seriously deficient, is capable of great acts of love when moved by God through the gift of wisdom.

By way of summary, faith, hope and charity have pride of place in the Thomistic view of the supernatural organism. They join the person to God. The gifts, especially wisdom, complete the theological and moral virtues by disposing the person to the divine impulse or movement necessary to complement the imperfection of the human mode.

Vanier's Understanding of the Heart

In articulating his understanding of the heart, Vanier does not use philosophical or theological language. His approach is quite simple and direct. However, the philosophical and theological traditions treated above have shaped his thought, and need to be kept in view if Vanier's understanding is to be fully appreciated.

For Vanier, heart describes the most fundamental dimension of the person. He understands the person as open to attraction, to be acted upon and influenced by another, and to be drawn to relationship and communion. That is to say, he views the person primarily as an affective being. This does not mean that the heart and human life are irrational. It is, rather, to say that understanding, deliberation and choice are given direction by the affect when it is developed properly. In itself the heart is unformed, ambiguous, dubious, even disordered because of human sinfulness. When it is purified by the action of the Holy Spirit within, it becomes the basis for contemplation (communication and communion with Christ in his mysteries) and action (service of one's neighbor).

In the active life, this attraction is formed as an openness to the weak, the wounded, and the handicapped. It requires that one be touched in one's own weakness. In contemplation this love of the weak is related to Jesus in his infancy, agony and passion as the disclosure of God.

Vanier contrasts the impurity and ambiguity of the human heart in and of itself with the heart renewed by grace. He recognizes a twofold purification of the heart. The first is by the activity of the Holy Spirit. The second occurs through participation in the life of a community in which one experiences the impact of love upon oneself.

Vanier is concerned with human needs of an affective sort. This concern helps him to understand the affective dimension of human nature, and also enables him to articulate that which is referred to in scholasticism by use of the notion *voluntas ut natura*. But for Vanier, this is better appreciated in terms of human needs, longing, affectivity, and their fulfillment. Further, his attention to human needs helps him understand that dimension of human nature which is touched and transformed by the gifts of the Holy Spirit.

Vanier speaks of the three great needs of the human person: the need for light, life and love. These needs might also be understood as the need for knowledge, freedom and love. Vanier's understanding of need is based upon experience, in which vulnerability and weakness are crucial, as is human affectivity. In speaking of the heart, Vanier is describing basic human needs, with attention to vulnerability and attraction to communion in love.

All of this is related to an understanding of grace which heals and corrects the affective (*gratia sanans*). This grace also disposes one to the movements of God in the most vulnerable region of the heart. These may come directly to the person or through others in community. As a result one can pursue the good through the active life, and likewise be disposed to the contemplation of God's love in the mystery of Jesus Christ.

In referring to the appeal to the heart, and the instincts or promptings of the heart, Vanier is in line with Thomas' understanding of the gifts of the Holy Spirit. However, he has his own particular view, namely, that God's grace and attraction touch one at the most vulnerable region of human existence, and it is response to this action that moves one to compassion, joy, celebration, forgiveness, and similar qualities of the heart. The heart is that which can be attracted, touched, moved, acted upon; the affective inasmuch as drawn, rather than moving toward, of its own motion. Consequently, those who act from the heart, when moved by God to compassion, become signs of God's love and tenderness.

Central to Vanier's thought on the heart is his understanding of love, and this he treats in terms of compassion and openness to the wounded and the weak. Love is of preeminence for Vanier as it reflects the very nature of God. It is the highest activity of the human person. From Vanier's Christian perspective, love sublates and nuances the Aristotelian virtues of justice, friendship and contemplation.

On the basis of this there is a reformulation of the understanding of justice, since in efforts to bring about the common good the needs of the vulnerable and wounded should have priority. Of crucial import in the carrying out of justice is the virtue of hope, which is related to freedom. In pursuing justice one needs to cultivate other cognate virtues, such as poverty, simplicity, and abandonment. Justice is the pursuit of the good for the many in obedience to the mandates of the heart transformed by grace. The exercise of justice is aimed at the establishment of an order in which *la connaissance du coeur* has an important place, and the weak, wounded and vulnerable have a certain priority.

The goal of knowledge given in contemplation is itself based in love, since it is rooted in the heart, and looks to the weak and vulnerable, or to the mystery of Jesus in the weakness of his infancy and hidden life, as well as to his agony and passion for the revelation of God. Contemplation is of the mystery of God revealed in the weak, and in the weakness of Jesus in his infancy, in his hidden life with Mary and Joseph of Nazareth, and in his agony and passion.

Friendship comes about by response to *connaissance d'amour* as one is prompted oneself by the attractions of grace and of the heart in another, making it possible for friendship to exist between any two persons, even those who in terms of human capacity are vastly unequal. Such a view of friendship is inconceivable in strictly Aristotelian terms.

Together with these, there continues to be a need for rational deliberation and prudence, as well as for the exercise of the moral virtues in efforts to realize the goals of the reign of God.

Vanier's Contribution to a Spirituality of the Heart

By way of conclusion, we can spell out in six points the contribution of Vanier and l'Arche to an understanding of the heart in Christian spirituality.

First of all, Vanier has retrieved the early Christian understanding of the heart as the basis and unifying foundation within the human person which is affective inasmuch as open to the attraction of God's love experienced directly through the prompting or impulse of the Holy Spirit, or through the attraction of love experienced with others.

Second, he has attributed positive significance to the inevitable human realities of woundedness, weakness, vulnerability, crisis and suffering by finding therein the possibility of the revelation of the divine and the capacity of the human heart.

Third, because the inspiration of Vanier's life has been the service of the handicapped, and it has been in conjunction with his work and life with them that his thought has developed and been given expression, Vanier offers insight into an understanding of "social" spirituality of service to the weak, and of peace built on recognition of vulnerability and openness to the transcendent.

Fourth, Vanier has managed to keep in focus the primacy of personal relationship with Jesus Christ and the gospel, thereby maintaining the quintessential value of the evangelical dimension in authentic Christian living.

Fifth, because of his focus upon significant others in human life and upon the need for community, as well as his analysis of human needs, especially affective needs, the interpersonal dimension of the spiritual life is explicated in Vanier's life and thought.

Finally, by establishing the heart as the basis and foundation within the human person, Vanier has made it possible to understand contemplation and action as unified through the gift of wisdom which resides in the deepest recesses of the one and same source.

NOTES

1. Jean-Pierre de Caussade, *Lettres Spirituelles*, ed. Michel Olphe-Galliard, I (=*LS*) (Paris: Desclée de Brouwer, 1962), p. 64.

2. Jean Vanier, *Le Bonheur: Principe et Fin de la Morale Aristotélicienne* (=*LB*) (Paris: Desclée De Brouwer, 1965).

3. Jean Vanier, personal interview held at the community of l'Arche (=PI) Trosly-Breuil, France, 15 June 1981.

4. Jean Vanier, introduction to Michael Downey, *A Blessed Weakness: The Spirit of Jean Vanier and l'Arche* (=*ABW*) (San Francisco: Harper & Row, 1986) p. ix.

5. Jean Vanier, *In Weakness Strength* (=*IWS*) Toronto: Griffin House, 1975. First published 1969.

6. Jean Vanier, *Be Not Afraid* (=*BNA*) (New York: Paulist, 1975).

7. Jean Vanier, *Eruption to Hope* (=*EH*) (Toronto: Griffin House, 1971), p. 46.

8. *EH*, p. 41, 42, 47; see also Jean Vanier, "Vivre avec le Pauvre à l'Ecole de Marie et de Joseph" (=*VP*), *Cahiers Marials* 129 (septembre 1981), pp. 205–216.

9. Jean Vanier (=NCC) "Normalization and Changing Concepts in Residential Care" (Mimeographed, 1972), p. 1.

10. Jean Vanier, "Spiritual Needs of the Handicapped" (=SNH) p. 2 (Mimeographed), Text in hand is a reprint from *Letters of l'Arche* 7 (Summer 1974), pp. 24–27.

11. "Jean Vanier's Account of the Evolution of His Concept of l'Arche" (=*JVA*), *Letters of l'Arche* 8 (Winter 1971/75) pp. 9–14, p. 10.

12. Jean Vanier, *Community and Growth*, trans. Ann Shearer (=*CG*) (New York: Paulist, 1979), p. xi; see also pp. 35–36.

13. *LB*, pp. 418–421; see especially Vanier's reference to "le don de l'Esprit Saint," p. 420, and "la loi nouvelle de l'Amour," p. 421.

14. See Michael Downey, "A Costly Loss of Heart: The Scholastic Notion of *voluntas ut natura*" (=*ACL*), *Philosophy and Theology* 1, no. 3 (Spring 1987), pp. 242–54; see also Downey, "Jean Vanier: Recovering the Heart" (=*JV*), *Spirituality Today* 38, no. 4 (Winter 1986), pp. 337–48.

15. For this treatment of the connection between the heart and the scholastic notion of *voluntas ut natura* I am indebted to Marie-Dominique Chenu, "Les Catégories Affectives dans la Langue de l'Ecole" (=*LCA*), in *Le Coeur*, Vol. 29 of the series *Etudes Carmélitaines* (n.p.: Desclée de Brouwer and Cie, 1950), pp. 123–128.

Annice Callahan, R.S.C.J.

Henri Nouwen:
The Heart as Home

"How can I be at home in my heart with myself, with others, with God, and the world?" This is a key question raised by Henri Nouwen, a Dutch priest, a clinical psychologist, pastoral theologian, and spiritual writer, who articulates a spirituality of the heart, that is, a life lived in the Spirit of Jesus Christ which draws its strength and center from the heart. In fact, the heart, for Nouwen, is home, the place where our thoughts and feelings and choices dwell in solitude, the place from which we reach out to others in ministry, the dwelling of Christ with us where we stand with open hands before our God in prayer.

Heart, for Nouwen, is more than the notion of the heart as the seat of the affections. It is the biblical notion of the heart as the center of the whole person, the center of consciousness and freedom, the center of affectivity and imagination, the center of our relational life. He describes the heart as the center or core of our being, as our "innermost self," as "that intimate core of our experience."[1]

His notion of the heart of Christ is biblical. His main image is the gentle, humble heart of the one who makes our burdens light. He describes the heart of Christ as the compassionate heart of God. Another expression he uses is "the first love," God loving us before we love God.[2]

Nouwen's spirituality is, above all, relational. He is constantly reflecting on how we can be more at home in our hearts, how we can move from loneliness to solitude, from hostility to hospitality, from illusion to prayer. In this concern, he names certain attitudes of heart which are counter-cultural to North American "habits of the heart."[3] He emphasizes compassion as the fellowship of the weak and a corrective to our ambition for power; gratitude as our openness to receive and a corrective to our tendency to identify ourselves with what we produce; and community as the fruit of solitude and a corrective to our rugged individualism. In these ways, Nouwen articulates an apostolic spirituality of the heart based on the integration of compassionate ministry and contemplative prayer, an ecumenical spirituality for all contemporary Christians since we are all called to serve God's people, and a eucharistic spirituality that celebrates gratefully the saving deeds of God in Christ.

In this chapter, I explore Nouwen's spirituality of the heart by describing six attitudes of heart, namely, solitude, service, and prayer, compassion, gratitude, and communion.

Attitudes of Heart

Solitude

For Nouwen, solitude enables us to experience our heart as home and ourselves as worthwhile: "In solitude we become aware that our worth is not the same as our usefulness."[4] The movement of reaching out to our heart is the movement from loneliness to solitude. It leads us to self-knowledge.[5] He himself experiences the cathartic power of solitude during a seven-month stay in a Trappist monastery at Genesee, New York, as he attests in *The Genesee Diary*.

Closely related to solitude is the healing power of silence. We need silence in order to respond rather than react: "Without silence we will lose our center and become the victim of many who constantly demand our attention."[6] With silence, we can be drawn into the calmness and quiet of contemplative prayer.[7] Following the way of the heart is following the way of silence in our preaching, counseling, and organizing.[8]

For Nouwen, solitude is not simply being alone, since we can be alone and daydream or mull over past hurts. Rather it is a quality of presence which enables us to respond creatively and compassionately to those whom we meet. Solitude is not our private time apart from community or from ministry when we relax and recuperate in order to get back into the fray. Rather solitude is a part of community life, intimacy, service, and prayer.[9] In fact, he calls solitude "the furnace of transformation" in which we are converted and purified to be compassionate.[10]

Service

The fruit of solitude is compassion which is the basis of all service. What does Nouwen mean by service? He integrated his own doctoral studies in psychology with theology and pastoral care.[11] He did not want the professional part of his life to be separated from the pastoral and the personal. In his book *Creative Ministry,* he begins to sketch lines of his spirituality of the heart, underlining the intrinsic unity between the apostolic and contemplative dimensions of our Christian lives, between ministry and spirituality. Ministry is not what we do, that is, teaching, preaching, organizing, but how we serve God's people, in other words, how we put our heart into our work. For example, he invites us not only to concentrate on the content of our lectures, but also to enter into a "redemptive process" of teaching that is evocative, bilateral, and actualizing.[12] This is in contrast to a competitive, unilateral, and alienating approach to teaching. By calling ministry "creative weakness," he sees it as the sharing of our weakness with others.[13]

This relational approach to service underlies his calling one who serves God's people "the wounded healer" and "the living reminder."[14] It characterizes a key movement in our interior life, the movement from hostility to hospitality. Hospitality opens us in friendship to our guest, to the other who enters our life and longs to find a home, if only temporarily, in our heart. From this perspective, Nouwen calls all service the movement of reaching out to our fellow human beings.[15] He is careful to argue against professionalism, which concentrates on advancing one's own career. At the same time, he maintains the need to be professional in one's service of others.[16] He contrasts compulsive ministers who are in constant need of affirmation from others with compassionate ministers who are purified for service in a solitude which grounds them in God's affirmation of their real identity.[17] He guards against a hierarchical view by reminding us that often our student becomes our teacher and our guest becomes the one who receives us.[18]

Prayer

Solitude enables us to get in touch with our hearts, where our loneliness is transformed. Ministry serves others from the centered place inside of us, transforming our hostility into hospitality. Prayer is the third movement of our relational life, our reaching out to God, which transforms our illusion into interiority.[19]

Nouwen argues against the performance of external rituals in the name of prayer, denouncing what he calls "word-magic."[20] Prayer only makes sense if it is viewed as absolutely essential. In his book *With Open Hands,* he reflects on prayer in connection with silence, acceptance, hope, compassion, and revolution. His image of prayer is that of being with open hands before God and others.[21]

He traces this movement as it unmasks the illusion in the life of Thomas Merton, who discovered that "The new name for the desert in which he saw many of his self-constructed ambitions destroyed was: compassion."[22] Nouwen also traces this movement in his own life, especially during his early years and his time at the Trappist monastery of the Genesee as an adult. He recalls spending hours in the chapel, reading many spiritual books as a little boy, and wanting to be a parish priest at the age of six: "God was so real for me. In fact, my spiritual life was more important for me than anything else, and my teenage years were characterized not so much by a desire to help people as to be with God."[23] In one of his prolonged stays at the Genesee, he evaluates his academic lifestyle and realizes that he needs to build in a definite time for prayer in his daily schedule in order to make it a conscious priority. Reflecting on the monks' lifestyle, he perceives the centrality of praise in their day. He experiences the power of contemplative prayer to reveal one's deepest identity and God's affirmation. At the same time, he experiences the power of intercessory prayer whereby we place our suffering friends in God's presence in the center of our heart.[24]

Later on, Nouwen continues to reflect on contemplative prayer. He views it as a valuable dimension of celibacy whereby our choice to be with God is not in competition with our choice to be with people, but rather it is our choice to be useless in God's presence, empty, with no need to justify this attitude. It is the discipline of contemplative life which opens us to receive nature, other people, and time as gifts. One way we can cultivate a contemplative life is to allow our unceasing thoughts to become unceasing prayer, drawing our mind down into our heart, inviting God into the details of our daily lives. Another way is through the Jesus prayer which leads to the prayer of the heart. Contemplative prayer enables us to see God in our heart. This growing sense of God's indwelling opens us to the world, since knowing God in the world requires knowing God "by heart."[25]

Intercessory prayer empties us of ourselves, our burdens, and our barriers to others, so that we can identify with others and mediate to them God's healing presence in our hearts. In this way, prayer is a discipline of compassion because intimacy with God includes a solidarity with all of God's people, with our enemies as well as with our friends and neighbors. It gives us a chance to plead for God's mercy on suffering and poor people in particular. One profound expression of our solidarity with others is the breaking of bread at which we celebrate together the presence of the Spirit in our brokenness. Here we can see how compassion, which is born of solitude, connects prayer and ministry: "The discipline of leading all our people with their struggles into the gentle and humble heart of God is the discipline of prayer as well as the discipline of ministry."[26]

The dynamism of Nouwen's spirituality of the heart is the triple movement into solitude, service, and prayer. He does not view these as things to do at the level of achievement, but rather as qualities of being, attitudes of heart at the level of relationship with ourselves, others, and God. Let us now explore three other attitudes of heart which seem to characterize his spirituality of the heart, namely, compassion, gratitude, and communion.

Compassion

It is possible and appropriate to call Nouwen's spirituality a spirituality of the compassionate heart because compassion is so central to his way of living, serving, and praying. It serves as the unifying principle behind the dynamism of solitude, ministry, and prayer. It assumes that we accept our weakness, that we are free to accept others in their weakness, and that we join with others in forming a "fellowship of the weak."[27]

Compassion is not pity which connotes distance nor is it sympathy which connotes exclusive nearness. It is born of prayer, our encounter with God who is also the God of our fellow human beings. It converts our illusions and pretensions into the truth of who we are before God. The authority of compassion is our possibility to forgive. Forgiveness is only real for those who have discovered their friend's weakness and their enemy's sin in their own hearts and are willing to be in solidarity with every human being. Christian ministers are wounded healers who can enter into others' pain because they have entered into their own, knowing that it is part of the basic human condition and believing that it is capable of being transformed by God into a source of hope and healing. One such wounded healer was Thomas Merton whose discovery of non-violent compassion in solitude led him to a solidarity with others based on his recognition that the roots of sin and violence are in his own heart.[28]

Closely related to compassion is care, which has to do with grieving, experiencing sorrow, and crying out with another. It does not mean that the strong take away weakness. It means rather that those who know themselves to be weak dare to be present to others who are weak, not to take their pain away but simply to be with them in the pain. In this way, caring people mediate God's compassion. Nouwen calls his mother's life a compassionate life because she felt others' suffering as her own in such a way that her death can also be seen as an act of dying with others.[29]

By saying that Jesus is the visibility of God's maternal mercy, Nouwen affirms that Jesus reveals to us a feminine face of God.[30] Writing to his father after his mother's death, Nouwen describes compassion as a feminine element of being: "You have found in yourself the capacity to be not only a father, but a mother as well. You have found in yourself that same gift of compassion that brought mother so much love and so much suffering."[31]

Our compassionate solidarity with others is rooted in God's compassionate solidarity with us in Jesus whose compassion is marked by a downward pull toward humble, obedient, self-emptying service rather than the upward pull toward competitive, individualistic achievement. Our discipleship implies voluntary displacement and voluntary community. By voluntary displacement, we move from what is familiar and comfortable in order to experience the brokenness of those who feel displaced and to identify with Jesus who voluntarily chose to be displaced. We do not displace ourselves in order to feel special or set apart, but rather to be closer to our fellow human beings in a non-competitive togetherness. By voluntary community, we choose to share life in faith with others. We identify with Jesus' self-emptying by affirming others' gifts which can benefit the community.[32] Nouwen articulated this spirituality of compassion with co-authors Donald McNeill and Douglas Morrison.

Nouwen has lived his concern for social justice in the praxis of his trips to Latin America. Each time he voluntarily displaced himself from the first world to the third world, choosing to live with poor people and to create with them a fellowship of the weak. In such a community, we confess our brokenness to one another, not as a form of complaint or excuse, but rather as a source of hope and healing. By focusing on the sharing of pain in faith rather than the removal of pain, Nouwen experiences an apostolic dimension of compassion, the apostolic value of what I would call our pierced heart experiences, that is, experiences of suffering which give life out of death. He writes: "Ministry is entering with our human brokenness into communion with others and speaking a word of hope."[33]

Closely related to the hunger for social justice are solidarity with poor people and peacemaking. At the same time that he was living in Central American countries sorely in need of peace, Nouwen began to articulate a spirituality of peacemaking based on prayer, resistance, and community as three ways of living a life of peacemaking. The context for prayer and resistance is a community of faith in which we forgive one another and so make the peace of Christ visible in our midst. In this way we express our hope that God's power can be made visible to one another and to the world. We are called not to destroy or deny life, but to share life with each other: "So we are *eucharistic* people and that is to be peacemakers."[34]

Gratitude

Receiving and giving life leads us to gratitude, another major characteristic of Nouwen's spirituality of the heart. It enables us to celebrate life by remembering the giftedness of life. It is evoked often by the dying and death of a loved one.[35]

Closely related to the Christian attitude of gratitude is the eucharist, about which Nouwen writes frequently. He emphasizes that the eucharist builds community, brings the past and the future together in the present, has transforming power, celebrates the sustaining presence and absence of the risen Christ, heals and strengthens, announces the new life of a loved one who has just died, and prepares us for death by proclaiming that Christ's death is life-giving.[36] He attests that the eucharist is the center of his life, the core of his priesthood, that from which everything else receives its meaning. He considers the eucharist as part of his primary identity: "My life must be a continuing proclamation of the death and resurrection of Christ. It is first and foremost through the Eucharist that this proclamation takes place."[37]

During his stay in Bolivia and Peru, Nouwen developed what I would call a spirituality of gratitude based on being able to receive from those we serve:

It is hard for me to accept that the best I can do is probably not to give but to receive. By receiving in a true and open way, those who give to me can become aware of their own gifts. After all, we come to recognize our own gifts in the eyes of those who receive them gratefully.[38]

Nouwen reflects on the significance of gratitude in mission work. In a former view, the missionary was to bring the gospel to poor people in order to enlighten their darkness. In the present view, the missionary is to help others recognize their own God-given talents and to make them visible as a source of celebration in the community. He perceives that the apostolic dimension of gratitude is an aspect of poverty of spirit: we serve most with our weakness since it opens us to receive from those to whom we are sent. He attests that gratitude is a visible characteristic of poor people since he is constantly being thanked by them and their thanksgiving is cause for them to celebrate. For them life is a gift to be celebrated and shared: "Thus the poor are a eucharistic people, people who know how to say thanks to God, to life, to each other . . . in their hearts, they are deeply religious, because for them all of life is a long fiesta with God."[39] In fact, he considers gratitude the treasure which Latin America can offer North America. This treasure is a voice crying out: "That voice calls us anew to know with heart and mind that all that is, is given to us as a gift of love, a gift that calls us to make our life into an unceasing act of gratitude."[40]

Nouwen's spirituality of compassion is a spirituality of social justice, peacemaking, and gratitude. While it is born in solitude, it grows only in the nurturing atmosphere of a fellowship of the weak. A life of compassion and gratitude can only be sustained by others who share and foster these values. Let us turn, then, to another attitude of heart which is pivotal in Nouwen's spirituality, namely, communion.

Communion

We have already seen the importance which Nouwen gives to communion in our reflection on previous aspects of his spirituality. For him, communion is an intrinsic element of the Christian life. It operates in a dialectic with solitude. One is not in competition with the other, but relies on the other for validation and growth. A community of faith, hope, and love is the context and goal of all ministry. Since ministry is hospitality, our service of others is about making them feel welcome and at home in their hearts and in our hearts. Communion is the touchstone of Christian prayer since prayer opens our hearts to God and to others. Intercessory prayer reveals the multi-dimensional nature of the communities to which we belong. We pray for our family and friends, for our neighbors and enemies, for poor and suffering people, for people who ask our prayer and for many people we never meet whose plight touches our hearts, for the living and the dead. The name that Nouwen gives a compassionate community is "fellowship of the weak." By this he means that our illusions of self-sufficiency block us from what we need most in order to accept ourselves and each other, namely, a solidarity of brokenness whereby we are not ashamed to be weak and to be in need of forgiveness and healing, to have to depend on the power of the Spirit. The Christian name for a life of gratitude is a eucharistic life. We become a eucharistic people by receiving and giving life to each other, by building community as we set about making peace.

Since Nouwen's spirituality is experiential, we can turn to his own life as the source of his spirituality of communion. His prolonged stays at the Trappist abbey of the Genesee gave him a new sense of community and he concludes: "The basis of community is not primarily our ideas, feelings, and emotions about each other but our common search for God."[41] More recently, his prolonged stays at the l'Arche community in Trosly-Breuil, France, and at Daybreak in Toronto, Ontario, have given him a strong sense of his heart as home.[42]

I propose that his contribution to a spirituality of communion is his notion of a fellowship of the weak.[43] Accordingly, we care enough for each other by sharing our pain, not by taking it away. But it is not only pain, weakness, and brokenness that we share with one another, but also faith, prayer, and talents. In fact, the source and climate of prayer is precisely a community of faith. In solitude, we come to realize that communion is a gift to be received, not a project to be completed. This discipline of community enables us to listen together to God. In prayer, we are freed from our compulsions in order to respond creatively and compassionately to those with whom we live. This response includes our encouragement of their gifts, our acceptance of their weakness, and our constant plea for their forgiving acceptance of our weakness. Community includes not only forms of the common life but also friendship, marriage, and family. It stretches us to invite into our hearts not only the people we find immediately attractive, but also people whose handicap reminds us of our own. It is a quality of heart which challenges us to let go of our individualism and to allow ourselves to be given our individual uniqueness: "The discipline of community makes us persons; that is, people who are sounding through to each other (the Latin word *personare* means 'sounding through') a truth, a beauty, and a love which is greater, fuller, and richer than we ourselves can grasp."[44]

Concluding Remarks

Henri Nouwen views the heart as home. He lives from the heart, integrating the professional approach of academia with the pastoral approach of a minister who sees himself as a wounded healer. His spirituality is a pastoral spirituality that combines the riches of scripture and the Judeo-Christian tradition with the poverty of serving broken people like himself in need of care and connectedness. It is a spirituality that speaks not only to the heart but also about the heart.

One of Nouwen's contributions, as I perceive it, is to treat each attitude of heart as a unifying principle for Christian living. For him, solitude is not something we do in a private time and place, but rather our openness to our real self which can be operative while we are engaged in our ministry or in prayer. Ministry is not the career we pursue during work hours, but rather our disposition of availability to those we serve, open to welcome them into the home of our hearts, open to share with them the strengths and weaknesses of our hearts. Prayer is not the time we set aside to be with God alone or in community, but rather our basic contemplative stance which learns to receive all in our daily lives as gift from God. In the geography of Nouwen's heart, we bring the people we serve and pray for into our solitude, we serve in solitude and prayerfulness, and we pray in a solitary way, solicitous of those we serve and certain that our prayer is part of our vital ministry. Compassion is not our feeling sorry for those less privileged than we are, but rather our conviction that it is a privilege to be with wounded people like ourselves who heal us as we care for them. Gratitude is not the ritual of thanking for a favor, but our way of accepting our weakness and need to depend on God and others for everything. Community is not activities we do together, but rather our commitment to help create communion among God's people. Notice how each attitude of heart unifies our life and integrates our experience.

Another contribution he makes is to show how each quality of heart is an intrinsic dimension of the other attitudes. Spiritual writers often discuss these topics as isolated units, urging us to emphasize seemingly one at the expense of others. For example, solitude can be viewed as more contemplative than community or ministry as more apostolic than prayer. This approach regards these as states of mind demanding options that exclude the others. Nouwen's approach regards these as habits of the heart that include and, in fact, rely on the others for support and challenge.

Nouwen's spirituality is not monastic, though he has lived in a monastery and has written a book on one monastic writer, Thomas Merton. It is apostolic in its Christ-centeredness and other-centeredness, with global implications for our intercessory prayer and compassionate solidarity with poor people. His books are written not exclusively for Roman Catholics, although he himself has been shaped by his own tradition and originally wanted to do formation work with Roman Catholic clergy. They speak to Protestants, Orthodox, and non-Christians as well, since their themes are so universal. The enthusiastic response of his reading public bears witness to his conviction that what is most personal is most universal. His writing is not directed to any one group or kind of individual. He writes for the lonely members of the rootless generation, for committed Christians who want to deepen their lives of prayer and service, for students preparing for ordained and non-ordained ministry in their churches, for handicapped people, for poor people, for people who are aging and those who care for them. His is above all a eucharistic spirituality that shares life and faith in the heart of Christ with all God's people proclaiming the hope that God's love is stronger than death.

Nouwen's spirituality of the compassionate heart makes a valuable contribution, not by giving us an easy solution to take away pain or even a ready formula about how to live with pain, but by inviting us to deal directly with pain, to feel it as it is, to accept it as part of the human condition, and to share it as a way of witnessing that God is with us in this part of our lives.[45] His approach to suffering and death speaks of the depth and sensitivity of heart-suffering which he himself has experienced. It touches on topics about which we often hesitate to speak, for example, loneliness, rootlessness, boredom, anger, and fear. By making his personal feelings and reflections available to us, he reveals their universal character and renews our hope that it is acceptable to have all human feelings and still be a believer.

His spirituality of what I call the pierced heart knows what it is like to be absolutely lonely, to feel restless, to make a solitary choice in faith without reward.[46] It dares to be vulnerable enough to acknowledge and accept the depths of its heart's movements toward anger and fear, tenderness and trust.

His spirituality of the heart is biblical, historical, and contemporary. He reveals that his own life of prayer is nurtured by the scriptures and he quotes from scripture in almost everything he writes. He is steeped in the history of Christian spirituality, especially fourth century desert spirituality.[47] He reflects the concerns and questions of people today, and refers often to other spiritual writers of this century.

Nouwen puts heart into ministry and spirituality. In fact, one of his most significant contributions is his attempt to integrate ministry and spirituality, service and prayer, to see them as integral to each other, to live them from the heart. In an era when ministry can fall prey to professionalism and spirituality can be reduced to individualism, he assures us that we can allow our wounds to be a source of healing for others, and receive their gifts as we share our own.

He rethinks the themes of Judeo-Christian western spirituality. Rejecting self-imposed austerities that damage the body and the psyche, he opts instead for a discipleship marked by traditional "disciplines": solitude and silence, self-emptying service, prayer, compassion, gratitude, and communal living. It is meaningful for him to speak also of the discipline of the church, of the book, and of the heart.[48] He strikes a balance in the practice of these disciplines, not emphasizing any one of them to the exclusion of any other one. This balance reveals his strong belief in the incarnation and vital sense of identification with Christ in his paschal mystery.

His prophetic voice speaks in a special way to North Americans. In our technological era when busyness and frenetic energy fill our lives, he invites us to attend to matters of the heart, namely, our relationship with ourselves, God, and others. In our times when fast foods and computers facilitate greater productivity, he reminds us that we are called to intimacy, fecundity, and ecstasy. Nouwen sees the need for our spirituality to be in dialogue with our first world culture, integrating it and confronting it. His voluntary displacement and his vision of the spiritual crisis we are suffering bridge the Americas. His global spirituality of peacemaking stretches our hearts to embrace all people on our planet.

His recent l'Arche experiences are enabling him to explore dimensions of prayer, service, and community life which he has only mentioned, for example, the role of our bodies and non-verbal communication.[49] He has not yet written of the intimate connection between leisure and contemplation, or, for example, what Margaret Farley calls "relaxation of heart."[50]

His spirituality of the heart points above all to the sacramentality of weakness and the giftedness of gratitude. Our solitude, ministry, and prayer enable us to accept weakness as the place of divine revelation. Our compassion, gratitude, and community life give us opportunities to share and celebrate weakness.

Nouwen's spiritual guidance reveals his own relational life. He humbly submits himself to be guided by soul-friends like John Eudes Bamberger and Jean Vanier. In his own spiritual direction, he does not preach, but rather tells us stories. He does not counsel esoteric spiritual exercises, but only the universal commandment of love. He does not hide his feelings, fears, faith struggles, and fantasies, but makes them accessible to us as the very stuff of prayer. His search has led him home, to the home of his heart. By speaking of the heart as the place of our shared weakness, he invites us to be at home with the truth of who we are, that is, always in need of God. By pointing us to his heart, he points us to our hearts and to the heart of Christ.

NOTES

1. For example, see Henri Nouwen, *Intimacy: Pastoral Psychological Essays* (Notre Dame: Fides Publishers, Inc., 1969), p. 19; *Creative Ministry: Beyond Professionalism in Teaching, Preaching, Counseling, Organizing, and Celebrating* (Garden City, New York: Doubleday & Co., Inc., 1971), p. 65; *The Genesee Diary: Report from a Trappist Monastery* (Garden City, New York: Doubleday & Co., Inc., 1976), p. 101; *Clowning in Rome: Reflections on Solitude, Celibacy, Prayer, and Contemplation* (Garden City, New York: Doubleday & Co., Inc., Image, 1979), p. 104; *The Way of the Heart: Desert Spirituality and Contemporary Ministry* (New York: Seabury, 1981), pp. 60–61; *A Cry for Mercy: Prayers from the Genesee* (Garden City, New York: Doubleday & Co., Inc., 1981), pp. 24, 26, 62, and 66; and *A Letter of Consolation* (San Francisco: Harper and Row, Pub., 1982), pp. 27 and 32.

In these endnotes, I give references in Nouwen's books and articles in chronological order in order to help the reader trace the development of his thought.

2. For examples of his use of the image of Jesus' gentle, humble heart, see *The Way of the Heart*, p. 70; *A Cry for Mercy*, pp. 66 and 157; and with Donald P. McNeill and Douglas A. Morrison, *Compassion: A Reflection on the Christian Life* (Garden City, New York: Doubleday, 1982), p. 57. See also Nouwen, foreword to Jean Vanier, *Man and Woman He Made Them* (London: Darton, Longman and Todd, 1985), p. xii, and "An Interview with Henri J.M. Nouwen," in Tilden Edwards, ed., *Living with Apocalypse: Spiritual Resources for Social Compassion* (San Francisco: Harper & Row, 1984), p. 22. For examples of his use of the image of the pierced side of Jesus, see *A Cry for Mercy*, pp. 78 and 135. For an example of his use of the image of the gentle, humble heart of God, see Nouwen, *The Way of the Heart*, p. 70. For examples of his use of the expression "first love," see *A Cry for Mercy*, p. 95; "A Spirituality of Peacemaking," unpublished transcript of 1983 tape, pp. 4–5; *Lifesigns*, p. 39; "A Conversation with Henri Nouwen," in *Living with Apocalypse*, p. 20; and Introduction to Yoshi Nomura, *Desert Wisdom: Sayings from the Desert Fathers* (Garden City, New York: Doubleday & Co., Inc., 1982), p. xii.

3. See Robert Bellah et al., *Habits of the Heart: Individualism and Commitment in American Life* (San Francisco: Harper & Row, 1985), in which the authors identify certain characteristics of North American culture from extensive interviews with people.

4. Nouwen, *Out of Solitude: Three Meditations on the Christian Life* (Notre Dame: Ave Maria Press, 1974), p. 22.

5. See Nouwen, *Reaching Out: The Three Movements of the Spiritual Life* (Garden City, New York: Doubleday & Co, Inc., 1966), pp. 13–44.

6. Nouwen, *Intimacy*, p. 152.

7. See Nouwen, *With Open Hands* (Notre Dame: Ave Maria, 1972), pp. 25–48.

8. See Nouwen, *The Way of the Heart*, pp. 42–49.

9. See Nouwen, *Clowning in Rome*, pp. 1–32.

10. See Nouwen, *The Way of the Heart*, p. 13.

11. See Seward Hiltner, "Henri J.M. Nouwen: Pastoral Theologian of the Year," *Pastoral Psychology*, 27 (Fall 1978), 4–7.

12. See Nouwen, *Creative Ministry*, pp. 2–14. Cf. Nouwen, "Living the Questions: The Spirituality of the Religion Teacher," *Union Seminary Quarterly Review*, 32 (Fall 1976), 17–24.

13. See Nouwen, *Creative Ministry*, pp. 112 and 116.

14. See Nouwen, *The Wounded Healer: Ministry in Contemporary Society* (Garden City, New York: Doubleday & Co., Inc., 1972), and *The Living Reminder: Service and Prayer in Memory of Jesus Christ* (New York: Seabury, 1977).

15. See Nouwen, *Reaching Out*, pp. 4–78.

16. See Nouwen, *Clowning in Rome*, pp. 18–23, and his response to John Robert McFarland in "The Minister as Narrator," *The Christian Herald*, 18 (January 1987), 20.

17. See Nouwen, *The Way of the Heart*, pp. 10–20 and 63–70.

18. See Nouwen, Introduction to Yoshi Nomura, *Desert Wisdom* p. xi, and Nouwen, "Called to be Hosts," *Faith/At/Work* (September 1976), 30–31.

19. See Nouwen, *Reaching Out*, pp. 80–117.

20. See Nouwen, *Intimacy*, pp. 5–20.

21. See Nouwen, *With Open Hands*, esp. pp. 92 and 94.

22. See Nouwen, *Thomas Merton: Contemplative Critic* (Notre Dame: Fides, 1972), p. 47.

23. Judd Anderson, "PW Interviews: Henri J.M. Nouwen," *Publisher's Weekly* (October 2, 1981), 3–4.

24. See Nouwen, *The Genesee Diary*, pp. 6–7, 73–4, 114–119, 149, 187.

25. See Nouwen, *Clowning in Rome*, pp. 53, 63–82, 91–106; *Prayer and the Priest* (Chicago: Franciscan Herald Press, 1980); and *Behold the Beauty of the Lord: Praying with Icons* (Notre Dame: Ave Maria Press, 1987). For other references to the Jesus prayer, see *The Genesee Diary*, pp. 155–56, *Reaching Out*, pp. 95–106, *Making All Things New* (San Francisco: Harper & Row, 1981), p. 78, *The Way of the Heart*, pp. 53–73, and *Lifesigns: Intimacy, Fecundity, and Ecstasy in Christian Perspective* (Garden City, New York: Doubleday, 1986), p. 40.

26. Nouwen, *The Way of the Heart*, p. 70. For other references on intercessory prayer, see Nouwen, *Clowning in Rome*, p. 32; *The Way of the Heart*, pp. 69–71; with Donald P. McNeill and Douglas A. Morrison, *Compassion*, pp. 103–115; *Gracias! A Latin American Journal* (San Francisco: Harper & Row, 1983), p. 11; *Love in a Fearful Land* (Notre Dame: Ave Maria Press, 1985), pp. 63, 85, 93, 96. For other references to the eucharist, see *Intimacy*, p. 147; *Clowning in Rome*, pp. 81–82; *The Genesee Diary*, pp. 18–20; *In Memoriam* (Notre Dame: Ave Maria Press, 1980), pp. 51–52; *A Letter of Consolation*, pp. 63–68; *Gracias!*, p. 147; and *Lifesigns*, pp. 78–79, 104–105.

27. See Nouwen, *Intimacy*, p. 30.

28. See Nouwen, *With Open Hands*, pp. 89–114; *The Wounded Healer*, pp. 40–47, 83–98; and *Pray to Live*, pp. 64–67.

29. See Nouwen, *In Memoriam*, pp. 29–30. See Nouwen, *Out of Solitude*, pp. 30–46, and *Aging: The Fulfillment of Life* (New York: Doubleday, 1979), p. 109. See also Nouwen, *The Genesee Diary*, p. 122, where Nouwen reflects on Abraham Heschel's insight into a feeling of compassion for God, and *The Way of the Heart*, pp. 19–26, where Nouwen writes of "A Compassionate Ministry."

30. See Nouwen et al., *Compassion*, pp. 15–17. See also Phyllis Trible, *God and the Rhetoric of Sexuality* (Philadelphia: Fortress, 1978), pp. 31–59, where she traces the journey of this metaphor in the Old Testament, and Monika Hellwig, *Jesus the Compassion of God: New Perspectives on the Tradition of Christianity* (Wilmington, Delaware: Michael Glazier, Inc., 1983), pp. 121–23, where the author emphasizes the passive and active aspects of genuine compassion, and calls Jesus the compassion of God.

31. Nouwen, *A Letter of Consolation*, p. 24.

32. Nouwen, *Compassion*, p. 133. See also Nouwen, *Letters to Marc About Jesus* (San Francisco: Harper & Row, 1988).

33. Nouwen, *Gracias!*, p. 18. See also *Gracias!*, pp. 11–18. Cf. "A Conversation with Henri Nouwen," *Harvard Divinity Bulletin* (April–May 1987), 8–10.

34. See Nouwen, "The Spirituality of Peacemaking," unpublished tape transcript of a 1983 lecture on the occasion of the celebration of the anniversary of the Norbertine Foundation in Paoli, p. 12, in Henri FJ.M. Nouwen Papers, Manuscript Group Series II, No. 43, Special Collections, Yale Divinity School Library. See also Nouwen, "Forum: Henri Nouwen's Plea for Nicaragua," *The National Catholic Reporter* (August 26, 1983), 9–11. See also Nouwen, *Love in a Fearful Land*, and the section on intimacy and solidarity in *Lifesigns*, pp. 43–51. Nouwen mentions another dimension of solidarity, that is God's solidarity with suffering people, in a conversation with Tilden Edwards; see *Living with Apocalypse*, p. 21.

35. See Nouwen, *Creative Ministry*, pp. 94–96, and *In Memoriam*, p. 7.

36. See Nouwen, *Intimacy*, p. 147; *Creative Ministry*, p. 98; *The Genesee Diary*, pp. 18–20; *The Living Reminder*, pp. 45–48; *Clowning in Rome*, pp. 81–82; *In Memoriam*, pp. 51–52; *A Letter of Consolation*, pp. 67–68; and "A Spirituality of Waiting: Being Alert To God's Presence in Our Lives," *Weavings: A Journal of the Christian Spiritual Life*, 2 (January–February 1987), 11–12. In his review of *The Living Reminder* in *Worship*, 52 (January 1978), 91–92, Terry Tekippe registers

his surprise that Nouwen does not develop more deeply the notion of eucharist as remembrance. I wonder if the reason is that, for Nouwen, the mystery of eucharist is much more a mystery of gratitude, and that is the form of remembrance which his worship takes.

37. Nouwen, *A Letter of Consolation*, p. 63.
38. Nouwen, *Gracias!*, p. 16. See also Nouwen, *In the Name of Jesus: Reflections on Christian Leadership* (New York: Crossroad, 1989).
39. Nouwen, *Gracias!*, p. 147. See also *Gracias!*, pp. 16–21, 55, 146–47.
40. Nouwen, *Gracias!*, p. 188.
41. Nouwen, *The Genesee Diary*, p. 188.
42. See Nouwen, *Lifesigns*, the series of articles in *New Oxford Review*, 53 (September–December 1986) and 54 (January–June 1987); *The Road to Daybreak: A Spiritual Journey* (New York: Doubleday, 1988).
43. For this notion, Nouwen was strongly influenced by Jean Vanier. For example, see Jean Vanier, *Community and Growth: Our Pilgrimage Together* (Toronto: Griffin House, 1979).
44. Nouwen, *Making All Things New*, p. 87. For references to his views on community used in this paragraph, see Nouwen, *The Genesee Diary*, p. 188; *Out of Solitude*, pp. 39–43; *Reaching Out*, p. 109; *Clowning in Rome*, pp. 1–32; *Making All Things New*, pp. 80–90; *Compassion*, pp. 49–61; and "A Spirituality of Peacemaking," pp. 8–12.
45. See Ann Belford Ulanov, *Receiving Woman: Studies in the Psychology and Theology of the Feminine* (Philadelphia: Westminster, 1981), esp. pp. 150–153, for a psychological approach to this spirituality of accepting pain. The similarities in vocabulary and perspective of these two authors is striking.
46. See Nouwen, *Heart Speaks to Heart: Three Prayers to Jesus* (Notre Dame: Ave Maria Press, 1985.) In this regard, I refer the reader to my book on *Karl Rahner's Spirituality of the Pierced Heart: A Reinterpretation of Devotion to the Sacred Heart* (New York: University Press of America, 1985). In particular, I see a connection between Nouwen's examples and the examples Rahner gives in his chapter of "Reflections on the Experience of Grace," *Theological Investigations*, Vol. 3, tr. Karl-H. and Boniface Kruger (New York: Seabury, 1974), pp. 86–90. I also see a parallel between Karl Rahner's image of the priest of the future as "a man with the pierced heart" and Nouwen's image of the minister of today as "a wounded healer." See Karl Rahner, "The Man with the Pierced Heart," *Servants of the Lord*, tr. Richard Strachan (New York: Herder & Herder, 1968), pp. 107–19.
47. For example, see the tapes of his class lectures on "Desert Spirituality" (September–November 1980), in Henri J.M. Nouwen Papers,

Manuscript Group No. 68, Special Collections, Yale Divinity School Library, 14 cassettes.

48. See "Spirituality and Ministry: An Interview with Henri Nouwen," *The Practice of Ministry in Canada*, 4 (Spring 1987), 11–13.

49. For example, see Nouwen, "To Meet the Body is to Meet the Word," *New Oxford Review*, 54 (April 1987), 3–7; *The Road to Daybreak*, pp. 150–51.

50. See Margaret A. Farley, *Personal Commitments: Beginning, Keeping, Changing* (San Francisco: Harper & Row, 1986), esp. pp. 58–66.

Annice Callahan, R.S.C.J.

Epilogue

This book has sketched fifteen spiritualities which reflect our search for and union with God in terms of the heart, affectivity, and desire. It has explored how the heart is a key symbol in the spirituality of several writers, namely, Catherine of Siena, Jane de Chantal, Francis de Sales, John of the Cross, Martin Luther, Madeleine Sophie Barat, Pierre Teilhard de Chardin, Jean Vanier, and Henri Nouwen. It has demonstrated how related notions such as affectivity, desire, and union with God have functioned significantly in the religious experience of other writers, for example, Bonaventure, Thomas Aquinas, Ignatius Loyola, and Teresa of Avila. It has also indicated how the holistic view of the human person to which the symbol of the heart points was held by early church writers such as Irenaeus and Augustine. Spiritualities of the heart have used religious experience as their point of departure for theological inquiry and insight. By so doing, they have demonstrated the significant contribution which spirituality makes to theology.

Will spirituality in the future continue to take account of people's religious experience? To trust our personal experience of God is to trust God and to claim our own inner authority. It is to listen to and follow the deep responses of our hearts to grace. It means that we rely on scripture and tradition not as external sources outside of ourselves, but as sources of God's revelation that mirror and nourish the word God speaks to us that is who we are. It also means that we avoid dangers in appealing to religious experience, such as individualism and sectarianism. It is quite easy to delude oneself into thinking that one hears God's word in what is in fact a soliloquy. To look to our corporate experience of God is to let our hearts be moved by the anguish and progress of humankind. It can lead us to surrender our struggles against injustice into the hands of God. And it can free us to accept our common humanity, our hearts, as a place of God's action in the world today.

Surely, Christian spirituality will continue to take account of the life, death, and resurrection of Jesus. Many Christians will continue to identify with the paschal mystery by describing their lives in the imagery of conversion, discipleship, becoming the body of Christ, intimacy and collaboration with Christ, living gospel values, giving glory to God, or openness to the Spirit. Some Christians may choose to interpret their lives as experiences of the heart. They will try to be in touch with their own hearts and with Christ's heart in order to invite others to do so.[1]

Will the practice of spiritual direction and the formal study of spirituality in the future continue to incorporate a positive view of the body, the feelings, the passions, and the unconscious? It is important to emphasize redemption as well as creation. We must integrate a sense of the pervasiveness of God's presence with a sense of our brokenness: both grace and sin are original to the human condition. Since the heart points to both the locus of God's action in our lives and the place of our fundamental option, it can serve as a symbol of God's self-communication and of human freedom.

The heart is both corporeal and spiritual. People are more aware of their bodies, their feelings, their passions, and their unconscious in their relationship with God. Will they continue to be so? Liturgical ritual engages not only our minds but also our senses and our relatedness to the others with whom we are worshiping. These experiences ground and shape our life of prayer. Spiritual direction can no longer take account only of the insights of the mind during times of formal prayer; it will more and more reflect on holistic insights, intuitions, and attractions which we are given in our everyday lives of faith. The formal study of spirituality is beginning to incorporate not only courses in the history of classical mysticism, but also times of leisure and creativity which rest and rejuvenate our bodies, psyches, and spirits. In the future, creative leisure will become a greater value as a shorter work-week and the time-saving devices of technology free us to attend more consciously to the inner journey.

Will there be spiritualities of the heart in the future? Will the heart serve as a key word, a key symbol in the future? Or will other words and symbols, for example, the womb, be more relevant ways of locating the place from which people relate to God?[2] One need not say that every major spiritual writer will have a spirituality of the heart. People who are conscious of having been given an experience of God, however, will continue to try to find an image or metaphor in which to make this experience communicable. In so doing, they look within to the place where they have tasted God's indwelling presence. Some will use the word "heart" to capture the locus of this dialogue between human and divine freedom. Others will speak of affectivity, desire, union with God, or life in the Spirit. Still others will talk of grounding themselves in their bodies, praying in their womb, or reflecting on their feelings and dreams. But all will point to their center of energy, depth, interiority, and integration. They will seek to describe a symbol of healing and transformation which expresses their growing presence to themselves, others, and God. It is in this larger sense that we have chosen to write about spiritualities of the heart which have an enduring relevance. This volume seeks to further this contemporary quest.

If we accept a spirituality of the heart, will there be an ongoing spirituality of the heart of Christ? This book clearly indicates that there has been a spirituality of Christ's heart in the history of Christian spirituality. This symbol of the heart reveals the mystery of the Trinity whereby the Spirit facilitates God's self-expression in Jesus Christ by the outpouring of grace and salvation. It captures the mystery of the incarnation, of the divine becoming human, of matter being transformed into spirit. It articulates the mystery of grace whereby God's self-communication is mediated by Christ's humanity in the Spirit. Will "heart" and "heart of Christ" be the key words that describe our Christian calling and commitment? Even if the "love of neighbor" is or becomes the key word, does it not find rich expression in these symbols?[3]

Will there be North American spiritualities of the heart? Native peoples have a rich religious tradition around the image of the moist heart.[4] A team of North American sociologists has investigated "habits of the heart" which mark our culture, for example, individualism, loneliness, and consumerism.[5] Already there are emerging movements in North American spirituality which support the transformation of these attitudes, for example, the black culture and spirituality, charismatic renewal, the peace movement, Hispanic culture and spirituality, Christian feminism, liberation theology, the new cosmology, and ecological ethics. These movements reflect group spiritualities of the heart in which the group experience has value and significance. People will continue to make "choices of the heart," choosing to stand in solidarity with poor and oppressed people. We are faced with massive and complex failure on this continent, in view of the situation of homelessness, the rate of unemployment, and the possibility of nuclear annihilation. How does the heart speak to this situation? Will we in North America continue to look to Europe and to the east for wisdom, or will we also look to our own hearts? Will we welcome the gift which our neighbors in Central and South America offer us, a gift of gratitude and compassion? Steeped in scripture, our heritage of Christian literature, and our own culture, we may find ourselves daring to risk exploration into God in undiscovered regions of our hearts, the new frontier of the future.

NOTES

1. For example, in Greek and Russian Orthodox spirituality, prayer of the heart is an essential element. See *Writings from the Philokalia on Prayer of the Heart,* tr. E. Kadloubovsky and G.E.H. Palmer (London: Faber, 1951).

2. For the use of the metaphor of earth-womb and woman as earth-womb, see Christian Lore Webber, *WomanChrist: A New Vision of Feminist Spirituality* (San Francisco: Harper & Row, 1987), pp. 8, 19, 48, 64–65, 67, 72–73, 142.

3. See Karl Rahner, S.J., "The Eternal Significance of the Humanity of Jesus for Our Relationship with God," *Theological Investigations* (=*TI*), Vol. 3, tr. Karl-H. and Boniface Kruger (New York: Seabury, 1974), pp. 35–46; "Priest and Poet," *TI* 3, pp. 294–317; " 'Behold This Heart!': Preliminaries to a Theology of Devotion to the Sacred Heart," *TI* 3, pp. 321–30; "Some Theses for a Theology of Devotion to the Sacred Heart," *TI* 3, pp. 331–52; "Reflections on the Unity of the Love of Neighbor and the Love of God," *TI* 6, pp. 231–49; and "The Man with the Pierced Heart," *Servants of the Lord,* tr. Richard Strachan (New York: Herder and Herder, 1968), pp. 107–19. Cf. Annice Callahan, R.S.C.J., *Karl Rahner's Spirituality of the Pierced Heart: A Reinterpretation of Devotion to the Sacred Heart* (New York: University Press of America, 1985).

4. See Jose Hobday, "Seeking a Moist Heart: Native American Ways for Helping the Spirit," *Western Spirituality,* ed. Matthew Fox (Santa Fe, NM: Bear & Co., 1981), pp. 317–29.

5. See Robert N. Bellah et al., *Habits of the Heart: Individualism and Commitment in American Life* (San Francisco: Harper & Row, 1986). Cf. Allan Bloom, *The Closing of the American Mind* (New York: Simon and Schuster, 1987).

Index